In very grateful memory of Carolyn Horne, an extraordinary teacher educator, a beloved colleague and a wonderful human being.

Primary Teacher Education:
High Status? High Standards?

Edited by

Colin Richards
Neil Simco
Sam Twiselton

UK	Falmer Press, 1 Gunpowder Square, London, EC4A 3DE
USA	Falmer Press, Taylor & Francis Inc., 1900 Frost Road, Suite 101, Bristol, PA 19007

First published in 1998

A catalogue record for this book is available from the British Library

ISBN 0 7507 0846 8 cased
ISBN 0 7507 0845 x paper

Library of Congress Cataloging-in-Publication Data are available on request

Jacket design by Caroline Archer

Typeset in 10/12 pt Times by
Graphicraft Limited, Hong Kong

Printed in Great Britain by Biddles Ltd., Guildford and King's Lynn on paper which has a specified pH value on final paper manufacture of not less than 7.5 and is therefore 'acid free'.

Every effort has been made to contact copyright holders for their permission to reprint material in this book. The publishers would be grateful to hear from any copyright holder who is not here acknowledged and will undertake to rectify any errors or omissions in future editions of this book.

Contents

Contents

Carolyn Horne: A Very Enabling Woman

I began by writing down some of the words I thought best described the very remarkable woman who had come to portray the essence of primary teacher education at St Martin's. The descriptors seem to fall into three categories:

enthusiasm, drive, energy;
colour, presence, poise

compassionate
gentle, non-threatening, understanding,

determined, difficult
outcomes and destinations superseded means of travel

The categories do not sit comfortably together, but then Carolyn was not a cosy sort of person; she was challenging. One would pause, mentally, before making a point, knowing that any inherent weakness would be picked up, just gently, but often to devastating effect. Her commitment to children, to primary schools and to primary teachers was total; quality was paramount and was not to be compromised. She was not good at accepting that economic considerations were important in this pursuit of quality.

My abiding memory of a superlative colleague is one of gentle flowing: her clothes, her hair, the ideas, the endless energy and work, the seamless robe of her professional responsibilities. One did not forget Carolyn after a first encounter. But the nice thing was, one did not want to forget, but looked forward to the next.

Ian Edynbry
Former Principal, University College of St Martin

Introduction: Primary Teacher Education: New Directions, New Issues, New Problems, New Opportunities

Colin Richards, Neil Simco and Sam Twiselton

Primary initial teacher education in the late 1990s is subject to intense scrutiny and tight control. To adapt a phrase from the Plowden Report this 'astringent scrutiny' is the outcome of increasing political involvement in initial teacher education beginning in 1984 and accelerating through the 1990s, resulting in wide-ranging changes to the arrangements for the preparation of the next generation of teachers. Symptomatic of this increased scrutiny are the inspection, follow-up inspection and reinspection of primary ITE courses with institutional and personal futures at stake depending on the outcome. Symptomatic of ever-tightening control is the introduction of the Government's National Curriculum for Initial Teacher Training (*not* Education) in which ownership of the detail of the curriculum is assumed by the Government. For the first time the fine grain of knowledge in English, mathematics, science and information technology is specified. The consequences for initial teacher education may well be as far-reaching as were those of the Education Reform Act of 1988 for primary schools.

This book takes its title quite deliberately from that of *Circular 10/97* which encapsulates these changes. It is written by a range of people mainly, though not exclusively, connected with the University College of St. Martin. The contributors share a number of characteristics. They accept that wide-ranging changes to teacher education *are* happening and that these present opportunities as well as problems. They do not defend some rosy-hued view of teacher education pre-1984, nor do they set out to be destructively critical of recent developments. While accepting the necessity to embrace change they do not ignore or play down the turmoil that has been, and is still being, felt in the teacher education sector.

The contributors believe in the importance of taking a proactive stance to change through constructively critical engagement with the reforms in order to fashion a renewed vision of teacher education. There is a need to both accommodate *to* reform and to innovate *within* reform. It is the latter that has proved so difficult in recent years as the sector has attempted to cope with an ever-accelerating pace of change. The book argues that the time is ripe for renewed innovation.

The contributors are optimistic not only about the possibilities of creative interpretation of current requirements (which will inevitably change) but also about the potential which teacher education has to produce a future generation of teachers characterized by highly developed technical competence and by knowledge and understanding of the intricacies of the contexts and processes of teaching and learning.

These qualities — a positive attitude, a desire for constructive engagement and a sense of optimism — characterized Carolyn Horne, a former colleague at St Martin's, to whom this book is dedicated. Even in the bleakest of moments Carolyn was accepting of the necessity to come to terms with reality and the very difficult problems it presented, without ever losing her vision of, or optimism for, the potential of initial teacher education.

The book endorses the opening sentence in Stewart Sutherland's report *Teacher Education and Training: A Study* (1997): 'Higher education plays a key role in the arrangements for training and educating teachers' but would want to add the phrase 'in partnership with schools'. The lack of contributions in the book from mentors or from those involved in SCITT schemes should not be construed as dismissing their important contribution. The book relates particularly to teacher education issues within institutions of higher education but many of the points it raises are also salient for those involved in school-based initial teacher education.

Throughout the book we have been careful to use the words 'student' 'student teacher' and 'initial teacher education', *not* 'trainee' or 'initial teacher training', except where official sources are quoted or official nomenclature is used. This is not backward-looking usage but reflects our conviction that the process of professional development, even within the Government's current regulations, is complex, demanding and when undertaken with appropriate regard for the nature of the teaching/learning enterprise can be deeply educative for both student and tutor. Both the DfEE and the TTA need to be convinced of this; the book makes a small contribution to that necessary process of reeducation.

The book falls into five main sections. The first considers the changing context both of primary education and of primary teacher education. The second provides a constructive critique of the National Curriculum for Initial Teacher Training. The third builds on the content-related chapters in the previous section by considering aspects of pedagogy in primary ITE. The next part reflects on mentoring issues from the perspective of higher education. The fourth section is concerned with the bridge between initial teacher education, induction and continuing professional development. The book concludes with an examination of primary education as 'a community of practice' in which members hold different but complementary roles.

The editors hope that this book with contribute in a small way to the further development of the primary community of which children, teachers, student teachers, researchers and teacher educators are members.

Part 1

The Changing Context of Primary Teacher Education

1 Changing Teacher Education — Genuine Partnership or Arranged Marriage?

Rob Hyland and Glynis Wood

In all the discussions and proposals for making the initial preparation of would-be teachers more effective, few concepts have been appealed to more often than that of the 'partnership' between schools and higher education. Often preceded by 'new', 'real' or 'genuine', it is difficult to resist the subtle or not so subtle discursive pressures exerted by such appeals; it is rather easier to dispute the attractions of motherhood and apple pie than it is to gainsay the merits of partnership. But tracing the developing use of the word illustrates the dynamic way in which *partnership* has taken on extended and particular meanings in the processes of policy generation and implementation. To be convinced of the necessity for a closer relationship between higher education and schools in the preparation of future teachers is not to be blind to ways in which 'partnership' may have served as a rhetorical device, masking the imposition of political control from the centre. A commitment to the desirability of a genuine partnership cannot obscure some of the real difficulties inherent in relationships forged under considerable pressure. The question is not whether partnership is desirable, but rather what sort of partnership can be achieved. Partnerships in teacher education are a matter of balancing interests as well as sharing commitments: for those working within schools and HEIs the balance achieved in the late 1990s seems at best precarious.

Long-standing Liaisons

For as long as some formal preparation beyond a rudimentary apprenticeship has been recognized as desirable, there have been links between schools and institutions geared to the specific preparation of teachers; and for just as long there has been debate about the desirable balance of influence (see, for example, Jones, 1924). In the early part of the long history of training teachers the school-based element was paramount, then the pendulum swung in favour of more education and training in institutions separate from schools. Though the McNair Report (1944) tried to give due weight to both elements, in the post-war era the details of their courses and the nature of their arrangements with schools for giving students practical experience were largely a matter for colleges and universities involved in ITT. The James Report (DES, 1972) tried to redress the balance of training and emphasize the particular contribution of schools and teachers, but most of its recommendations were quickly lost sight of as successive governments struggled to reduce ITT numbers in line with falling school rolls. Whilst there were many structural changes, and though students' 'teaching practice' was commonly redefined as 'school experience', the essential relationship between HEIs and schools was undisturbed. Within very broad guidelines, ITT institutions and schools were free to enter into such liaisons as they saw fit.

There had always been some calls for more practical training and the greater direct involvement of serving teachers in ITT. In the late 1970s and early 1980s a number of projects, some funded by the DES, developed models of ITT involving closer links with schools (Ashton et al., 1983; Tickle, 1987; Furlong et al., 1988). Much of the impetus for such initiatives came from the professional communities of teachers and teacher educators. An HMI discussion document reflected these debates and recommended:

> Partnerships between schools and initial training institutions should be strengthened at all levels, and in all aspects of the students' training. (HMI, 1983, p. 17)

Thus far the debate was essentially a professional one in which the sorts of recommendations made by HMI, including those about 'partnership', enjoyed considerable support from HEIs and the Universities Council for the Education of Teachers (UCET).

Accredited Relationships

Indication of a general change in political climate came with the White Paper *Teaching Quality*; this did not just advocate increasing 'the active participation of experienced practising school teachers' in ITT, but also proposed a new body to accredit teacher training (DES, 1983). The Council for the Accreditation of Teacher Education (CATE), established in 1984, had to approve all ITT courses. DES *Circular 3/84* set out the arrangements; its annex set the tone and language of much of what was to come. Under 'Links between training institutions and schools' it was clear that 'courses should be developed and run in close working partnership with . . . schools' (para 3). Not only were 'experienced teachers from schools' to be involved in the 'planning, supervision and support of students' school experience', but they should also 'be given an influential role in the assessment of students' practical performance'. At this stage there was no suggestion that teachers should be *directly* responsible for the training of students in school, but they should be involved 'in the training of the students within the institutions' (i.e. HEIs). Such involvement is likely to have been identified as good practice in many ITT institutions at that time; somewhat more controversially, ITT staff were to be given 'opportunities to demonstrate their teaching effectiveness in schools' (para 4).

When CATE was reconstituted, DES *Circular 24/89* replaced *Circular 3/84*. The requirements (the 'CATE criteria') were adjusted and amplified, but there was also a subtle change of tone in sections detailing the relationships between HEIs and schools which further extended the language of partnership:

> Close cooperation between schools, local education authorities and initial teacher training institutions leads to better training of student teachers for their future careers and provides valuable staff development for institutions and schools. Where possible, institutions should build long-term partnerships with individual schools which will foster collaboration and training opportunities. (*Circular 24/89*, Annex B, para 1)

Whereas *Circular 3/84* talked of 'sharing responsibility', *Circular 24/89* was more directive:

> The assessment of students should be a shared judgment, in which the views of both serving teachers and teacher trainers are given full weight. (ibid, para 3)

Serving teachers were also to be directly involved in interviewing candidates (ibid, para 4) and not restricted to drawing up selection guidelines. *Circular 24/89* also extended the requirements of 'school experience for ITT tutors' (paras 7–9).

Leading Partners

Secretary of State Kenneth Clarke's speech to the North of England Education Conference, January 1992, signalled the firm direction of policy:

> Student teachers need more time in classrooms guided by serving teachers and less time in the teacher training college. (Clarke, 1992, para 19)

> The essence of school-based training is that the partnership is one in which the school and its teachers are *in the lead* in the whole of the training process, from the initial design of a course through to the assessment of the performance of the individual student. (ibid, para 22, emphasis added)

Perhaps the most crucial signal of intent however, was that ITT institutions 'will have to reimburse the schools for the additional costs' involving 'a considerable shift of funds from colleges to schools' (ibid, para 29). Nevertheless, Clarke maintained his proposals were:

> designed not to take teacher training away from higher education, but to reaffirm that the objective of the training is to prepare the student for a career as a teacher in a school. (ibid, para 44)

There was another clear message: training institutions should select the 'best schools' as partner, those 'which command the greatest confidence in academic and other aspects of measured performance' (ibid, paras 31–2).

A Consultation Document, prepared by CATE, followed immediately (DES, 1992). Premised on the view that the 'quality of the teaching force' would be raised by measures 'to give the best teachers real responsibility for training new members of their own profession' (p. 2), the far-reaching proposals were designed to reform all of ITT and make it more 'school-based'. The document was clear:

> In future, the whole process of teacher training will be based on a more equal partnership between school teachers and tutors in higher education institutions, with the schools themselves playing a much bigger part. (ibid, p. 7)

The partnership would involve a contract between HEI and school and 'a considerable shift of funds . . . to schools' (ibid, p. 3). HEIs, however, would be 'expected to associate as partners with the best schools' and use 'performance indicators' to determine these (ibid, p. 7). The structure of the partnership would be part of CATE's accreditation brief, as would the further specification of professional competences. New draft criteria for secondary courses were appended whilst another consultation document on primary ITT was promised in the accompanying 'Dear colleagues' letter from the DES. In characteristic fashion, that letter gave two months for reply, 'if you have any comments on the Secretary of State's proposals' (Whitaker, 1992).

Within HEIs the 'dear colleagues' had plenty to comment upon: Gilroy's rather intemperate language, 'the political rape of initial teacher education', reflected the depth of feeling in ITT (Gilroy, 1992). The disjunction between gentle words of 'more equal partnership' and the repetition of Clarke's unequivocal statement that the schools would now be 'in the lead in the whole of the training process' was noted. There were dire predictions about universities withdrawing from initial training, but the reforms were pushed through. Secondary courses were restructured in line with the criteria of *Circular 9/92*; primary courses awaited the outcome of further consultation.

'Mutual Trust and Willing Cooperation'

In June 1993, 'new criteria for course approval' for primary ITE were set out in a draft circular. Drawing attention to the reports of the 'three wise men' (Alexander et al., 1992) and the follow-up by OFSTED (1993), with their emphasis upon curricular subject knowledge and practical teaching competences, the draft circular stressed the National Curriculum as the 'framework for teaching and learning' and therefore 'the basis for ITT requirements' (DFE, 1993a, p. 6). Though recognizing that the 'nature and extent' of partnerships between HEIs and primary schools would 'vary with local circumstances', there was a clear transfer of responsibilities to schools (ibid, p. 14). Just in case any HEIs thought they could dupe their primary school partners over 'an adequate transfer of funds', the Secretary of State proposed to 'monitor and make public' the details of such arrangements; though naturally partnerships would be 'on the basis of mutual trust and willing cooperation' (ibid, p. 15). Should this not be enough:

> the Secretary of State reserves the right to withhold approval from an institution's courses of ITT if there is evidence that individual schools have been treated arbitrarily or unreasonably. (ibid)

The criteria (annex A) set out the details of the aims, course hours and conditions for ITE courses; it also included 33 'competences expected of newly qualified teachers'.

The Teacher Training Agency and Circular 10/97

Circular 14/93 formalized the draft criteria and established school-based training on the partnership model as the basis of primary ITE. An increased role in the delivery of the training of students was given to teachers in school and some of the funding was devolved accordingly. But even as it was being implemented, further reforms were set in motion with *The Government's Proposals for the Reform of Initial Teacher Training* (DFE, 1993b). This document summarized progress to date, but most significantly proposed 'a new statutory body, the Teacher Training Agency'. Its remit was to be more all-embracing than that of CATE; most noticeably it would 'administer all central funds for initial teacher training in England (ibid, p. 6).

The Teacher Training Agency was established in September 1994. The TTA would now regulate the framework of partnership between HEIs and schools and draw up new standards for the training of teachers. Following consultations, *Circular 10/97* was eventually issued. That the policy of school-based training based on partnerships was now established is clear:

> In the case of all courses of ITT, higher education institutions and other non-school trainers must work in partnership with schools . . . (DfEE, 1997b, p. 45, para 3.1)

Though schools are to be 'fully and actively involved' where they 'fall short' it is 'providers' who must 'demonstrate that extra support' is given to ensure the quality of training. If this quality 'cannot be guaranteed', then the HEI (or 'other non-school trainers') must implement their 'procedures . . . for the deselection of schools'. It is a 'quality assurance requirement' that:

> only those schools and teachers who can offer appropriate training and support for trainees are used to provide ITT. (ibid, p. 46)

The new Circular continues the transfer of training to schools, but leaves quality assurance firmly in the hands of the higher education institutions. Far from solving the problems of teacher training, this precarious balance of responsibilities in school–based partnerships has given rise to many contentious issues for schools, individual teachers, HEIs and tutors.

Theory and Practice

As Glenny and Hickling (1995) observe:

The notion of partnership generated by recent educational policy indicates a determination to challenge the traditional role of higher education in the initial training of teachers. This has resulted in a rather truncated debate about partnership, focused primarily on the allocation of power and resources between schools and higher education, and has obscured the more fundamental shared core purpose of improving the quality of teaching and learning for children. (p. 56)

The 'rather truncated debate' concerning the location of initial teacher training sometimes descends to an argument over the relative merits of *theory* and *practice*, with schools providing the latter and higher education institutions the former. Such a practice/theory divide is simplistic. As Beardon et al. (1995) observe:

The difference between the training institution and the school is that in the former the theories are more likely to be very explicit and to be underpinned by some academic or research-based rationale, whereas in the latter the theories tend to be more explicit or taken for granted as good practice derived from the long experience of the supervising teacher. All practice is grounded in some kind of theory: it is impossible to get rid of theory simply by emphasizing practice or a particular location for that practice. (pp. 81–2)

Evidence gathered from our work with mentors suggests some reticence on the part of mentors to teach the students anything linked to formal 'theory'. This was generally due to a lack of security in up-to-date academic literature and a lack of time to read current research. Many mentors were very able to explain their practice, and inevitably discussed some of their underpinning theory, but they contrasted this with:

the sort of heavy theory you do in college, like all the stuff I did when I was a student, you know the latest info about the curriculum, orders from the DfEE or OFSTED, or about people like Piaget, Skinner. (unpublished fieldwork)

Whilst it is true that practice and theory are inextricably linked, it would be rather naive to assume that mentors are in a strong position to draw out all the aspects of educational theory which are related to students' practice. In practical terms there needs to be an agreement about which aspects are best taught where and by whom; in the longer term there needs to be a more fundamental partnership between teachers in higher education and schools. If the old theory/practice dichotomies are simply recreated, albeit in different settings, then the learning experience of the student must suffer.

Roles and Responsibilities

A major assumption underlying the new model is that schools actually desire to be 'in the lead'. The TTA appears to have taken little heed of recent research demonstrating that many teachers and headteachers may not want significantly greater responsibility for ITE. John Furlong, commenting on a five-year research project which focused on partnerships, concluded:

> Despite the misgivings of Government agencies over the style and quality of teacher education provided by universities and colleges, most heads think higher education is a better initial teacher training ground than the classroom. (*THES*, 19 July 1996, p. 4)

Even where schools are committed to being closely involved in the professional preparation of new teachers, in the final analysis training must be a secondary function. For most schools, receiving students in training remains an undertaking to be negotiated year-by-year; this in itself makes it difficult for them to take a longer term, proactive view, particularly against a background of continual educational change.

It remains the task of higher education institutions to recruit the overwhelming majority of would-be trainees and to be responsible for their suitability. In seeking placements for students, ITE institutions have always made some professional judgments about the quality of schools, but these judgments are now to be much more rigorous and public. HEIs are now in the invidious position of being directly accountable to OFSTED and the TTA for the selection of partner schools. Directives to use OFSTED inspection reports, or other performance indicators, to inform decisions about the selection of partner schools impose yet more central control upon the partnership relationship (OFSTED/TTA, 1996; DfEE, 1997b). This will also brings its own anomalies: some schools receiving a good OFSTED report may not be sympathetic to the learning and training needs of students; schools receiving less than glowing reports may still have much to offer in 'pockets' of good quality.

Mentors at the Centre of Partnership

Whilst the education of pupils remains their first obligation, and teachers' conditions of service continues make the participation of individual teachers in ITE 'entirely voluntary' (DfEE, 1997c, p. 18), many teachers have welcomed greater involvement. They have appreciated the professional development that mentor training and taking responsibility for students have provided. Under the mentoring system the student is likely to receive more direct supervisory support than under the traditional models of college supervisor who saw only 'snapshots' of the student experience. This is a strength of the newer model, but it is not without its costs. Evidence from our work with mentors clearly demonstrates the tensions experienced in fulfilling their multi-task role. The learning needs of the student and the immediate needs of the pupils are not always easily reconciled. This frequently results in overwork for mentors whose professionalism may not allow students or pupils to suffer from receiving anything less than their best efforts.

As the role of mentor has been given some status, and sometimes financial recognition, it is proving to be a career springboard for promotion. Nias's (1989) work on personal perspectives and career stages shows how a 'mid-career' change can be extremely productive both for the individuals concerned and for the institution. This certainly appears to be true from the experience of mentor training to date. In our research, teachers assuming the role of mentor have frequently perceived a rise in status in the school as well greater professional recognition from the college. Few mentors wished to hand the role to another member of staff within the school, though this appears to be changing as the role of mentor becomes more accepted as a career stage. With their newly acquired or recognized skills many mentors have been prompted to apply for new posts, frequently citing mentor accreditation as part of their marketing strategy.

Some mentors choose not to continue, often due to additional pressures from their work load, and schools lose or need to change mentors for a variety of reasons. Given this turnover, the formal contract between the higher education institutions and the school may not reflect the real partnership which is often reliant upon individual mentors. Although it is not difficult to specify the formal requirements of the role, in practice effective mentoring rests upon the capabilities and personalities of individuals. The selection and training of mentors needs to ensure a certain level of competence in order for all trainee teachers to have a high standard of in-school training. Higher education institutions have sought to develop initial and ongoing mentor training and to guarantee quality within the programme. In the recent round of inspections, HMI asked how higher education institutions will ensure the high level of training observed in specific schools is sustained and how this level of provision can be assured across *all* the schools used. This is clearly a problem facing HEIs who remain responsible and publicly accountable for quality assurance within the partnership model. The choice, training and deployment of mentors can all be sensitive issues for partner schools and HEIs within partnership arrangements.

Relationships Under Pressure

The Government deliberately created a system which left the responsibility of financing school-based training with the HEIs. But the new partnership schools see the system as anything but transparent. Many, feeling they were promised 'real money' and realizing the time, commitment and responsibility partnership training entails, now feel disappointed in the funding they receive. Some claim it does not cover costs and governing bodies are asking hard questions; in some areas it has become a competitive market with schools taking the best offer going. Many HEIs now experience more difficulty placing students *with* the funding than they ever did when relying upon professional goodwill and ensuing mutual professional development.

If, as John Furlong concludes, 'Partnerships are dangerously dependent on the goodwill of the partners' (*TES*, 19 July 1996, p. 5), then there are very obvious pressures upon that goodwill. The more involved, rigorous and demanding the requirements become, the more difficult it will be to bring schools into partnerships and, more importantly, to keep them in the relationship. With the new National

Curriculum for ITT, the requirements, objectives and procedures will need to be fully understood and implemented by all partners. There is a real question here:

> Will the colleges' partner schools take one look at the increased workload and abruptly terminate their involvement with training? (TES leader, 4 July 1997, p. 20)

Sustaining Partnerships

There is no doubt that the partnership approach to teacher training will continue. David Blunkett, Secretary of State for Education and Employment has emphasized the Government's commitment to continue shifting the emphasis from teacher training institutions to schools. The recent White Paper, *Excellence in Schools*, is clear:

> We shall seek to strengthen existing partnerships between schools and higher education training institutions to ensure that teacher training is firmly rooted in the best classroom practice. (DfEEa, 1997, ch. 5, para 13)

But if 'partnership' is to be a justified description of the relationship between school and HEIs, then it must be more than just a term for a set of enforced administrative arrangements. Effective partnerships must recognize the distinctive contributions of the different partners and convey mutual benefits. The prime responsibility of schools must remain the education of their pupils, whilst ITE institutions remain accountable for the training of effective teachers.

All the changes in ITE have taken place within a context of unprecedented school reform. Despite some shortcomings, the quality of what has been achieved in constantly shifting circumstances is testimony to the professionalism of those directly involved both in schools and higher education institutions. The many vested interests in teacher education may make it impossible to achieve unanimity; the best that may be hoped for is a more fully negotiated working consensus, the basis of many long-standing relationships. Teachers in schools have always had a professional commitment to the preparation of the next generation of teachers. That commitment is still very evident today. Without such commitment the Government imposed reforms would have brought the system to its knees.

References

ALEXANDER, R., ROSE, J. and WOODHEAD, C. (1992) *Curriculum Organisation and Classroom Practice in Primary Schools: A Discussion Paper*, London: DES.

ASHTON, P.M.E., HENDERSON, E.S., MERRITT, J.E. and MORTIMER, D.J. (1983) *Teacher Education in the Classroom: Initial and In-service*, London: Croom Helm.

BEARDON, T., BOOTH, M., HARGREAVES, D. and REISS, M. (1995) 'School-led initial teacher training', in KERRY, T. and SHELTON MAYES, A. (eds) *Issues in Mentoring*, London: Routledge.

BINES, H. and WELTON, J.M. (eds) (1995) *Managing Partnerships in Teacher Training and Development*, London: Routledge.

CLARKE, K. (1992) 'Check against delivery', speech to the North of England Education conference, Southport, 4 January.

DES (1972) *Report of the Committee on Teacher Education and Training* ('The James Report'), London: HMSO.

DES (1983) *Teaching Quality* (Cmnd 8836), London: HMSO.

DES (1984) *Initial Teacher Training: Approval of Courses (Circular 3/84)*, London: DES.

DES (1992) *Reform of Initial Teacher Training: A Consultative Document*, London: DES.

DFE (1993a) *The Initial Training of Primary School Teachers: New Criteria for Course Approval* (draft circular), London: DFE.

DFE (1993b) *The Government's Proposals for the Reform of Initial Teacher Training*, London: DFE.

DfEE (1997a) *Excellence in Schools* (Cmnd 3691), London: HMSO.

DfEE (1997b) *Teaching: High Status, High Standards (Circular 10/97)*, London, DfEE.

DfEE (1997c) *Schools Teachers' Pay and Conditions of Employment 1997 (Circular 9/97)*, London: DfEE.

FURLONG, J. and SMITH, R. (eds) (1996) *The Role of Higher Education in Initial Teacher Training*, London: Kogan Page.

FURLONG, V.J., HIRST, P.H., POCKLINGTON, K. and MILES, S. (1988) *Initial Teacher Training and the Role of the School*, Milton Keynes: Open University Press.

GILROY, D.P. (1992) 'The political rape of initial teacher education: A JET rubuttal', *Journal of Education for Teaching*, **18**, 1, pp. 5–21.

GLENNY, G. and HICKLING, E. (1995) 'A developmental model of partnership between schools and higher education', in BINES, H. and WELTON, J.M. (eds) *Managing Partnerships in Teacher Training and Development*, London: Routledge.

HMI (1983) *Teaching in Schools: The Content of Initial Training. An HMI Discussion Paper*, London: DES.

HMI (1992) *School-based Initial Teacher Training in England and Wales: A Report by HM Inspectorate*, London: HMSO.

JONES, G.E.L. (1924) *The Training of Teachers in England and Wales*, Oxford: Clarendon Press.

NIAS, J. (1989) *Primary Teachers Talking: A Study of Teaching at Work*, London: Routledge.

OFSTED (1993) *Curriculum Organisation and Classroom Practice in Primary Schools: A Follow-up Report*, London: DFE.

TICKLE, L. (1987) *Learning Teaching, Teaching Teaching: A Study of Partnership in Teacher Education*, London: Falmer Press.

TIMES EDUCATIONAL SUPPLEMENT (1997) 'Prepare for the primary polymaths', *Times Educational Supplement*, 4 July, p. 20.

WHITAKER, J.W. (1992) 'Reform of initial teacher training' (letter accompanying DES *Reform of Initial Teacher Training: A Consultative Document*), London: DES.

2 The Teacher Training Agency, Higher Education and the Professionalism of Initial Teacher Educators

Kate Jacques

Teaching is the fundamental profession. There is no more important job that can be done in opening the understanding and appreciation of life for our people. (The late Labour party leader John Smith, speaking to pupils, staff, parents and governors at John Kitto Community College, Plymouth, shortly before his death.)

... we need a new professionalism. For this, we need a profession which has the confidence grounded in its indispensable place in society — without teaching there would be no other professions. We need a profession whose skilful practitioners are recognised and rewarded ... We need a profession that sees the quest for improvement as a never-ending task. And, above all, we need a profession which displays its willingness to embrace new ideas and its desire to seek perspectives from outside itself. (Anthea Millett, Chief Executive of the Teacher Training Agency, Annual Lecture, *Teaching: The Challenges Ahead*, December 1997.)

The Teacher Training Agency was formally established as a non-departmental public body on 21 September 1994. Its primary purpose, 'to improve the quality of teaching, raise the standards of teacher education and training and to promote teaching as a profession in order to improve the standards of pupils' achievement and the quality of their learning', is both ambitious and far reaching, but it unites teachers and teacher educators with the TTA. One 'central aim' is to promote teaching as a profession. In pursuit of this aim the TTA's first Corporate Plan established a number of objectives:

To establish a centrally controlled programme to promote teaching as a profession.

To encourage teachers to promote teaching as a profession.

To keep under review the image of teaching as a profession.

To encourage a diversity of routes into teaching in order to meet the varying needs of prospective teachers.

To establish strategies to help prevent teacher shortages. (TTA, 1995b)

In the four years of its existence the TTA has constantly referred to teaching as a profession and to teacher professionalism. It is important to assess the extent to which the TTA recognizes the significance of the concept and whether its pronouncements and policies have enhanced the professionalism of teachers and teacher educators. What is understood by 'professional' is complex because there is no one accepted interpretation. The term is employed formally and casually to convey different and subtle messages about occupational group membership, status, prestige, behaviour, attitude, reward and especially work practices. In relation to teaching the meaning of professionalism is evolving at a rapid pace. Here it is argued that inevitably a 'new professionalism' is replacing traditional definitions. This new conceptualization has to be bound with the new circumstances of teacher educators where the TTA is a major and powerful stakeholder. Teachers, teacher educators and the TTA will need to develop a spirit of cooperation and trust in identifying agreed standards and work practices to provide a professionalism which does improve standards and quality in schools.

The Struggle for Status

While there is no one single agreed definition of what is a professional, despite the extensive and diverse literature (Etzioni, 1964; Perkin, 1983; Downie, 1990; Eraut, 1994), it is possible to identify the six most frequently mentioned characteristics of an ideal type of professional.

(i)   A base of theoretical, esoteric knowledge which influences professional practice.

(ii)   A prolonged period of education and socialization to acquire the knowledge base.

(iii)   A desire to serve according to a clear code of ethics.

(iv)   Testing of competence.

(v)   Autonomy and self-regulation over recruitment, training and standards of practice.

(vi)   Disciplinary powers over the colleague group and powers to enforce a code of ethical practice, (Leggatt, 1970; Perkin, 1983).

The concept of teacher professionalism continues to be the focus of wide debate. It has been argued (Downie, 1990) that, when matched against the traditional professions of law and medicine, teachers and teacher educators emerge as semi-professionals, making progress towards full professionalization as their qualification base and conditions of service improve. Arguably the development of teaching as an all graduate profession, the local management of schools and the increased salary scales for senior managers have enhanced the professional status of teachers but not yet invoked autonomy or self-regulation.

In practice, progress has been uneven; there have been setbacks along the way. Teachers and teacher educators have a long history of struggle in which Government control, salary levels and their sheer numbers have contributed to constraining their feelings of professionalism and perceptions of their social status. They have had difficulty in articulating a distinctive body of knowledge, lacked autonomy or formal self-regulation and been subjected to continuous intervention by a number of Government agencies. Much greater emphasis is placed on 'common sense' knowledge and competence rather than specialist knowledge. Efficiency and value for money are put before professional values and the long processes of becoming qualified (Eraut, 1994). Government has intervened in the form of charters to protect citizens' rights and to ensure accountability of clients. For teachers, the introduction of the National Curriculum, supplemented recently by the literacy and numeracy strategies, have eroded those areas where, traditionally, teachers made decisions. Similarly in teacher education, Government intervention by Circular has contributed a centralizing tendency in the persistent tension between autonomy and control.

Tutors in universities and colleges have, over the years, enjoyed a relatively higher professional status than that of school teachers. Until relatively recently teacher educators shared in that enhanced professional status. Before 1984 they held significant control over the curriculum and assessment of teacher education and managed the education and training of teachers independently. Consequently and deliberately considerable diversity existed across the sector.

> It was possible for a student to receive a training in which the disciplines of education still featured prominently or a training in which the school was regarded as 'central' and in which curriculum courses took precedence over educational theory. (Wilkin, 1996, p. 135)

At the time choice and diversity were perceived to be a strength of the system and ironically contributing factors to the strengthening professionalism of teaching and teacher education.

Until the early 1980s teacher educators did well in terms of Leggatt's criteria for the ideal type of professional. Teacher educators appeared to have a large measure of professional freedom to determine the knowledge base of teacher education courses, inducting entrants into a specific department of education culture that their freedom and control made possible. However this was not to last.

Throughout the 1980s the work practices of all professionals was being questioned and none more so than state employed professionals A new managerial ideology challenged the accountability of these occupational groups and began to question assumptions about expertise, competence, efficiency and control. Doctors, teachers, social workers and civil servants all became the subject of scrutiny as publicly funded services were 'reinvented' (Osborne and Gaebler, 1992) The vocabulary of professionalism began to change to incorporate strong ideas about productivity, competition, value-for-money, efficiency, performance and success. Resistance to this 'reinvention' of professionalism was interpreted as the preservation of self-interest.

Though strongly defended, the freedom enjoyed by teacher educators was always vulnerable to political intervention. A publicly funded service has to satisfy the national interest and national objectives. The link between education and the economy and the belief that education was connected inexorably to the nation's well-being gave Government an interest in teacher education and legitimized its intervention. Public and political disquiet about standards in schools quickly moved on to include teacher education. In the absence of consistency and coherence across HEI providers of teacher education, much of the public debate was based more on myth than detailed knowledge but it made allegations of poor practice, in the context of the standards debate. The publication of *Circular 3/84* and the establishment of the Council for the Accreditation of Teacher Education (CATE) signalled the start of a regulatory regime designed to exercise greater control over teacher education, including the content of courses.

CATE activity in implementing a succession of Government circulars (4/84, 24/89, 9/92) had profound effects on teacher education. The amount of main subject study was defined, the time students spent on practical teaching was detailed and the content of education courses indicated, albeit in fairly broad terms. A precise number of hours were to be allocated to the preparation of students to teach English and mathematics. Teachers were increasingly expected to play a more prominent part in training. Initial teacher training firmly replaced initial teacher education as competences, or outcomes, provided the only acceptable evidence of whether a course was effective.

CATE had a limited remit and limited resources. It could do little other than check course details. It could prevent, but could not initiate or lead, change in teacher education. The standards debate would not relent and in the late 1980s the debate suggested a crisis and fuelled further doubts on teacher education (O'Hear, 1988; Hillgate Group, 1989; O'Keefe, 1990; Lawlor, 1990). More decisive Government intervention appeared inevitable. Enter the TTA.

The Teacher Training Agency

From the day of its inception the TTA has had an impact on teaching and teacher education. The task here is not to evaluate that impact but to consider the effect on the perceived professionalism of teacher educators. The sector has been transformed in ways not anticipated.

> Since its origin the TTA has generated a whirlwind of initiatives. These have impinged on every stage of teacher education and professional development . . . There is no aspect of the occupational and professional lives of teacher (educators) not affected by the Agency. Few question the dynamism and energy the TTA has brought to its activities. More concern has been expressed about the procedures through which these initiatives have been, and are being, established and implemented. (Mahony and Hextall, 1997, p. 270)

In order to achieve its overriding aim the TTA has to be active across all aspects of teacher education provision. To succeed it had to control, to lead, to reward and to punish. The threat to established professionalism posed by CATE pales into insignificance. The TTA undermines classical professionalism in a big way.

Professionals control their own destiny. The TTA controls the destinies of teacher educators. Teacher educators feel powerless, made worse by misgivings about the TTA's intentions regarding the future of HEIs in teacher education and training. The Government and the TTA have promoted a variety of routes into teaching, the most significant of these being school-centred initial teacher training (SCITT). SCITTs not only pose a local threat, taking schools out of HEI/schools partnerships, they represent a bigger danger that ultimately the future of teacher training will be entirely in schools. Both the Government and the TTA have given repeated assurances that HEIs have a place, but lack of specific detail about the significance or size of that place have only served to add to the suspicion that TTA policies have been designed to encourage HEI teacher education provision to wither away. Lack of control over events, inability to prevent what might be extinction, has given any debate about professionalism a hollow ring.

The unease remains but after four years the HEIs are still there, so that concern has abated somewhat. Nevertheless, after four years of TTA policy making, the professionalism debate has moved on. For the TTA the issue is about standards and quality of provision according to criteria set by the Secretary of State for Education.

Funding Teacher Education and Quality

The TTA's Chief Executive speaks of the need for a new professionalism. New professionalism is increasingly about accountability, meeting criteria, performance and competence. The use of the term initial teacher training is a small semantic issue for some; for years the terms 'teacher education' and 'teacher training' have been used interchangeably. For many in HEIs, however, the insistence on training represents a significant change of direction that undermines the distinctive body of knowledge that the profession possesses. Similarly, the term 'provider', used to refer to both HEI/schools partnerships and to SCITTS, emphasizes the diversity in provision and does not recognize the special place of HEIs within ITT. In a competitive system there are no automatic 'special' places.

In its 1995 Corporate Plan the TTA set out a range of new initiatives designed to manage the teacher education sector and make it overtly accountable to the Agency. A major initiative focuses on the allocation of student numbers and funding. The TTA declared its intention to

> develop a methodology for allocating student numbers and funding which rewards quality, promotes cost effectiveness and diversity and which reflects the key aim of the TTA to improve the quality of teaching and teacher training. (Corporate Plan, TTA, 1995b, p. 10)

Following a wide ranging consultation in which a number of options could be considered, there emerged a complex system of bidding to the TTA for student numbers over three years. Subsequently numbers are allocated to providers based on the principle of rewarding quality. Evidence from OFSTED inspections, together with further information and performance indicators determined by the TTA, result in a categorization of providers according to the quality of their provision. Different categories are allocated different bidding opportunities, with good quality providers having the opportunity to expand and poor quality provision facing the possibility of a nil allocation.

The impact of this strategy is considerable and has confirmed the extent to which the TTA has seized control of the sector. The formula applied to the bidding and allocation round means that the TTA, and to a lesser extent OFSTED, determines what is meant by quality and where expansion or reduction, or even ultimately closure, takes place. Student intake numbers are allocated for a three-year period but can be altered by recent inspection evidence or by revisions to the teacher supply calculations. For some HEIs the unexpected drop in numbers has serious consequences for their ability to deliver their full portfolio. For those HEIs rewarded with new courses and additional student numbers, the need to extend partnership arrangements, find new school mentors and more school places brings a different set of pressures. The effect overall is one of instability and unpredictability.

Any profession must have a quality standard but to sustain a claim to professional status that profession must have a major, even a determining, say on what constitutes quality. Peer review reconciles quality judgments and professional integrity. Peer review is practised throughout most of higher education, outside teacher education. DfEE Circulars, with their criteria, competences and standards, have removed providers from the quality debate. OFSTED makes its quality judgments solely on the basis of how well the Secretary of State's criteria are met. The new inspection framework (*Framework of the Assessment of Quality and Standards in Initial Teacher Training*, OFSTED/TTA, 1996, 1997), over which providers have had little influence, omits key areas teacher educators consider to be essential to strong and effective teacher education. The inspection process does not allow professional dialogue with inspectors about anything outside the framework criteria which itself is felt to erode professionalism.

Even though the sector dislikes the means, the outcome has resulted in a system which is public, open and understood. Winners and losers have been created where as previously, only players existed.

Accreditation of Teacher Education

One of the most serious actions that any professional body undertakes is the removal of a professional colleague from the approved list of practitioners. Self-regulation determines who is qualified to practise and what happens to those who fail to meet the high standards set. Teacher educators along with teachers have no overt mechanism for challenging under performing colleagues.

TTA policy on poor performance is clearly stated and unambiguous. OFSTED evidence demonstrating poor quality, non-compliance in terms of the requirements of *Circular 10/97*, brings with it the threat of the withdrawal of accreditation from the provider. Individuals are not punished but institutions are. The withdrawal of accreditation is a thorough and systematic process, and does allow for remedial action and reinspection. If a provider is unsuccessful at reinspection the effect is final and irreversible. Clearly, public money cannot be used to support poor provision, but there is no opportunity for the profession to be involved in the process. The result is the perception, and for some the experience, of a punitive system, which denies real professional dialogue by which flaws might be addressed, and which punishes alike those responsible for the poor quality and those whose own professional practice is perfectly satisfactory. Strong signals about collective professional responsibility for 'good practice' issue from the TTA.

The most unsurprising but professionally damaging effect of the introduction of this ultimate sanction is to inspire fear and some lack of integrity to the inspection process. It is not in the provider's interest to declare problems and concerns, or engage with inspectors in discussion of areas of sensitivity. There can be a cautiousness, a lack of openness and perhaps even a tendency to conceal, that offends professional dignity but are necessary for survival. A new professionalism might encourage collaboration in tackling issues of compliance.

The National Curriculum for Teacher Education and Training (Circular 10/97)

The introduction of a National Curriculum in each of the core subjects and in information communications technology (ICT) marks the TTA's most contentious policy initiative. It constitutes a fundamental challenge to the claim to special knowledge that lies at the heart of professional status.

Part of the TTA's remit is to advise the Secretary of State and others on matters concerning teacher education. DfEE *Circular 10/97* (*Teaching: High Status, High Standards*) represents the result of such advice and includes the initial teacher training National Curriculum for English (annex B) and mathematics (annex C). These will be followed by ITT national curricula for science and ICT. The Circular sets out new criteria which all teacher education courses must meet and specifies what English and mathematics *must* be taught to *all* trainees on *all* primary ITT courses. The criteria set out the standards of knowledge, understanding and skills which all trainees must demonstrate in order to complete a course of ITT and be eligible for qualified teacher status. New teachers cannot be admitted to the profession if they fail to meet the standards.

The consultation that preceded the publication of the new standards created considerable disquiet. Teacher educators expressed a number of major concerns. First, there was disagreement about the efficacy of the content and knowledge base in the English and mathematics curriculum. Second, there was concern about the tight timescale for the implementation of the new standards. Third, there were, and are, anxieties about the effects of the regulations on the rest of the ITE primary curriculum.

The extent to which the new standards are achieved are assessed during OFSTED inspections the results of which are reported to, and used by, the TTA. For its part the TTA has presented the new core subject and ICT requirements as rather modest. In her 1997 annual lecture the Chief Executive (Anthea Millett) explained that;

> In developing the new National Curriculum for initial teacher training we have sought to keep this to a genuine core, not to prescribe everything.

In practice, the dominant curriculum position occupied by the core subjects severely restricts the non-prescribed area of work. Also, the implementation of the standards on the one-year PGCE programme has created an overcrowded curriculum with little time for scholarship, only time to do and demonstrate competence.

Areas of the ITE curriculum considered essential by teacher educators have been eliminated and a reductionist curriculum of the bare essentials prevails.

Nevertheless what is signalled is the lack of trust in teacher educators to agree on what a basic literacy and numeracy curriculum should be. The new professionalism argues for a standardization and consistency which assures children of a basic entitlement and newly qualified teachers of an appreciation of that entitlement. The TTA has focused the teacher educators on basic skills deliberately.

Research into Teacher Education

Most TTA policy initiatives are characterized by clarity of purpose. The TTA policy regarding research in education is, by contrast, shrouded in ambiguity. There is little money to support research but what there is, is awarded to teachers to conduct research in schools. The TTA is committed to 'the investigation and dissemination of key features of classroom practice and training practice' (TTA, Corporate Plan, 1995). The TTA endorses the view 'that educational research should and could have much more relevance for, and impact on, the professional practice of teachers than it now has' (Hargreaves, 1996). The TTA supports teaching as a research-based profession but is not clear how this is to be achieved. School teachers are able to apply for funding for various research projects; a recent one focuses on support for newly qualified teachers. HEI providers may be involved in the research but cannot lead it or deploy the resources allocated to undertake it.

The TTA appears to distrust HEI-led research. This may be due, at least in part, to the belief that researchers in higher education produce jargon-laden, qualitative research of dubious reliability, validity and relevance; impenetrable and inaccessible to teachers (Hargreaves, 1995). There have been complaints also that theories about teaching and learning are ideologically driven rather than evidence based (McIntyre, 1997). However, in failing to recognize the professional research skills that can be found in higher education, the TTA is in danger of failing to provide an adequate research base for the improvements that it wants to see in teacher education and in schools.

If higher education was involved more, it is probable that the TTA would meet with limited collaboration. Researchers located in higher education may prefer to turn to their own, established, funding bodies but keep the TTA at a distance. There is a distrust of research contracts designed to support Government or TTA policy and a suspicion that the TTA prefers 'common sense' solutions to the evidence of research (Reid, 1994). However, if research is going to be employed to contribute to a body of evidence which can help to explain what constitutes successful teaching and learning, the TTA will have to recognise the professionalism of higher education-based researchers and include them more directly in leading the research that it is able to fund.

Conclusion

This chapter has explored professionalism in teacher education. At the start attention was drawn to the TTA's intention to promote teaching as a profession. In all areas discussed power and control exercised by HEIs have been eroded, and have been replaced by mechanisms designed to make providers more accountable, more conforming, more transparent and more open to challenge. Despite this deliberate strategy to undermine the autonomy of HEIs, changes have taken place rapidly. Providers felt, and continue to feel, threatened, insecure and unsure of the real policy agenda. But what has been achieved in moving teacher education forward and modernizing the sector has been done because many providers themselves knew what the issues were and, even before the foundation of the TTA, were beginning to deal with them. For example priorities in training and education were misjudged:

> Increasingly it was clear that the understanding about teaching expertise which underlay that system was misguided; theory had been wrongly privileged over practice and necessary tensions between theory and practice ignored; teachers' practical expertise had not only been neglected but had wrongly been assumed to be transparently accessible . . . (McIntyre, 1997)

The higher education ITT sector was in the process of reassessing its practices and recognizing that changes were necessary. Prior to the TTA initiatives many HEIs were forming successful partnerships with schools and were involving teachers in the delivery of courses and the assessment of students. From the perspective of Government and its policy agenda progress was too slow and uneven across the sector.

Teacher educator providers have felt uncomfortable with the increases in control and direction and compromised by the tone and manner in which the TTA has gone about its business. The frequency of OFSTED inspections and the punitive nature of the TTA's use of inspection evidence has generated hostility but not lack of cooperation. At each stage teacher educators have responded because despite the uncomfortable relationship the profession of teacher educators endorse the work on the ground and there is considerable optimism about the role of teacher education as a change agent in schools. A new professionalism is emerging which, while different, corresponds to some extent with the professional characteristics of Leggatt and Perkin as detailed on page 15. It develops thus:

(i)   A new body of knowledge is growing around mentorship and school-based teacher education;

(ii) Recruits to teaching prefer extended training in higher education, SCITTS and other schemes outside higher education have not flourished and show little sign of doing so.

(iii) Recruits to teaching and in teacher education remain largely driven by a strong desire to serve the community and to do well by children and students. Altruism remains a firm feature of its professionalism along with a strong ethical view on education.

(iv) The testing of competence is much harder edged, endorsed by the profession, and now a central feature of all courses.

(v)   Autonomy and self-regulation over recruitment, training and standards of practice have been taken over by the TTA and will be supported by HEIs largely because such a large system demands it.

(vi) Finally disciplinary powers over the colleague group are not in place but teacher educators are more informed in their selection and appointment procedures.

Old definitions of teacher education have to be reconceptualized. What is encouraging is that the TTA have here injected new life and refreshment into a system suffering from extensive internal tension. What needs to be kept in focus is what the TTA is trying to do and what HEIs are trying to do. The TTA, however, could reflect on the concept of professionalism and its operational relationship with teacher education. Much is to be gained from a dialogue of respect, of trust and professional collaboration from both sides of the equation. The spirit of cohesion might profitably be replaced by a spirit of cooperation.

References

ADAMS, A. and TULASIEWICZ, W. (1995) *The Crisis in Teacher Education: A European Concern?*, London: Falmer Press.

APPLE, M.W. (1996) *Cultural Politics and Education*, Milton Keynes: Open University Press.

BINES, H. and WELTON, M. (eds) (1995) *Managing Partnership in Teacher Training and Development*, London: Routledge.

DfEE (1997) *Teaching: High Status, High Standards*, London: DfEE.

DOWNIE, R.S. (1990) 'Professions and professionalism', *Journal of Philosophy of Education*, **24**, 2.

ERAUT, M. (1994) *Developing Professional Knowledge and Competence*, London: Falmer Press.

ETZIONI, A. (1964) *Modern Organisations*, New York: Prentice Hall.

GILROY, P. and WILCOX, B. (1997) 'OFSTED criteria and the nature of social understanding: A Wittgensteinian critique of the practice of educational judgement', *British Journal of Educational Studies*, **45**, 1, pp. 22–39.

GRAHAM, J. (1997) *Initial Teacher Education: TTA/OFSTED Framework, Occasional Paper no 9*, London: UCET.

HALPIN, D. and TROYNA, B. (eds) (1994) *Researching Education Policy: Ethical and Methodological Issues*, London: Falmer Press.

HARGREAVES, D.H. (1996) 'Teaching as a research-based profession: Prospects and possibilities', *British Educational Research Journal*, **23**, pp. 141–61.

HILLGATE GROUP (1989) *Learning to Teach*, London: Claridge Press.

LAWLOR, S. (1990) *Teachers Mistaught*, London: Centre for Policy Studies.

LEGGATT, T. (1970) 'Teaching as a profession', in JACKSON, J.A. (ed) *Professions and Professionalisation*, London: Cambridge University Press.

MAHONY, P. and HEXTALL, I. (1997) 'Problems of accountability in reinvented governments: A case study of the Teacher Training Agency', *Journal of Education Policy*, **12**, 4, pp. 267–83.

McINTYRE, D. (1997) 'A Research Agenda for Initial Teacher Education', in McINTRYRE, D. (ed) *Teacher Education Research in a New Context*, London: Paul Chapman Publishing.

McINTYRE, G. (1991) *Accreditation of Teacher Education: The Story of CATE 1984–1989*, London: Falmer Press.

MILLETT, A. (1997) 'Teaching: the challenges ahead', Chief Executive's annual lecture, London: TTA.

O'HEAR, A. (1988) *Who Teaches the Teachers?*, London: Social Affairs Units.

O'KEEFE, D. (1990) *The Wayward Elite: A Critique of British Teacher Education*, London: Adam Smith Institute.

OSBORNE, A. and GAEBLER, T. (1992) *Reinventing Government: How the Entrepreneurial Spirit is Transforming the Public Sector*, Reading, MA: Addison Wesley.

PERKIN, H. (1983) 'The Teaching Profession and the Game of Life', in GORDON, P. (ed) 'Is teaching a profession', Bedfordway Papers 15) London Institute of Education, University of London.

REID, I., CONSTABLE, H. and GRIFFITHS, R. (eds) (1994) *Teacher Education Reform: Current Research*, London: Paul Chapman Publishing.

TAYLOR, P. and MILLER, S. (1996) *The Primary Professional, A Study of Professionalism in Primary Education*, London: Educational Partners.

TAYLOR, W. (1994) 'Teacher education: Backstage to centre stage', in BECHER, T. (ed) *Government and Professional Education*, London: SRHE.

TEACHER TRAINING AGENCY (1995a) *Conduct of the Teacher Training Agency's Business*, London: TTA.

TEACHER TRAINING AGENCY (1995b) *Corporate Plan Promoting High Quality Teaching and Teacher Education*, London: TTA.

TEACHER TRAINING AGENCY (1996) *Corporate Plan*, London: TTA.

WILKIN, M. (1996) *Initial Teacher Training: The Dialogue of Ideology and Culture*, London: Falmer Press.

3   Primary Teaching: High Status?
High Standards?
A Personal Response to Recent Initiatives

Colin Richards

Wonderland?

'When we were little' the Mock Turtle went on at last, more calmly, though sobbing a little now and then, 'we went to school in the sea' . . .
'I only took the regular course.'
'What was that?' inquired Alice.
'Reeling and Writhing, of course, to begin with' the Mock Turtle replied, 'and then the different branches of Arithmetic — Ambition, Distraction, Uglification and Derision'. (Carroll, 1995, pp. 93–94)

These have been, and remain, major components of the core curriculum for initial teacher education (ITE) and for primary education both for some years before, and now after, the publication of the 1997 White Paper, *Excellence in Schools*, and of *Circular 10/97, Teaching: High Status, High Standards*. Uglification and derision have characterized public pronouncements of both sectors, particularly before and, to some extent after, the 1997 General Election. Though not based on even reasonably conclusive evidence criticisms of English primary schools for failing to teach 'basic skills' effectively have also been used to castigate training institutions. Tellingly, the TTA's announcement in 1996 of its determination to move towards a National Curriculum for Initial Teacher Training took place in the context of a critical (and later much criticized) OFSTED inspection report on the teaching of reading in three inner London LEAs (1996) which badly misrepresented progress, performance and practice in the schools (Mortimore and Goldstein, 1996; Richards, 1997). Practice in primary ITE is not, of course, without its shortcomings but, to quote the findings of OFSTED's primary sweep, when grudgingly published, 'standards have been found to be mostly sound or good' — an overall judgment that could be made of primary education more generally.

Why then a process of uglification? Almost certainly, part of the answer lies in ambition on the part of individuals, either personal ambition to be leading players or institutional ambition to ensure that their organizations are positioned to play robust parts in the 'driving up' of standards both in schools and in ITE.

The result is reeling and writhing on a massive scale in both in schools and higher education institutions. In the latter staff are reeling with having to meet the insatiable appetite for data from a TTA bureaucracy trying desperately to understand and to regulate the teacher education sector. Even more than their colleagues in school they are reeling with the pressures of almost continuous inspection — a massive distraction, for the most part, from their commitment to improving the quality of initial teacher preparation. Preparation for inspection, the long drawn-out inspection process itself, and coping with the aftermath are all taking tolls — on staff morale, on preparation time for teaching (whatever happened to research?) and on links with schools and mentors — as well as on rainforests, printers and printing ink. The 'high status' nature of inspections with personal and institutional futures at stake results in acute mental discomfort (one definition of 'writhing'), a resignation to play the game by OFSTED's rules (while often being uncertain about their changing nature), an unwillingness to express public dissent from a deeply flawed and unfair inspection regime, and a determination to hide from inspectors, both HMI and attached inspectors, problems and difficulties which a more sensitive, less punitive, inspection and advisory system might help resolve. Similar issues arise in relation to school inspections.

Rhetoric

The picture painted above (some might say in garish colours!) draws parallels between the current predicament of primary ITE and of primary education itself. This paper attempts to draw further parallels — occasioned by the publication of the Education White Paper, *Excellence in Schools* (DfEE, 1997a), and *Circular 10/97 Teaching: High Status, High Standards* (DfEE, 1997b). Both these documents are intended to improve the quality of education and to raise both standards and the status of teachers but both need to have their assumptions analysed, their language contested and their proposals critiqued. This chapter focuses on the first two of these; other contributions to the book provide a constructive but critical commentary on the proposals.

At one level those involved in initial teacher preparation are not in dispute with the Government, the DfEE or the TTA. There is virtually universal support for the Government's 'determination to raise standards across the education system and to ensure that all pupils have access to the high quality teaching they deserve' (DfEE, 1997b, p. 3). There is widespread support too for the need to give priority to primary education and to raising standards of literacy and numeracy. Similarly, those involved in initial teacher preparation would agree that 'to raise the standards we expect of schools and teachers, we must raise the standards we expect of new teachers' (ibid). But such statements are rhetorical and such support is rhetorical. Such propositions are the educational equivalent of virtue, motherhood and apple pie. Would anyone seriously advocate their opposites: vice, matricide and food-poisoning? Policy for both primary and teacher education needs to be built on a firmer foundation than rhetoric; this chapter contends that there are fundamental problems with some of the assumptions on which policy is being based.

Assumptions

Unsatisfactory Standards

The first major assumption is that 'standards' in both primary and teacher education are unsatisfactory in a very significant proportion of institutions. In relation to primary schools that assumption was made explicit some years ago in HMCI's Annual Report for 1994/95 where it was stated that 'it is evident that overall standards of pupil achievement need to be raised in about half of primary schools' (OFSTED, 1996, p. 8), despite the report's highly economical use of registered inspectors' judgments and its very dubious interpretation of its own rating scale (Richards, 1997). The criticism, though more muted, continued in the next Annual Report: 'About two-fifths of the schools have some strengths but they also have weaknesses that hamper the achievement of higher standards . . . Overall standards are judged to be poor in about one in 12 schools in Key Stage 1 and one in six in Key Stage 2. Standards in these schools need to be substantially improved' (OFSTED, 1997, p. 11). This down-beat assessment of primary standards is the implicit back-cloth for the 1997 White Paper's assertion that 'Excellence at the top is not matched by high standards for the majority of children' who are judged to be 'not achieving their potential' (p. 10). The assumption is one of considerable underperformance by schools.

In relation to teacher education OFSTED's overall assessments have been rather more positive, though still guarded, as in the 1994/95 report which claimed that 'Early indications are that the training of students to teach mathematics and English and to conduct assessment and recording in primary schools is sound in the majority of HEIs and that it is often good. In a significant minority of cases, however, there are shortcomings related to students' competences in school' (OFSTED, 1996, p. 62). In the report no indication is given as to what 'the majority' means (51%, 99%?) or how large the 'significant minority' might be (5%, 49%?). The following Annual Report implicates teacher education in the moral panic over standards in numeracy and literacy — 'serious concerns continue to be expressed about standards of numeracy and literacy, and, indeed, about how well students are trained' (OFSTED, 1997, p. 7). This overt criticism becomes more muted and indirect in the 1997 White Paper but is presupposed by the claims that 'we must raise the standards we expect of new teachers' and that 'improving the skills of our new teachers in these areas is critical to achieving our numeracy and literacy targets' (ibid, p. 47).

In relation to primary schools how can such a derisory, negative picture be reconciled with other evidence (not made publicly available by OFSTED) that in 1995/96

- standards of achievement were judged satisfactory or better in 95% of sessions in nursery schools and classes and in 93% of reception classes;
- in Key Stage 1 standards were satisfactory or better in 87% of lessons;

- in Key Stage 2 standards were satisfactory in 83% of lessons;
- the quality of teaching was good or very good in 41% of lessons and satisfactory or better in 83%?

Such figures (and others could be quoted) give no cause for complacency but nor do they suggest that standards in 'a significant minority' of primary schools give serious cause for concern.

OFSTED has not published or made available any comparable data on standards or the quality of teaching in teacher education despite its extensive database supposedly open to interrogation by the research community. Instead it prefers to damn by faint praise and use of innuendo, as in the much delayed report of the primary sweep which did its best to put on a sad (as opposed to a brave) face on undoubted achievements in the laconic words 'standards have been found to be mostly sound or good. There was some very good quality work as well as some clear weaknesses' (OFSTED, 1996) Tellingly, no data was published on the quality of the 'training' observed. Judging from UCET's reanalysis of institutional inspection reports this would certainly have yielded evidence of high standards of teaching, even in the areas of literacy and numeracy where HMCI had reported 'serious concerns'.

It is crucially important for the future of the teacher education community that it persuades the Government in its 'new spirit of openness' to pressurize OFSTED into releasing the aggregate data from the Primary Follow-Up survey so that the data can be debated and its significance (and weaknesses) assessed rather than the sector having only to rely on, and react to, OFSTED's or the TTA's summary interpretation of what the data reveal.

Unfavourable International Comparisons

A second assumption is that standards of attainment in English primary schools compare unfavourably with those in our 'competitor' countries and that inevitably initial teacher education is implicated in that relative failure. This general overall assumption is made explicit in relation to numeracy and literacy in the White Paper:

- too many children have poor literacy and numeracy skills;
- we have fallen behind many other developed countries in numeracy;
- our performance in literacy is behind a number of comparable English-speaking countries. (DfEE, 1997a, p. 19)

Putting aside the enormous methodological problems surrounding comparative studies of educational achievement well summarized by Reynolds and Farrell (1996), it needs to be stressed that there have been no such studies conducted for most areas of the primary curriculum — history, geography, design technology, information technology, art, music, physical education or religious education. For English there has been only one study involving English primary-aged pupils — in written composition conducted in 1984/85 — but subject to severe methodological problems which render its findings highly suspect. Over the last quarter of a century no international surveys of reading attainment at primary level involving English pupils have been undertaken. It is impossible to see how research findings can possibly support at primary level the claim in the third indent above.

Two studies conducted in the 1990s into children's achievement in mathematics have received considerable attention in the media, have underpinned the criticisms in the White Paper and have contributed, more indirectly, to the decision to introduce the National Curriculum for Primary Initial Teacher Training (NC for Primary ITT). Both Foxman (1992) and TIMMS (Keys, 1997) focus on the performance of 9-year-olds (note only that age group) and both reveal overall lower than average performance compared with most other Western European countries as well as states such Taiwan and Korea. However, as Keys (1997) points out in relation to TIMMS, this lower than average performance characterized some areas of mathematics such as number operations but not others — '9-year-olds in England, together with those in Australia and Hong Kong came "top" in geometry and . . . scored above the international mean score on data representation and analysis' (p. 20). Interestingly, other comparative data. published in 1997 showed English 13-year-old pupils scoring well above average in the application of number to everyday problems. English pupils may be less proficient at number operations than their counterparts in many countries but they appear to be far better at applying their knowledge in real-life contexts! Are these findings sufficient to fuel the moral panic behind the proposed numeracy strategy and the detailed requirements of the NC for Primary ITT?

Such reservations are given extra force by the results of two similar surveys (Foxman, 1992) and TIMMS (Keys, 1997) also carried out in the 1990s into 9-year-olds performance in science which showed well above average results despite the tests focusing on scientific knowledge and understanding rather than scientific investigation, a major emphasis of the English primary science curriculum. Why then the necessity for a very detailed prescriptive NC for ITT in primary science? Shouldn't initial teacher education be implicated in the success, rather than in the failure, of primary science?

Or is the assumption of the comparative failure of English primary and teacher education too deeply embedded in the collective psychology of the DfEE, OFSTED and the TTA?

Unexamined Language

The language of the White Paper, of *Circular 10/97* and of the TTA is instructive in uncovering further, contestable assumptions about the purpose of primary (and thus teacher) education and about the nature of teaching.

In relation to what it calls 'the foundations of learning' the White Paper is clear and unequivocal:

Investment in learning in the 21st century is the equivalent of investment in the machinery and technical innovation that was essential to the first great industrial revolution. Then it was physical capital; now it is human capital. We need to build up the store of knowledge and keep abreast of rapid technological development if we are to prepare the future generation. Our children are our future as a civilised society and a prosperous nation. If they are to have an education that matches the best in the world, we must start now to lay the foundations, by getting integrated early years education and childcare, and primary education, right.

Note the language of economics — of 'investment', 'technical innovation', 'capital', 'store of knowledge', 'technological development', 'prosperous nation'. Why these particular guiding metaphors? Why the emphasis on an economic rather than a personal or cultural calculus? The importance of primary education to the economy is at best indirect and partial (despite supposed evidence from competitor countries) so why emphasize the economic dimension at the expense of others? The assumptions behind the use of such language need debating by the education community, though such issues form no part of the TTA's *training* curriculum and are unlikely to be debated by students preparing to be teachers.

Indeed the TTA shares a similar language and similar assumptions — drawn in particular from mechanics, 'the science of machinery' which is put to work for economic ends. Note the technical/mechanical nature of the language used by the TTA's Chief Executive, tellingly taken from an article entitled 'Bringing a new professionalism (*sic*) into teaching':

> We cannot *unlock* teachers' potential if we do not *equip* them, as part of their initial *training*, with the *toolbox* of *skills* they need to be *effective*. At the moment there is a danger that some new teachers may never even find out what *tools* are supposed to be in the *toolbox*, let alone acquire the *skills* to use them effectively. (my italics) (Millett, 1997, p. 12)

Do the ideas of primary education as primarily economic investment and initial teacher preparation as essentially skilling-up technicians or mechanics do justice to the nature of both primary and teacher education as many practitioners conceive them? Is teaching *simply* (sic) a straightforward if complicated technical activity concerned with delivering a pre-planned curriculum with clearly defined, agreed targets rather than with the making of complex, contestable judgments and undertaking intelligent action in the complex ecology of classroom and school to foster that most intangible of outcomes — children's learning? Are there ethical, interpersonal, intellectual and cultural dimensions untouched by the use of 'economic' language? Shouldn't these dimensions also feature in any defensible NC for primary ITT?

Best Practice?

Another instructive aspect of the 1997 White Paper (DfEE, 1997a) is its frequent reference to 'good' or 'best' practice. Ironically the phrase has been resurrected by central Government and its agencies at the very time when its long-standing use in primary education has been successfully (and justifiably) challenged. In relation to teaching methods the White Paper intones:

> We must make sure that all teachers understand the *best* methods of teaching and know how to use them. (p. 9)

> All primary teachers need to know how to teach reading in line with *proven best* practice. (p. 19)

In terms of the curriculum

> A good education . . . offers opportunities to gain insight into the *best* that has been thought and said and done.

In terms of partnerships

> We shall seek to strengthen existing partnerships between schools and higher education to ensure that teacher training is firmly rooted in the *best* classroom practice. (p. 47) (my italics)

And so on.

But 'best' for what? 'Best' or 'good' in respect of which set of values? 'Best' in terms of what conception of education? What is 'best' or 'good' involves value judgments, not factual generalizations; it is inevitably and inherently contestable; it cannot simply be asserted as self-evident without justification. The use of 'best' or 'good' practice in the White Paper implies a straightforward, value-free view of education, presumably based on the 'common sense' view of the Government and its agencies. Dissent from this view or challenge to what is construed as 'best' seems to be construed by central agencies such as the TTA and the DfEE as resistance based on professional self-interest, rather than as reasoned opposition based on a rather different set of values or conceptions of what primary and teacher education are about.

Proven Research?

Unlike its predecessor which placed almost no reliance on educational research, the new Government seems far too wedded to its supposed benefits. The honeymoon with school improvement research (and its leading proponents) may not last long but at present at least the DfEE, the Standards and Effectiveness Unit and, to a lesser extent, the TTA seem to assume that the keys to educational improvement are value-free (see previous section), clear and 'proven' through research. Notions such as 'proven best practice' are used to make claims which most educational researchers would disavow. There is no hint in the official literature that research findings are at best suggestive, are never definitive, and are valuable, not as blue-prints to effective practice, but as sources of useful insights and possible lines of enquiry or practice to pursue. The notion of research or inspection providing clear 'proven' answers ties in with a technicist approach to teaching — research as a kind of applied pedagogic mechanics establishing 'what works' and what does not. It is naive to believe that research, in particular school improvement research, is value free and that it provides ready-made transferable solutions to educational problems, whether in primary education or teacher education.

Hard Times?

This chapter has attempted a critique of some of the assumptions underlying recent 'official' pronouncements about primary education and teacher education. Though in *Circular 10/97* the notion of 'competence' (with its utilitarian, down-beat overtones) has been replaced by that of 'standard' (with its qualitative, up-beat overtones) the notion of teaching as a value-free if complicated technical activity remains the dominant assumption. With its embodiment in the standards required for qualified teacher status it represents, not the reprofessionalization, but the *de* professional-ization, of teaching. Official views are informed by a Victorian model of training concerned with 'turning out' technicians, rather than embryonic professionals.

This chapter began with a quotation from a Victorian classic, *Alice in Wonder-land*. It ends in *Hard Times* with Dickens' description of the *training* received by Mr Choakumchild, close in basic intent and, amazingly close in terms of some of its English content, to that expected of current (note the term) 'trainees':

> He and some 140 other school masters had been turned out at the same time, in the same factory, like so many pianoforte legs. He had been put through an immense variety of paces, and had answered volumes of head-breaking questions. Ortho-graphy, etymology, syntax and prosody, biography, astronomy, geography and general cosmology, the sciences of compound proportion, algebra, land-surveying and levelling, vocal music, and drawing from models were all at the ends of his 10 chilled fingers. He had worked his stony way into Her Majesty's most Honourable Privy Council's Schedule B, and had taken the bloom off the higher branches of mathematics and physical science, French, German, Latin and Greek. He knew all about the Water Sheds of all the world (whatever they are) and all the histories of all the peoples, and all the names of all the rivers and mountains, and the produc-tions, manners and customs of all the countries, and all their boundaries and bearings on the two-and-thirty points of the compass.

Very tellingly, (prescient of the current obsession with 'subject knowledge'?) he concludes:

> If he had only learnt a little less, how infinitely better he might have taught much more! (Dickens, 1994, p. 7)

References

CARROLL, L. (1995) *The Penguin Selected Works of Lewis Carroll*, London: Claremont Books.

DEPARTMENT FOR EDUCATION AND EMPLOYMENT (DfEE) (1997a) *Excellence in Schools*, London: HMSO.

DEPARTMENT FOR EDUCATION AND EMPLOYMENT (DfEE) (1997b) *Teaching: High Status, High Standards (Circular 10/97)*, London: HMSO.

DICKENS, C. (1994) *Hard Times*, London: Penguin Books.

FOXMAN, D. (1992) *Learning Mathematics and Science (The Second International Assessment of Educational Progress in England)*, Slough: National Foundation for Educational Research.

KEYS, W. (1997) 'Behind the headlines: What do the results of TIMMS really tell us?', *Education Journal*, September.

MILLETT, A. (1997) 'Bringing a new professionalism into teaching', *Education Journal*, March.

MORTIMORE, P. and GOLDSTEIN, H. (1996) *The Teaching of Reading in 45 Inner London Primary Schools; A Critical Examination of OFSTED Research*, London: University of London Institute of Education.

OFSTED (1996) *The Annual Report of Her Majesty's Chief Inspector of Schools: Standards and Quality in Education 1994/95*, London: HMSO.

OFSTED (1997) *The Annual Report of Her Majesty's Chief Inspector of Schools: Standards and Quality 1995/96*, London: HMSO.

REYNOLDS, D. and FARRELL, S. (1996) *Worlds Apart? A Review of International Surveys of Educational Achievement involving England*, London: HMSO.

RICHARDS, C. (1997) *Primary Education, Standards and OFSTED: Towards a More Authentic Conversation*, Occasional Paper, Centre for Research into Elementary and Primary Education, University of Warwick.

Part 2

A New National Curriculum for Primary Initial Teacher Education

4   Circular 10/97: Its Context and Implications for Course Design and Development

Jack Hogbin and Karen Jarmany

Provision in Context

Following the 1944 Education Act there were fundamentally two routes to becoming a qualified teacher: the first was to gain a degree (not necessarily followed by a one-year PGCE course) and the second was to follow a two-year teachers' certificate course. A shorter emergency training scheme for those who served in the armed forces was established; while many sound teachers with much experience were trained, the scheme was discontinued in 1951 and the two major routes remained. Teachers with degrees taught mostly in grammar schools or independent schools; those with teachers' certificates (following the old elementary school tradition) taught in primary or secondary modern schools. The teachers' certificate was regarded by many as a second class qualification. Two significant moves were made to change this position: firstly, the BEd degree was introduced, initially, as a one-year top-up for a three-year certificate course but eventually becoming a coherent four-year course; secondly, the PGCE was made compulsory for all graduates entering as teachers into all state schools. The principle of an all graduate profession was widely endorsed. The work of the CNAA contributed to the widening of provision of the BEd degree and the PGCE, beyond the traditional universities. In more recent years, the pattern of provision has widened further to include a relatively small number of two-year BEd degree and PGCE courses and most recently the Teacher Training Agency has introduced a Graduate Teacher Scheme and a Registered Teacher Scheme.

Provision since 1944 has taken place largely in universities (including the Open University) and colleges, formerly teacher training colleges, now more commonly called (university) colleges of higher education. Throughout the period there have been tensions between teacher supply on the one hand and the quality of provision on the other. For many years the development of the BEd degree and the PGCE took place in the context of a need to increase teacher supply; however, in the 1970s major contraction of teacher education took place. While a shortage in certain secondary subjects has persisted, and still persists, the prediction of supply needs has been notoriously unreliable. The issue remains a lively one, with the recent report of the House of Commons Select Committee (1997) offering a detailed investigation of the subject. Their conclusions continue well established themes:

- a welcome to the Government's commitment to raising standards in schools;
- the need to ensure sufficient numbers of able, motivated teachers in post;
- the need for an adequate number of high-calibre people to train as teachers each year;
- a belief that the Government must act to prevent serious shortages worsening.

While the recruitment to BEd courses is currently holding up, there are signs that this situation may well not continue. It is widely recognized that teacher supply does relate to patterns of economic prosperity. Nevertheless this favourable position is balanced by concerns for financial stringency. The present issue of the funding of students and the introduction of fees may have a significant effect. In particular, the exemption from fee paying of postgraduate (PGCE students) but not at present undergraduate BEd/BA (QTS) students marks a significant priority. While Government statements refer to a shortage of funds as an explanation, the discrimination against the undergraduate route may have less obvious and more sinister implications — this may well relate not only to the length of BEd or BA (QTS) courses of three or four years, but to the priority of postgraduate over undergraduate courses as a favoured model.

The length of the vast majority of PGCE courses (one-year) makes them readily adaptable in terms of increasing or decreasing teacher supply. However, other significant factors arise. A key question to be faced is whether both routes offer outcomes of comparable quality in terms of the level of professional competence achieved by students who complete them. In general, given the different starting points in terms of age, experience and academic knowledge/skills of entrants to the two routes, many in teacher education would regard the standards of achievement as broadly comparable. There have, however, been those who have been critical of the BEd degree as offering an inferior product or as not giving good value for money. The numbers entering the PGCE primary courses have, however, been encouraged to grow steadily over recent years.

In theory *Circular 10/97* (DfEE, 1997) is intended to embody the standards of achievement that apply to all courses of initial teacher education. In this sense it should offer a guarantee that whatever route is chosen by a student, a minimum or threshold level of competence has been achieved by all those who are successful. This is marked by the award of qualified teacher status (which is separate from any academic award which is given). Currently, an induction year after completion of the training course is being introduced (following the abolition of the old probationary year in 1991). As Chapter 18 points out, it is currently a matter of discussion as to whether or how QTS might be awarded (or confirmed) at the end of the induction year. While the standards relate directly to the award of QTS and the parallel inspection document (the Quality and Standards Framework, 1997) relates to initial teacher education, the extension of the award of QTS to the end of the induction year, could significantly affect the overall content and pattern of provision in the courses which lead to the award. Much would depend upon the role that higher education providers would exercise in the induction year and which course elements are identified for location within that year. The principle of the full involvement of higher education in the initial education and training of teachers has been most recently endorsed by the Sutherland Report and by the professional associations, following concerns that the fundamental link between them, including the principle of the all graduate profession, has been under threat. While at the level of structural provision this threat may have receded for the time being (for example, those entering the registered teacher scheme must be reading for a degree and successfully complete the undergraduate course) nevertheless, comparability of standards depends also on consistency in their assessment. In this respect, the involvement of experienced higher education tutors in the assessment process is a key requirement.

Standards in Context

Whatever the issues concerning teacher supply or the pattern of course provision and their interactions, the matter of standards is a substantive 'concern' that needs to be analysed separately. It was in 1976 that James Callaghan initiated what was called 'the Great Debate'. Some key issues were raised at that time which continue to be of importance in terms of the current Circular and its implementation. Callaghan and others regarded 'subjects' as fundamental to education; they also considered that knowledge needs to include basic literacy, numeracy and understanding of scientific and technological areas; 'progressive teaching methods' were thought to have failed and teacher educators were thought to be too far removed from the classroom. These concerns later resulted not only in the introduction of a National Curriculum, following the 1988 Education Reform Act (with three core and six/ seven other foundation subjects and a sharp focus on assessment), but fundamental changes in the provision of teacher education.

DES *Circular 3/84* represented the Government's direct intervention into teacher education by the establishment of the Council for the Accreditation of Teacher Education (CATE). The introduction of CATE was to ensure higher standards and control diversity. The different Secretaries of State for Education have, via the work of CATE and various circulars, (previously 3/84, 24/89, 14/93 and now 10/97) sought to establish requirements for courses and criteria for the award of QTS. Validation (the academic process) and accreditation (the CATE process) were clearly distinguished. In principle, this distinction, if placed as a central issue, had the potential (and still has) to drive a wedge between academic and professional achievement. The dilemma manifests itself, as we shall see, in the nature of *Circular 10/97* and its implementation. The professional dimension came to reflect the development (some years after CATE) of the National Curriculum, following the 1988 Education Reform Act. There has not been in the past, and nor is there at present, any principled articulation of the relationship between the Secretary of State's 'requirements and standards' for teacher education and the National Curriculum. While consideration of the National Curriculum for 2000 and beyond is under current consideration, no public structures exist for the pattern and nature of that interrelationship to be considered, despite the fact that providers are currently educating teachers for the millennium and beyond. It seems likely that hasty, ill considered and last minute demands could once again be placed upon teacher education when decisions are reached. A key issue already emerging is the balance of the National Curriculum and the consequences for the provision of courses, including the implementation of *Circular 10/97*.

Curriculum Balance: Its Implications

James Callaghan identified the importance of English, mathematics and science and these were later accorded core subject status in the National Curriculum and in *Circular 14/93* the time to be allocated to each of them on the recommendation of CATE increased from 100 to 150 hours. *Circular 10/97* has removed the time requirement. Moreover, the Circular describes standards as the minimum required and points out that other content may be added. However, the descriptions of the content required (reinforced by the rigour of the inspections that are part of the Primary Follow-Up Survey) are extensive and extremely detailed. Moreover, as Richards, Harling and Webb (1997) argue they do not represent a balanced or coherent programme for ITE in either mathematics or English (science is at the time of writing yet to be published). Hence, the removal of the time requirement is itself irrelevant given the scale and detail of what is required. This difficult situation is made more problematic by the developments in schools arising from the national projects in literacy and numeracy, including such expectations as the literacy and numeracy hours. A further complication is the increasing importance of information and communication technology (ICT) which has within *Circular 10/97* what TTA officers have called 'a marker for standards' ie level 8 of the National Curriculum. As Chapter 9 points out, it is not yet clear just what this will entail for meeting the standard set but informal indications are that the detail is extensive in terms of personal skills and professional applications. Given this situation, despite the claimed pruning of the National Curriculum (Dearing, 1993), it raises questions about the balance of time and requirements of the whole school curriculum and in turn, the pattern of course provision in ITE courses. The implication of this set of changes means less time for the remaining subjects of the National Curriculum. In January 1998 the Secretary of State announced his intention to introduce, from September 1998, new arrangements for the National Curriculum. The proposals will enable schools, if they so choose, to give more time to the teaching of literacy and numeracy. Sir William Stubbs, Chair of the Qualifications and Curriculum Authority (QCA) wrote to headteachers: 'The flexibility will be achieved by modifying the requirements of the statutory orders in history, geography, design and technology, art, music and physical education, so that schools will not be required to follow the programmes of study in these six subjects at Key Stages 1 and 2 for the period September, 1998 — September 2000'. The QCA is currently conducting a national consultation (a two page questionnaire!). Those parts of the curriculum supposedly directly linked to wealth, creation and commerce appear to have a greater priority than subjects or approaches related more to civilizing values and the quality of life.

Patterns of Teacher Education Courses

The significance of these issues is clearly seen in the provisions made in *Circular 10/97*. They are reflected both in the pattern of courses and the nature of the content of the courses where this is identified. In terms of the courses which may be offered in the primary field, these include courses (whether undergraduate or postgraduate) which relate to the following pupil age ranges: 3–8 years, 3 or 5–11 years, 7–11 years and perhaps 7–14 (Key Stage 2/3 courses). There are different requirements relating to each of these courses and perhaps different unstated assumptions. The range represents some significant changes or emphases. The traditional 5–11 pattern remains, but there is the emphasis on early years with 3–8 or 3–11 on the one hand and new programmes relating to 7–11 and 7–14. This presages greater potential diversity of provision. Significantly, there is an emphasis on the three core subjects in all these patterns together with a specialist subject. However, only in relation to 3–8 courses is there a requirement that courses should equip prospective teachers to teach '*across the full primary curriculum*'. Such a requirement is not made in relation to courses for other age ranges, implying that full subject-coverage is not required. It is made clear that *full age range* coverage is required within the emphasis on 3 or 5 to 8 years or 7 to 11 years in the case of 3 or 5–11 years courses.

The introduction of 7–11 years courses as a distinct provision reflects a view expressed by a number of people, including officers of the TTA, that there is a problem in Key Stage 2 of teachers being unable to cope with the levels of specialist knowledge required to implement the National Curriculum (OFSTED, 1997). An assumption is that the BEd/BA (QTS) degree although it usually includes a specialist subject has not been effective in producing the required specialist standards. This may arise from that minority of undergraduate courses which have not included study of a specialist subject. Alternatively it may imply a preference for a PGCE (primary) route. However, admission tutors for the PGCE as a consequence of the Circular may be required to focus sharply on the nature of an applicant's first degree. OFSTED inspection practice has implied a need for rigorous audits of subject knowledge and remedial action in course programmes. Given the extensive and detailed expectations of the standards, how far such demands can be met in a meaningful way on a one-year course (even of 36 weeks) is a key question in implementing the Circular. OFSTED inspectors have gone so far as to enquire what additional preparation courses may include for graduate specialists in the core subjects. The TTA appears also to be moving steadily towards target allocations to primary courses that are related to recruitment based on subject-based student numbers. However, it is far from clear just what is intended by the concept of a specialist subject. It is significant that the requirement of previous circulars that in undergraduate courses 50 per cent of course time should be allocated to a specialist subject at a level appropriate to higher education has been dropped. The earlier requirement was consistent with one and two-year courses where degree equivalence of study was defined to permit their shortened pattern; this provided equivalences in the context of three and four-year BEd/BA degrees incorporating

QTS. However, it is not clear that specialism means beyond GCE 'A' level. Moreover, the issue of the level of subject knowledge is manifest in the requirement which states:

> for any specialist subjects students must have a secure knowledge of the subject to at least a standards approximating to GCE Advanced level in those aspects of the subject taught at KS1 and KS2.

This, it can be argued, represents a reduction in standards compared with two years' equivalent subject study post GCE 'A' level, a characteristic hitherto of many BEd/BA (QTS) courses.

Recently, the issue of subject knowledge in relation to professional preparation within a PGCE course has been raised. It is highly improbable that many academic shortcomings can be made good within the constraints of a PGCE course beyond those closely related to pedagogic matters. Just what the relationship is between subject knowledge and pedagogic skill is itself a highly problematic issue. Just how far audits of subject knowledge or tests to establish improvements in subject knowledge are satisfactory or can be positively related to the levels of teaching competence is far from clear.

Given a National Curriculum based on a subject rationale, the standards expected in all subjects, especially non-core, non-specialist subjects is also an important issue. A footnote to the standards makes clear the position:

> Where providers choose to offer more non-core, non specialist subjects in addition to the specified minimum, trainees being assessed for qualified teacher status should be able to demonstrate secure knowledge of the subject to a standard equivalent to at least level 7 of the pupils' national curriculum . . . if necessary with the support of a teacher experienced in the subject concerned . . . The newly qualified teacher's Career Entry Profile can indicate priorities for induction in each of these subjects. Providers may also wish to offer more limited coverage of other subjects than that required for non-core, non specialist subjects e.g. a few hours of taster training in a foundation subject . . .

The relation between hours provided and level 7 is itself far from clear. What counts as 'a few hours' is also unclear. However, there is the key issue of the balance of subject coverage implied in this footnote. A significantly large number of teacher educators and headteachers have expressed major reservations regarding the implications of this pattern of provision. The principle of educating and training teachers who are 'generalists with a specialism' is put at risk, especially in relation to Key Stage 2 students. Certainly, the assumption that shortcomings can at present be put right during induction or later must be seriously questioned. Of course, if following the Secretary of State's announcement, the balance of the primary curriculum changes significantly in favour of core subjects and ICT, then these assumptions may fall in line with what could arguably be said to be appropriate.

Implications for Early Years Training

A further issue arising from the proposed pattern of courses relates to the provision for students to teach pupils aged 3–4 years. The emphasis on this age group and its integration with the education and training for wider age ranges (rather than in isolation) is very much to be welcomed. However, the standards in the Circular are far from adequate. UCET (1997) in its response to the TTA consultation on standards, drew detailed attention to the shortcomings including lack of attention to:

- multi-professional relationships;
- a sound knowledge of child development;
- knowledge and respect for cultural and social similarities and differences;
- observational skills and the knowledge and ability to assess and evaluate the programmes of work offered;
- knowledge of the law relating to families.

The Issue of Standards Overload and Prescription

Clearly the incorporation of early years requirements of a more extensive nature on courses intended to train teachers for the 3–8 or 3–11 years, aggravates the more general problems of an overloaded set of standards and a shortage of specialist nursery expertise among teacher educators. Such problems arise from the Secretary of State's strong desire to control course development by imposing a largely uniform pattern of standards and to reduce the scope for diversity, distinctiveness of courses and the power of providers to respond to the needs they perceive as important in a rapidly changing educational context. It is, however, possible to conceive ways of formulating standards that offer alternatives, support greater worthwhile diversity, encourage innovative practice and respond to the priorities of providers. Such an approach is likely to raise standards, not reduce them.

The significance of these comments is sharpened by the approach adopted towards the standards expected. The Circular makes two key statements:

> All providers must:
> ensure that courses involve the assessment of all trainees against all the standards specified for the award of qualified teacher status
> ensure that trainees meet all the standards specified for the award of Qualified Teacher Status before successfully completing a course of ITT. (2.1.3 and 2.1.4)

Between 80–90 standards which apply generally are itemized and at least as many for mathematics and English are listed in addition. This represents an unprecedented level of direct intervention in the knowledge, skills and attitudes that are to be taught to students. Nothing as prescriptive has ever before been introduced into British higher education. Indeed, it could be said that the demands of the Circular echo the problems associated with the National Curriculum for pupils: it is overprescriptive, overloaded and overassessed. Moreover the prescription is backed up by an inspection process and framework in which failure to meet even one of the standards represents, at least theoretically, non-compliance and puts at risk the provider's accredited status. Whether the draconian imposition by external regulation and control of a uniform and, generally questionable set of standards is the best way to improve quality is a fundamental issue. So is the nature of the standards themselves.

Standards and Competences

How far can the standards presented in *Circular 10/97* be implemented in terms of students' professional development? Standards in the Circular represent discrete statements of what students are expected to know, understand and do. Many of them are best described as competences. Previous circulars have sought to identify criteria or competences and used these in the context of the professional preparation of teachers. This approach is itself controversial. A report in 1993, by the Department of Education in Northern Ireland (DENI, 1993) drew attention to the differences between a view of competences related to observed behaviour broken down into discrete parts and a more holistic view attaching much greater importance to knowledge, understanding and attitudes as central to the whole process of developing professional competence. The report went on to attempt a description of competences related to initial teacher education, induction and continuing professional development. The authors pointed out that the former approach to discrete competences is more straightforward for assessment purposes but also commented that this approach is open to the criticism that 'such a varied and diffuse activity as teaching cannot properly be seen as nothing more than the sum of a number of discrete behaviours'.

   If course designers take the view that a holistic approach to teaching based on a student's professional development is essential to achieving high standards of competence then this has to be reconciled with a view of standards that emphasizes discrete components since this is broadly the assumption within the Circular. Indeed, the Circular makes it quite clear that all the standards are to be assessed. Just what is implied by assessment? Some course designers may be led to produce a check list of competences related to teaching competence and training (reflecting the basic distinction in the OFSTED Quality Framework) and seek to show how each of these is formally tested in a variety of ways. This could lead to a highly bureaucratic system of assessing, recording and reporting. Other course designers may adopt a more holistic view of tasks which contribute to assessed assignments and prioritize key holistic perspectives, drawing upon selected standards and relying on a monitoring process which uses key statements at particular stages of course progression (rather like end of Key Stage statements in the pupils' National Curriculum). This system has the advantage of modelling student practice in relation to the National Curriculum. Central to the implementation of these approaches is how course designers seek to support, promote and record the student's professional development, a process which culminates in the production of a career entry profile. For some this may involve students in a continuing individual review of their progress via a series of personal tutor meetings. For others, each course area for example, core subjects or school experience, may seek, within its own time allocation to provide opportunity and the means to review progress. A sophisticated system may embrace both of these procedures. Whatever system is adapted there is likely to be tension between a pattern of progression determined by course structures and the personal, perhaps uneven, pattern of a student's professional development throughout a course. The place of a supervisor is central in enabling each student to overcome such problems and to do so in a context of rigorous intellectual and practical challenge. Tutors themselves face a difficult challenge in enabling students to understand their professional identities in terms of well thought out beliefs, attitudes and values.

Conclusion

A consequence of an education dominated by instrumental perceptions of the value of learning is likely to result in pupils at the end of their careers expressing views succinctly expressed recently by one sixth-form pupil on his preparation for GCE 'A' level history: 'I would like more practise essays at home, fewer seminars which are useless for "A" level . . . I do not care for variety or interest so long as I pass the examination'. Such statements send shudders through the hearts of those who value education for something much more than the values expressed in such comments. Education is about the enlargement of our personal horizons, about the central convictions that motivate us as responsible human beings in a rapidly changing, diverse and morally challenging world. It is worthy of note that the standards in *Circular 10/97* make no reference to Europe, never mind any global perspectives that embody the moral and social values needed for the twenty-first century. The importance of non-violence, respect for life, solidarity, a just economic order, tolerance, truthfulness, equal rights, even a need to provide opportunities for a transformation of personal consciousness have not been the kind of values that have informed either the pupils' National Curriculum or the model of teaching that informs Government thinking. If such priorities were to be taken seriously we would be unlikely to face circulars of the kind that have become increasingly familiar. We need to seek fundamental changes if we are to prepare effective teachers for the twenty-first century.

References

DEARING, R. (1993) *The National Curriculum and its Assessment* London: SCAA.
DENI (1993) *Review of Teacher Training in Northern Ireland*, Belfast: HMSO.
DES (1984) *Initial Teacher Training: Approval of Courses* (Circular 3/84) London: HMSO.
DES (1989) *Initial Teacher Training: Approval of Courses* (Circular 24/89) London: HMSO.

DfEE (1993) *The Initial Training of Primary School Teachers, New Criteria for Courses* (*Circular 14/93*), London: HMSO.

DfEE (1997) *Teaching: High Status, High Standards* (*Circular 10/97*), London: HMSO.

HOUSE OF COMMONS SELECT COMMITTEE (1997) *Education and Employment Committee First Report: Teacher Recruitment: What Can Be Done: Vol. 1*, London: HMSO.

OFSTED/TTA (1997) *Framework for the Assessment of Quality and Standards in Initial Teacher Training 1997/1998*, London: HMSO.

OFSTED (1997) *Using Subject Specialists to Promote High Standards at Key Stage 2*, London: OFSTED.

QCA (1998) *The National Curriculum in Primary Schools* (letter from Sir William Stubbs (13 January).

RICHARDS, C., HARLING, P. and WEBB, D. (1997) *A Key Stage 6 Core Curriculum?* London: ATL.

UCET (1997) *Response to the TTA Consultation on the Training and Curriculum Standards for New Teachers*, London: UCET.

5   A Key Stage 6 Core Curriculum?
A Critique of the National Curriculum
for Initial Teacher Training

Colin Richards, Paul Harling and David Webb

Introduction

Fifteen years ago there was no National Curriculum. Within the constraints of professional and public opinion primary schools were free to determine their own curricula except for the legal requirement to teach 'religious instruction' (widely disregarded in practice). There was no national system for the assessment of pupils and no pressure from the centre to adopt particular teaching methods, ways of grouping or modes of curriculum organization.

Fifteen years ago higher education institutions and departments concerned with initial teacher education (ITE) were free to determine the content and methodology of their courses provided they met the requirements of the universities or the Council for National Academic Awards who validated their courses and qualifications and who themselves held academic freedom as sacrosanct.

Fifteen years ago central Government had no means of influencing curricular provision in ITE except indirectly through the professional advice offered by Her Majesty's Inspectors, themselves free from the necessity to adhere to any policy. At that time, partly as a result of reports from HMI, central Government was increasingly conscious and concerned at the diversity of provision within both school education and ITE, the relevance of that provision to what it deemed 'the world of work' and the wide differences in the quality of education provided in different schools and institutions. In what in retrospect seems an unduly timorous way central Government was stirring itself to intervene decisively in what was seen as two 'secret gardens' one tended by primary school gardeners and the other by higher education horticulturists.

Fifteen years on, English primary schools are required to follow a National Curriculum of 10 subjects plus locally determined religious education. This curriculum especially in the 'core' subjects of mathematics and English and the rather lesser 'core' subject of science, is more closely prescribed than similar curricula in many other countries. National systems of pupil assessment and school inspection have been instituted, in part to provide central Government with data on standards of attainment and quality of provision. There is powerful pressure (as yet short of legislation) from the centre to adopt particular (politically correct?) forms of curriculum organization, grouping and teaching methods. The curricular (and less the pedagogic) world of primary schools has changed and changed dramatically.

Fifteen years on, higher education institutions and departments concerned with initial teacher education (ITE) have to provide courses which meet not only the requirements of validating universities but also multiple, every more tightly pre-scribed criteria laid down by central Government (see Leather and Langley–Hamel Chapter 6 below, and David, Hamel and Rowley, Chapter 8 below). They are subject to almost continuous inspection by HMI working under the auspices of a non-ministerial Government department, the Office for Standards in Education (OFSTED). Their reports are made available to a Governmental agency, the Teacher Training Agency (TTA) who amongst other matters has the responsibility 'to secure a divers-ity of high quality and cost-effective initial teacher training which ensures that new teachers have the knowledge, understanding and skills to teach pupils effectively' (TTA, Corporate Plan, 1996, p. 12). It was the TTA who, nine years after the establishment of the National Curriculum for schools, proposed the introduction of the Initial Teacher Training National Curriculum for primary English and for primary mathematics from September 1997 and for primary science and IT from September 1998 — a kind of 'Key Stage 6' core curriculum for intending primary school teachers. That curriculum was incorporated into *Circular 10/97* setting out 'a full and detailed codification of requirements for new teachers'.

The National Curriculum for Primary Initial Teacher Training: An Overview

In introducing the National Curriculum for Primary Initial Teacher Training and other standards for the award of qualified teacher status, Anthea Millett, the Chief Executive of the TTA pointed out that 'It is the first time ever that we in education have set down clearly and explicitly what we expect of our new teachers, in terms of what they must know, understand and be able to do.' (Millett, 1997). Never before has central Government described in such detailed 'black and white' the knowledge and understanding trainees (note the term) need in order to develop pupils' competence in English, science and mathematics, the teaching and assess-ment methods they are to use, and the knowledge and understanding of the subject matter they need to underpin their teaching. The proposals herald a sea-change in teacher education/training similar to that experienced in schools with the imple-mentation of the National Curriculum after the Education Reform Act of 1988.

Whatever the merits of the National Curriculum for Primary Teacher Training (and it does have merits!) there are a number of general points which raise important issues for both teacher education and the teaching profession in general. Much *could* be made of the way in which the proposals were produced — by anonymous working groups operating to an impossibly tight timescale and in consequence not involving adequate consultation during the drafting process. However, here more substantive issues of curriculum design and structure are raised.

Most fundamentally, the TTA has not provided any rationale for the curriculum. No statement of purposes has been provided; no reasons have been offered for the content prescribed; no attempt has been made to discuss the nature and purpose of the English or mathematics intending primary teachers are to teach. There has been no attempt to 'locate' the proposed training curricula in relation to either the curriculum followed by students in school prior to their training or to the process of induction or continuing professional development following it. The proposals are presented as straightforward educational 'common sense' in no need of justification and self-evidently 'right' for the next generation of primary teachers. Neither providers nor trainees are expected, let alone encouraged, to question their basis. Perhaps the proposals are 'right' but not entirely so? There is a direct parallel with the National Curriculum for schools; it too has been provided with no detailed rationale apart from the highly general, vague clauses of section 1 of the Education Reform Act. The key questions remain: 'Why this particular set of detailed proposals? What are they designed to do? Are they appropriate as parts of higher education courses where, presumably students are to be encouraged to question and challenge rather than meekly accept educational "commonsense".'

The design of the proposed National Curricula is instructive. There is only one element: a detailed specification of the content to be taught which is provided in a valuably detailed and direct form. Apart from the inevitable ambiguities inherent in the English language and the scope for a degree of diverse interpretation they provide, the proposals set out a reasonably clear and useful programme of work. Interestingly, the structure and terminology of the school National Curriculum are avoided: there are no attainment targets, no reference to programmes of study, and no assessment arrangements and 'levels'. The absence of assessment requirements is particularly noteworthy. There are formidable problems related to the valid, reliable assessment of teaching competences or standards but as Richard Daugherty (1997) points out 'The National Curriculum for ITT neatly sidesteps such problems by not having an assessment model at all'. Why is the proposed structure of the ITT curriculum so different from that of the school curriculum? Is the Government or, at the very least, the TTA unhappy with the latter? Does this presage a change following the review currently being conducted by Qualifications and assessment Authority? Are the proposed curricula for teacher training 'throwbacks' or 'throw forwards'?

The curricula are intended to cover only the 'core' subjects of English, mathematics science and IT, though other parts of *Circular 10/97* concerned with the standards required for qualified teacher status, have many implications for other aspects of training courses. Anthea Millett argues 'We have set out the priorities, the core elements of what we believe initial teacher training should cover . . . There is still plenty of scope for flexibility, variation and innovation'. No one would deny the importance of the core subjects but why is there no intention to spell out the training requirements of the remaining seven foundation subjects of the school National Curriculum and of religious education? Are there no essential elements in these subjects which all teacher-trainees ought to be taught? Is this yet another manifestation of the current political obsession with so-called 'basics' and the education system's supposed neglect of these?

By concentrating only on the 'core', by specifying this in detail and by not prescribing the length of such courses in those subjects, the TTA has left providers of initial teacher training with an extremely difficult, perhaps intractable, problem of fitting curricular quarts into narrow-necked, regularly inspected pint bottles. Nor do the proposals take due account of the very different contexts (especially constraints) of one-year postgraduate courses (involving a maximum of 20 weeks tuition) and three or four-year initial degree courses. Especially in relation to the very short PGCE courses are there the necessary 'degrees of freedom' to promote the innovation and flexibility trumpeted in the TTA's rhetoric? The very detail of the proposals, one of their strengths, serves to exacerbate design problems. The difficulties schools faced when attempting to manage the overprescriptive, unmanageable pre-Dearing National Curriculum are in danger of being paralleled in the initial teacher education sector.

Initial Teacher Training National Curriculum for Primary Mathematics

Background

The major basis for the National Curriculum for ITT in mathematics appears to have been the schedules used in the 'sweep' inspection of provision for mathematics, English, assessment, recording and reporting and quality assurance within teacher education which took place in 1995 and 1996. In these schedules were detailed lists of common criteria against which to inspect the quality of teacher education. The schedules used by the inspectors were made available to all the parties involved in teacher education and, in effect, immediately became an unofficial form of National Curriculum for Initial Teacher Training — parallel to some extent to the 'OFSTED curriculum' taught in many schools prior to their inspection.

Close inspection of the current document *Initial Teacher Training National Curriculum for Primary Mathematics* reveals that it contains little that was not already available in documentary form, or which could not be implied from recalling the questions posed to individuals and groups during the inspection process itself. Indeed, large parts of it directly reflect the content, style and structure of courses which were inspected and found to be of 'high quality' in relation to the statutory criteria.

This part of the paper is not intending to explore the way in which the *Initial Teacher Training National Curriculum for Primary Mathematics* was produced. Just as the National Curriculum for schools evolved into its current form 'in mysterious ways' there is no doubt that this document also will change and develop over the next few years. The rest of this section will therefore explore some of the issues that are raised by the content of this document as it relates to mathematics and mathematics education.

Critique

Fundamentally the curriculum needs a rationale to accompany the raw statements of required content. It fails to provide a clearly defined purpose or a set of goals appropriate to the future of mathematics *education*. Of course it is possible that a rationale has been deliberately omitted so that each provider can 'do its own thing', but such a ploy has immense potential dangers when the expected benchmark competences of trainees are so precisely defined and expected to be delivered to students by all providers.

Coverage

The expected 'standards' required of new teachers with regard to the teaching and assessment of mathematical concepts and skills are extensive and seem to be expanding exponentially with each new Government directive. Almost 10 years ago there was an immediate outcry at the expected breadth and depth of coverage of the National Curriculum for schools. When the contents of the original statutory orders for National Curriculum mathematics were eventually unveiled the amount of mathematical material included was a long way beyond the expectations of everyone except possibly the authors. Two extensive revisions were needed before the current, and to a large extent workable, model was in place. However, it should be noted that very little of the *breadth* of content was removed. Instead it was the *depth* of treatment of the content which was altered. Will the same process happen with the ITT National Curriculum for Primary Mathematics?

It is important to stress that 'good' courses in primary mathematics for student teachers include all the elements listed in the document, to a greater or lesser degree. We have yet to meet anyone involved in teacher education who feels that they would like to see the removal of any substantive aspects of the section devoted to 'the development of pupils' competence in mathematics', or the section outlining 'effective teaching and assessment methods'. Indeed, the general comment has been that some *additional* aspects should have been included.

However there is no indication in the curriculum of a desirable ethos or philosophy related to the development of the competences of student teachers. The current curriculum seems to regard teacher education as a series of 'culture-free' skills and items of knowledge to be learned. That fact alone will cause major problems as each provider will seek (and will certainly find) its own model, emphasizing its own view of the most desirable elements and de-prioritizing others. This may be deliberate, so that each provider is able to, or is being forced to, develop its own philosophy, but the price to be paid is a degree of inconsistency in the actual experience of trainees.

It is disappointing that the curriculum makes no mention of the following:

- mathematics has a major role to play in everyone's lives;
- the quality of each person's mathematical education is fundamental to any definition of 'being educated';
- mathematics has a unique identity, and unique concepts, skills and processes;
- mathematics is concerned with making sense of the world;
- mathematics is an essential tool of communication;
- mathematics is a powerful tool for understanding phenomena, processing information and carrying out practical and logical tasks;
- mathematics has coherence and elegance in its form and use.

It also makes no reference to trainee 'teachers':

- personally enjoying teaching mathematics;
- learning how to encourage a sense of enjoyment of mathematical activity in children;
- learning how to encourage children to take responsibility for their own mathematical development;
- learning how to engender investigative skills, and the techniques related to solving problems;
- understanding the cultural and historical origins of mathematics;
- holding expectations of pupils' performance appropriate to their needs and situations;

and so on.

Without such statements coverage in the curriculum remains fundamentally incomplete because it does not recognize the essential need for teachers to get to grips with the subject as a whole and be active learners while being trained and later while in post. Understanding the 'culture' of mathematics is essential if students are to find ways to introduce pupils to that culture. Mathematics is not culture-free or value-free and neither is the education and training of the next generation of teachers.

In this context a further observation can be made. The document refers only to 'trainees', never to students or student teachers. Is this an indication that future teachers are to be taught to be 'technicians' without encouraging them to be reflective, analytical and critical evaluators of their own actions and the actions of others? If this is *not* true, then a document which determines the quantity, quality and content of teacher education must provide clear indications of what the whole subject of mathematics, and indeed the whole profession of teaching, entails.

One other feature related to coverage is of particular significance. The explicitly stated requirement that all students on 'primary' teacher training courses are trained in the content and methods appropriate to *both* Key Stage 1 and Key Stage 2 is of profound importance. This requirement should ensure that students are able to validly and appropriately teach pupils across a much wider range of abilities and ages. However the requirement has implications for course design and delivery which all providers will need to address.

Progression

The requirements that all students on 'primary' teacher training courses are trained in the content and methods appropriate to *both* Key Stage 1 and Key Stage 2, and know how to take account of the individual needs of pupils, have made it doubly essential that the issue of progression is addressed in an ITT National Curriculum for primary mathematics.

Any attempt to emphasise progression would need to include details of the earliest stages of learning, should contain material which demonstrates what a learner progresses from, and should indicate a target amount of learning, stage or level to reach. Additionally it would be useful if the key aspects of mathematics (hopefully the most fundamental concepts) are 'separated-out' and discussed. The structure of the curriculum does not do this adequately. There are a number of problems.

Firstly minimal attention is given to the fundamental stages of mathematical education. The whole of 'Early Mathematics' takes up 12 lines only viz:

> Trainees must be taught how to ensure very young pupils acquire the basic mathematical concepts necessary for later progression in mathematics, including the knowledge, understanding and skills needed to:
>
> (a) count, understand the value of small numbers and combine them;
> (b) compare, as a basis for recognizing relationships in, for example, measures and transformations;
> (c) order, as a basis for understanding number, spatial relationships and measures;
> (d) sort and identify properties of numbers and shapes as a basis for classification;
> (e) establish invariant properties as a basis for work in number, measures and shape.

Even as a summary of the very important groundwork on which subsequent mathematical competence is based this can only be regarded as very inadequate. It is caught between an attempt to list detailed expectations with regard to students' experiences, and an attempt to highlight some general principles. Because of this inconsistency it greatly undervalues the importance of early mathematical learning. As it stands it appears to be an afterthought, slotted into the document after the notes concerning general progression in pupils' mathematics have been written.

A similar problem arises in the subsequent part, summarizing with a rather spurious sense of detail, a series of notional starting (and finishing) positions for each major aspect of the mathematics National Curriculum for schools.

e.g.   Trainees must be taught the key aspects of progression in pupils' mathematical development, including how to ensure that pupils:

- progress from using informal mathematical vocabulary to using precise and correct mathematical vocabulary, notation and symbolism;
- progress from counting, ordering and sorting with small numbers and understanding their value to using and approximating numbers within the extended number system and using the number operations to calculate accurately and efficiently;
- progress from guessing unknown numbers as a basis for trial and improvement and forming simple statements with unknowns, e.g. $53 = ? + 36$, to solving simple equations using inverse operations, manipulating algebraic symbols, and constructing general expressions;

The curriculum says little or nothing about *how* progression can be achieved and this is surely a major omission. As with the section outlining early mathematics what is needed is *either* a full statement of the curriculum *or* a brief list of the principles of progression within mathematics.

The curriculum also includes a list of 'key aspects of mathematics underpinning progression'. With some modification to selected items and a clearer use of terminology in order to make them understandable the list provides a sound set of fundamental mathematical concepts and skills. However, given the previous comments about the level of detail concerning 'early mathematics' and 'progression in pupils' mathematics' this list needs to *either* be placed in a section on its own *or* included in the section on 'Knowledge and understanding of mathematics' of the document. It could then form the basis of a checklist of students' competence to know, recall, understand and use the most fundamental ideas of mathematics while teaching.

Effective Teaching and Assessment Methods

The curriculum contains a long and detailed section setting out a particular, and mainly valid, framework for the teaching of mathematics.

The first part is as much a list of 'what to teach' as 'how to teach'; content is smuggled in under the guise of methodology. In terms of its requirements for teaching methods the document runs counter to earlier publications such as *Mathematics 5–11* (HMI, 1979), *Mathematics Counts* (DES, 1982) and *Mathematics 5–16* (HMI, 1985). The stance of those papers which was to allow, even encourage, a broad range of teaching styles appears to be missing or, at the very least, deemphasized in the ITT curriculum. Here there is an emphasis on tight teacher control and leadership of classroom activity, rather than a willingness to recognize the teacher as at least in part a 'facilitator of learning'. Many in higher education will see this as a welcome emphasis. However, with such a strongly advocated approach to mathematics education some care is required. To our knowledge there is as yet no definitive research evidence which proves unequivocally that any single approach is more effective than others which are not afforded a mention in the document.

The curriculum lacks clarity about the use, albeit within a teacher-led system, of investigational approaches. It gives inadequate attention to the knowledge, skills and approaches required to effectively teach the elements of Attainment Target 1 of the schools' National Curriculum. Indeed, its suggested approaches are rather mechanistic.

Despite the emphasis on assessment, recording and reporting of attainments in the school National Curriculum, the framework for its development within the ITT National Curriculum is notable for its lack of detailed guidance. Is the assumption being made that the issue has been 'taken care of' elsewhere? Should we be expecting another set of materials concerning assessment offering training guidance in the same way as SEAC attempted to retrain serving teachers when the schools' National Curriculum was introduced? Should we read anything into the fact that the document does not mention formative assessment when all SCAA and previously SEAC documents have highlighted the fact that the fundamental role of assessment is to inform teachers' curriculum planning? Should we read anything into the major emphasis on testing rather than using a wide range of techniques of assessment and evaluation of learning which have a long pedigree?

Subject Knowledge Requirements

The inclusion of a requirement to enhance students' personal mathematical knowledge as a part of all primary mathematics courses leading to the award of QTS is a crucial, positive and forward looking development which has the *potential* to significantly improve the quality of the teaching of mathematics at Key Stages 1 and 2.

It will do this by, amongst other things:

- increasing the level of confidence students have in their own abilities as 'mathematicians';
- enabling them to understand some of the reasons why particular aspects of mathematics are taught to young children;
- increasing their personal knowledge, understanding and skill related to aspects of mathematics previously misunderstood and therefore acting as barriers to confidence when teaching mathematics at Key Stages 1 and 2;
- in conjunction with their training in the pedagogy of the subject, exploring ways of presenting and learning about relatively abstract mathematical concepts and recognizing links within and between concepts;

However, the question is whether the particular listing of required 'mathematical knowledge and understanding' is appropriate. There has to be some doubt as to whether the chosen items fit the bill, given that there is no definitive and conclusive evidence that knowing and understanding selected aspects of mathematics previously studied for GCSE will *directly* enhance the teaching of a conceptual prerequisite of that aspect.

The ITT National Curriculum for Primary Mathematics has found itself in a 'catch-22' situation. If no detail is offered then the document looks vague and the competences required will be open to interpretation. If a significant amount of detail is offered the list provides an 'Aunt Sally' for every critic of the notion of enhancing students' personal mathematical knowledge and understanding.

This is not the place to begin a detailed examination of each item on the list of required knowledge and understanding, nor of the validity of the notional connection between it and the concepts and skills included in the school National Curriculum for mathematics. Suffice it to say that a student entering a course leading to QTS who has merely scraped a grade C at GCSE (at the bottom of the top 30 per cent for attainment in mathematics) will not have even met, never mind understood, some of the items of knowledge and understanding shown in the list. Perhaps there *is* a serious argument in favour of raising the minimum entry qualification to a grade B in mathematics, but that is a discussion for another time and place.

Areas of Trainees' Knowledge to be Audited

Directly related to the previous section are the issues of auditing students' knowledge of mathematics on entry to a course leading to QTS and, presumably, of developing a system for evaluating the quantity and quality of students' gain in subject knowledge.

An audit on entry is likely to do little to alleviate, or even stabilize, students' anxieties about their personal mathematical knowledge and understanding. However, the *subsequent* attainment of the required knowledge and understanding of mathematics by the conclusion of the course should reduce anxiety, but only if the process of enhancing knowledge and understanding is handled professionally and with purposes clearly explained to students. The need to enhance personal knowledge of a subject should not be a stick with which to beat people. Rather it should be pursued by providers developing professional attitudes to learning in students.

With this in mind the curriculum suggests that this enhancement of knowledge can be achieved through supported self-study. There is much merit in this, particularly since it would not need to use increasingly precious 'contact hours'. However, the emphasis must be firmly on the word 'supported' rather than on the phrase 'self-study'.

Initial Teacher Training National Curriculum for Primary English

Background

One difference between the background to the mathematics and the English curriculum concerns politics. There are periodic bursts of anxiety about standards in mathematics, but they are as nothing compared with the frequent and intense hysteria about English. People feel strongly about language. Language is central to our sense of our identity, and, in a culture preoccupied with social class, how people speak (and to a lesser extent how they write) places them socially. To many people, the failures of others of conform linguistically feel subversive, and threaten their sense of identity. It is therefore not surprising that English has always been contested ground on the political battlefield.

Much in the events which surrounded the genesis of the English National Curriculum for schools illuminates the arguments which are half-hidden behind the surface of the English National Curriculum for ITT. Those not directly involved in education, those journalists and right wing politicians trapped in the linguistics equivalent of the pre-Copernican view of the universe, had expected the Kingman Committee Report (DES, 1988a) to advocate the teaching of Standard English and traditional Latinate grammar. Brian Cox, famous as editor of the supposedly right wing Black Papers, and therefore thought to be safely traditionalist, was expected to put things right. The Cox Committee Reports followed (1988/89). It included the first version of the English National Curriculum which with little alteration was implemented for 5-year-olds in 1989 and 11-year-olds in 1990. Cox, too, disappointed many in Government and the press, but his report was unexpectedly, despite many controversial components, welcomed by most of those actually involved in education.

However it was not long before the National Curriculum Council produced *The Case for Revising the [Cox] Order*. It was worried that not enough attention was being paid to Standard English, that the composing aspects of writing were elbowing out 'grammar', and that phonics in the teaching of reading was being neglected. These themes recurred. Periodic assertions about a crisis in the teaching of reading echoed throughout this period, even though the claim of a decline in reading standards remained unproven. Critics attributed the supposed decline to modern teaching methods and 'trendy' teacher trainers. It needs to be stressed that there was no research or inspection evidence of 'trendy teaching' or its implication in reading failure, HMI reported in 1990 that 'phonics were taught almost universally' and that there was 'a clear and balanced approach in the vast majority of primary schools'.

The story with Standard English and 'grammar' is similar. Following Kingman and Cox, the Language in the National Curriculum (LINC) project (1989–91) was set up to disseminate to teachers the increased knowledge about language which they recommended should be taught. LINC geared itself up to teach what modern linguistics knew about Standard English and grammar, but it was shut down promptly by the Government, and its materials were denied official publication. Old battles illuminate much in the National Curriculum for ITT English, as we shall see.

Critique

The English document possesses many of the features already discussed in relation to mathematics but in contrast to the latter it also raises a number of very contentious issues — about the nature of the subject, about Standard English and grammar — which need to be discussed critically and in some greater detail.

Structure of the Document

Many of the comments made about the mathematics document also apply to the English one. In particular there is an equivalent need for a rationale and for the technical terms about language to be placed in a coherent justifiable and precise description of English.

Coverage and Level of Detail

As with mathematics, the requirements here are extensive, and fit a now familiar pattern of increasing range and specificity in the instructions about teaching English in official documents. Without doubt many of the major elements required have been included, if in varying detail.

Tutors of English accept the idea that the key terms of English need to be learned, as the National Curriculum document suggests. They know that understanding the language or discourse of a subject is central to its mastery. A document which brings greater consistency and terminological precision to their work should be welcomed. There is, however, a common misunderstanding about the nature of subject knowledge which is evident in the ITT English Curriculum. Subject knowledge tends to be seen as just content, a collection of objective facts 'out there'. Terms from the language of the subject are thought to exist meaningfully outside the minds of the community of experts and learners who make up the subject. It follows that any reasonably intelligent person can just teach the terms effectively one by one without any grasp of the subject as a whole. It needs to be said again and again that the terms of the discourse of a subject only fully have meaning within the context of the subject and its culture as a whole. Of course learners need to be inducted into the discourse of the subject, but that induction is a complex process requiring expertise in both the subject — its concepts, skills, values and attitudes — and in its induction (see Clayden and others, 1994).

All intending teachers need to be imbued with some of the culture of English. They must be helped to take into themselves the traditional English concern with literature and the imagination, with self-expression, and with ways of responding to the self and the world in words which combine feeling and thought. They need to recognize the importance of *how* things are expressed (*form*) and not just focus on what is being said (*content*). They need to be brought to feel that, just because they speak, read and write, they do not know all they need to know about language. The ITT English Curriculum discourages any attempt to teach these things. It is a collage of technical terms and named skills. It feels more like the basis of a training manual for technicians than for educating teachers in a subject.

This view of the proposed curriculum as emphasizing those aspects of English and English teaching which can be presented with lists of technical terms for the technician-teacher comes over most clearly from the different levels of detail in the exemplification offered in different parts of the document. Although it is made clear that the document 'does not attempt to cover everything that needs to be taught to trainee teachers', inevitably those aspects of English which are dealt with in detail will be seen as more important than other matters which are just mentioned briefly or omitted altogether.

In the document's treatment of reading the extensive and detailed exemplification of the terminology of phonic teaching with only cursory treatment of other aspects of reading inevitably suggests that joy in reading, the complex critical and discriminatory skills and the insights which mature reading can require, and the capacity to enter in imagination into the world of a book and empathize with its characters are not much valued. This amounts to a tragic disregard of the *uses* of literacy. Whatever happened to those essentials which got prominent mention in the earlier National Curriculum English documents for schools, to 'enthusiastic, independent and reflective readers', to 'opportunities to read a wide variety of literature', to extending pupils' ideas and their moral and emotional understanding, to 'imagination' to 'poetry' and to 'enjoyment'?

The section on writing invites a similar criticism about emphasis. It gives extensive attention to mechanical details and easily identified and label-able gobbets of knowledge (spelling patterns, syllabification, prefixes, suffixes, pen grip, letter orientation, use of imperatives and connectives etc.). As with the material on phonics, all these skills and items of knowledge ought to be covered by intending teachers. Where, however, is the emphasis on writing for real purposes, to learn, to persuade, to entertain, to express feelings, to capture on the page the fruits of the imagination, to create a thing of beauty in words and to discover more about one's self?

At least the treatment of reading and writing covers several pages and is evidence of their significance in the eyes of the DfEE and TTA. How important then are speaking and listening given that they are given just a quarter of a page? Or is the old distrust of oracy still at work?

Drama is not a separate subject in the National Curriculum, and because of that is likely to be neglected in many schools, and in the preparation for teaching of many students. It needs to be included explicitly in the primary English teacher education curriculum. Drama has proved its value in helping children to learn across the whole curriculum, and it also has a special contribution to make to English. For all children (and especially those who are not yet reading fluently) it can supply some of the key experiences which literature and writing provide, those experiences which the English teacher training document is sadly reticent about: creating or enjoying stories, the pleasure of imagining yourself into other situations and people, and using language creatively.

Further, drama is particularly valuable in filling out the lack of specificity in the section of the curriculum which deals with speaking and listening. This is territory where students and many teachers would welcome help. Merely 'requiring' pupils to 'be articulate and coherent', 'to adapt their speech for different purposes and situations using different registers as appropriate', 'to listen attentively' and 'to participate effectively' in discussions, as the curriculum does, will not make it happen. Students need familiarity with drama to equip them to design effective tasks to do these things. Drama also provides ways of assessing pupils' confidence in speaking and listening. It falls within the category of 'essential core knowledge, understanding and skill which every primary trainee must be taught and be able to use' (to use the words of the Introduction to the English curriculum).

Another major problem is the lack of sufficient attention given to English as an Additional Language (EAL). The English National Curriculum for ITT needs to insist that students are taught about progression in learning English for these pupils. Students need to be taught about typical EAL developmental errors, and how some of these characteristic errors indicate progress and need to be regarded positively. Work needs to be done with students on adapting teaching methods and materials for these pupils so that their language development is fostered. Children can be helped to develop their own sense of identity through the classroom valuing of languages other than English and stories from other cultures. For all these intending teachers need substantial teaching about EAL language and a range of literature and stories from other cultures. It is more 'essential core knowledge'.

Progression

The document adds nothing to the various versions of the English National Curriculum for schools which have long been indispensable frameworks for teacher education. As with mathematics, defining progression in some key areas is fraught with difficulty, and in these areas the National Curriculum for schools falls back on vagueness. What counts as better writing or more demanding reading defies easy description. In fact, to settle such questions, a teacher needs be to imbued with the culture of the subject English and, as argued above, the culture of the subject is a serious blind spot in the document. If the document is seen as insisting for the sake of comprehensiveness that intending teachers learn about progression, then who could object? What it does say is unexceptionable, as far as it goes.

Effective Teaching and Assessment Methods

What the curriculum has to say about effective teaching and assessment methods neither adds to, or changes much from, the prescriptions already contained in the various versions of the school National Curriculum, the schedules used in the 'sweep' inspections of 1995–96 or the criteria in the OFSTED/TTA framework for the assessment of ITT.

Subject Knowledge

The document is absolutely right to stress the need for intending teachers to have subject knowledge. This is particularly important in a subject like English for two reasons. First, despite the National Curriculum in school there are many students wishing to become teachers whose own literacy is suspect. Uncorrected, these students will damage children's progress and attainment. Second, English is not a subject where students can simply be given some material to 'deliver' and instructions on ways of doing it. Children are 'doing English' all the time they are constantly talking, and reading and writing. The key is to know enough to intervene appropriately to help them progress, and that requires deep, wide, confident subject knowledge.

It is in the language area that the TTA's treatment of subject knowledge is suspect. The agency needs to dissociate itself explicitly from a still widely believed set of superstitions about language, but it fails to do so. Linguistics is research based; much of what it teaches is not a matter of opinion. The term 'grammar' is often put into inverted commas because what 'grammar' used to mean, and in some quarters still does, has been discredited by twentieth century linguistics. When the specialists in the field say grammar they mean something different. 'Grammar' (traditional grammar) includes all sorts of unsubstantiated 'rules' which derive ultimately from the schoolrooms of centuries ago. Whereas modern research-based grammar looks at and attempts to analyze what people actually say and write, traditional grammar is prescriptive (it tells us what we ought to write) rather than descriptive. Because the classics had such high prestige in the classrooms of earlier centuries, many of the 'rules' derive from classical Latin and do not fit English at all.

Ill-informed people speak of grammar as if there were only one grammar and as if it were an objective set of indisputable facts 'out there'. From the perspective of research-based linguistics this is a mistaken view. Linguistics specialists have produced a variety of different grammars, written for different purposes and embodying different principles, as Ronald Carter (1995) explains. These grammars may well use terms which are unfamiliar to those who think they know about grammar because they 'learned grammar at school', or use familiar terms in new ways. So when the TTA English document speaks of just 'grammar', as if there was only one grammar, it displays a certain ignorance, or perhaps an unwillingness to offend those who are politically powerful and who hold fast to traditional grammar.

For a document which purports to help trainees and training providers gain a common understanding of requirements, the curriculum is inconsistent in its own use of key terms. For example it refers to 'a variety of forms of language'. Are 'forms' grammatical or to do with genre? It refers to 'language sounds, structures and patterns'. Are the 'structures and patterns' grammatical or of other kinds? Its list of types of sentences which 'trainees' must know about is a curious mixture of grammatical and functional terms.

Perhaps the DfEE and TTA do not know that many of the definitions and formulations of traditional grammar are intellectually flawed and confuse children. Traditional definitions which emphasize and muddle together content or meaning with form are notoriously confusing. Tell a child that a verb is a 'doing word', for instance, and she will have to search hard for a verb in 'John seemed old'. Further-more, talk to her as if all words belong in particular word classes whatever the context, and, faced with 'the washing machine' in a sentence for analysis, she will deduce that 'washing' is a verb, because washing is doing. It is not surprising that too many children become discouraged and say they are no good at English, because they are quite rightly confused by traditional grammatical definitions. Whatever its source, this unwillingness to reject traditional grammar will do dam-age in classrooms by encouraging traditional grammar to continue to be taught. The National Curriculum needs another LINC project to produce a respectable recom-mended grammar to be used in teacher education and in schools.

When politicians, colleagues and parents speak of 'bad English' or 'bad gram-mar' they are often actually complaining of moments when writers deviate from standard English into their regional dialect. Though the ITT English Curriculum for teacher education is careful not to speak ill of dialects, it is possible to catch glimpses of a discredited view which seems to lie behind the text, for example when the curriculum talks of 'errors and misconceptions', including 'subject/verb agreement' and 'verb tenses'. Certainly children (and highly educated adults) some-times forget the number of the subject and what tense they are using, and this is a worthwhile topic for an English lesson. The commonest cause of this kind of mistake, though, is a lapse from the grammar of Standard English into that of local speech; '*we was* going down the shop', for instance.

Standard English is widely seen by specialists in linguistics as a damaging term. It suggests that there is one correct English and that all other varieties are inferior. It is a myth that regional dialects are not grammatical (or are 'lazy' or 'sloppy'). They have their own grammars, different in some ways to that of Stand-ard English. These grammars are just as consistently used and just as complex as the grammar of Standard English. For these reasons, linguistics specialists argue that it is a mistake to speak as if there is one correct English, and that teachers should go instead for the concept of appropriateness.

The National Curriculum requires children to be taught Standard English, and that is quite appropriate, but for social, not linguistic, reasons. There are social contexts for which Standard English is required. It is needed to do well in educa-tional contexts and to get the more interesting and mostly better paid kinds of jobs. However, teaching Standard English is not best done by disparaging dialects. Chil-dren quite understandably construe criticism of their language on this basis as an attack on their very identity and on the family and the community from which they come. It is better to set them to investigate their own regional and other dialects positively, and thus to help them to understand the differences between them and Standard English, including when the use of each is appropriate.

There is no longer opposition to teaching grammar. It is accepted that children and teachers need a metalanguage, a language about language, to talk about writ-ing; otherwise children, unless they somehow pick up the generalization intuitively, can only experience hundreds of individual *ad hoc* suggestions for particular im-provements to their writing. It is acknowledged too that teachers need to know much more about grammar than they will teach the children explicitly in order to assess the readability of texts for children and to understand children's writing fully and to help them make progress. So it is not the presence of grammar in the curriculum which is unfortunate; it is the way grammar is used in the document and the way it is taught by those holding traditional views.

The ITT Curriculum implies that there is a single simple right answer in English, that it is always and everywhere correct and that it has to be learned by heart. Instead, the curriculum needs to encourage investigative work on language with children and to do so unequivocally. Work on language can be fascinating, but not *via* rote learning. The differences between Standard English and regional dialects, and when the use of each is appropriate, and what used to be called parts of speech, can all be taught by investigations and games, and taught in these ways they are fun. If the National Curriculum English document remains as it is in this respect, a checklist of dull labels which seem to want to be learned and applied mechanically, without specifying the use of investigative approaches to language, such work will be discouraged.

Implications for Schools and Higher Education

Course Design

The section of this chapter providing an overview of the proposed National Curriculum for Primary Initial Teacher Training has outlined a number of important general issues for the design of course programmes.

However, in relation to English and mathematics specifically, few institutions will need to add or change much because there is remarkably little in the proposed ITT curriculum which is not implied by the documents which already govern the preparation of primary teachers. Much hard work will be needed to devise and implement an effective audit of students' subject knowledge and to devise suitable ways of remedying deficiencies, but as it is vital that teachers' knowledge of mathematics and English is good, the DfEE's insistence that this should be done is welcome.

The proposed curricula for mathematics and English are likely to be undermined by the shortage of time available for the subjects. The same error which marked the original National Curriculum for schools has been made. There is no doubt that some of the various requirements will have to be met very perfunctorily. (The situation is particularly acute on one-year postgraduate courses which are even more desperately overloaded than four-year undergraduate courses.) It is very strange then that the 150 hours of contact and directed time for mathematics and English specified by DFE *Circular 14/93* have been dropped. Already in higher education institutions there are mutterings from other departments about reducing the time given over to the subjects. Further, given the difficulties touched on below in making sure that a focus on subject learning happens when students are in school, it seems inappropriate to risk damaging the agreements between schools and HE about directed time, which have recently been negotiated.

Mentoring and Supervision in Schools

Post *Circular 14/93* subject knowledge is a problem in primary teacher education, when student teachers do a much larger part of their learning in schools (see Twiselton and Webb, Chapter 14 below). It has also been seen as a worry in primary schools, even without the problems of teacher education. Providing subject–based supervisors for student school experience in primary teacher education is also a problem of long standing. Even in the days when supervision of school experience was done entirely by college tutors, they had their own subject allegiances, and, when discussing with student teachers lessons from other domains, they fell back often on to matters of general classroom management. School-based teacher education has not solved the problem. Teacher mentors are also unlikely to provide support across the whole curriculum, and there is no evidence to suggest that subject curriculum coordinators are being brought extensively into the mentoring process to fill any gaps in subject mentoring. Indeed finding the range of subject expertise on the staff to provide subject coordinators for all subjects and to monitor subject learning effectively across the range of subjects is hard, particularly in small or medium sized primary schools.

Recent research (for example, Edwards and Collison, 1996) has found that scant attention is paid to subject learning in dialogues between teacher-mentors and student teachers and that issues related to classroom management crowd out discussion of what and how the pupils are learning in subject terms. A common national curriculum for mathematics and English in teacher education, shared between HE and school staff involved in preparing intending teachers for the profession should help. It should foster a proper focus on subject knowledge and the proper use of a terminology which expresses that knowledge in school and higher education, but it requires as an essential pre-condition: that mentors in schools get more support in their subject mentoring role.

The proposed curriculum can only be welcomed if money is found to release teachers from school and to set up extensive (and expensive!) CPD for mentors where they can work with HE tutors towards a shared understanding of the contents and how they may be taught to intending teachers. Otherwise the new curriculum will destabilize partnerships and foster that dangerous and delusive snare, 'we do the practice in school and they learn the theory in college'. This CPD would bring those primary teachers who were not mathematics or English specialists into the community of teachers of these subjects, able to criticize and develop the discourse of the subjects from the inside.

A shared vocabulary enshrined in a well designed curriculum and joint work with mentors and higher education staff to ensure shared understanding and priorities is essential. Directed subject time in school, with suitable tasks devised and scrutinised in college is necessary but not enough. As the Edwards and Collison research implies, it will not automatically solve the problem of ensuring that students focus on subject learning. Quality assurance (except in some SCITTs) is the responsibility of higher education within partnerships. It is for HE staff to devise and negotiate ways forward.

A Necessary Ongoing Debate

Whatever the merits or demerits of the current National Curriculum for ITT, the debate of which it is a part will continue — not just the officially-sponsored debate about the content of initial training courses and the roles, responsibilities and accountabilities of the various providers and agencies, but also the more fundamental debate about the purpose and nature of teacher *education* or *training* with its focus on the kinds of teachers needed to educate future generations. Does Britain need an army of *basic instructors* to staff its primary schools and inculcate pupils with necessary skills and knowledge? If so, the current National Curriculum for Primary ITT could, pared down, provide the instruction needed for the instructors. Does Britain need a cadre of *skilled technicians* able to deliver the school National Curriculum programmes of study to pupils in an efficient and effective way? If so, the current training curriculum has the makings of a very useful and detailed training manual for would-be technicians. Or does Britain need a profession of imaginative, creative teachers whose informed professional judgment leads to intelligent action? If so, the training curriculum will not suffice as it stands. It lacks imagination and vision; it embodies, rather than opens up to scrutiny, a straightforward, value-free common sense view of education, teaching, English and mathematics. Its simplistic approach belies the complexity of the educational enterprise whether in school or college. It will certainly provide would-be teachers with important knowledge and skills but it will fail to provide them with the understanding, or to develop *with* them the necessary attitudes and values, which they need to make *educational* judgments and undertake intelligent action to foster their children's learning. It *will* provide a Key Stage 6 core curriculum but not one which, to quote Section 1 of the ERA, 'promotes the spiritual, moral, cultural, mental and physical development' of future teachers.

References

CARTER, R. (1995) *Keywords in Language and Literacy*, London: Routledge.

CLAYDEN, E., DESFORGES, C., MILLS, C. and RAWSON, W. (1994) 'Authentic activity and learning', *British Journal of Educational Studies*, **XXXXII**, 2.

DAUGHERTY, R. (1997) 'Bright ideas that will lead to a primary shortage', *Times Educational Supplement*, 11 April.

DES (1982) *Mathematics Counts*, London: HMSO.

DES (1988a) *Report of the Committee of Inquiry into the Teaching of English Language*. ('The Kingman Report'), London: HMSO.

DES (1988b) *English for Ages 5–11: Proposals* ('The Cox Report'), London: HMSO.

DES AND WELSH OFFICE (1989) *English for ages 5 to 16* ('The Cox Report'), London: HMSO.

EDWARDS, A. and COLLISON, J. (1996) *Mentoring and Developing Practice in Primary Schools*, Buckingham: Open University.

HMI (1979) *Mathematics 5–11*, London: HMSO.

HMI (1985) *Mathematics 5–16*, London: HMSO.

HMI (1990) *The Teaching and Learning of Reading in Primary Schools*, London: HMSO.

MILLETT, A. (1997) 'Bringing a new professionalism into teaching', *Education Journal*, March.

NATIONAL CURRICULUM COUNCIL (1992) *National Curriculum English: The Case for Revising the Order*, London: NCC.

TEACHER TRAINING AGENCY (1996) *Corporate Plan*, London: TTA.

6   Primary ITE English National Curriculum: Model Standards or Standard Model?

Bob Leather and Kath Langley Hamel

Writing in the *Sunday Express* in 1989, the then Secretary of State for Education and Science, Kenneth Baker, confidently proclaimed that the new English National Curriculum for schools:

> means clear standards for reading, writing, spelling, punctuation, grammar and handwriting . . . Common sense is winning out. Common sense is back in fashion. Standards of English must improve. Baker (1989)

This might have been the preamble to *Circular 10/97*. But, and it is a big 'but', everybody in education remembers the fate of the first National Curriculum for English. Between 1992 and 1995 'common sense' became very uncommon and 'sense' was replaced by the nonsense of endless debates in the media about the need to improve standards by scrapping the 'progressive' National Curriculum with one that returned to basics. We have got to hope history is not repeated with the National Curriculum for ITE. Our aim in this chapter is to raise questions about the validity of some of the assumptions underlying *10/97* (no doubt common sense assumptions) before suggesting (somewhat tentatively) how we might interpret some of the standards in order to avoid a new, even more prescriptive document in two or three years' time.

An initial response to *Circular 10/97* suggests that the omens are not good. Significantly, it fails to provide any rationale or context within which to read the document and plan courses for students. The document is referred to by its authors as: 'a full and detailed codification of requirements for new teachers'. The use of a legalistic term here suggesting as it does a list of rules or laws and the lack of a coherent rationale make this very much of a 'What' document. There is little attempt to answer critical questions such as 'Why?' or 'How?' The authors of *10/97* disclaim all responsibility for these kinds of questions; it is up to providers to make what sense they can of the document and to 'provide coherent, intellectually stimulating and professionally challenging courses of primary ITT'.

The failure to provide any clear indication of the thinking and philosophy behind the Circular can only leave us to suppose that Governmental and quasi-Governmental organizations no longer feel they have to explain themselves. It was a noticeable part of the history of the original schools' National Curriculum that the rationale behind it (*English for Ages 5 to 11* and *English 5 to 16*) quickly became, as Brian Cox himself points out: 'no longer easily available to teachers and new entrants to the profession (Cox, 1991). Memorably, of course, when *English 5 to 16* was published in June 1989 the sections containing the rationale (Chapters 1–14) were placed after those with the attainment targets and statements of attainment (Chapters 15–17). The risible explanation for this was to ensure 'ease of reference', whereas the real reason would appear to have been a desire to ensure a foregrounding of what the Government of the day considered the real meat of the document.

The intrusion of political agendas into the world of the English curriculum is not new, of course. From the early decades of the twentieth century, teachers of English have had to contend with a series of official reports which have reflected changing ideologies as masters from different sides of the political divide have sought to dress the subject in their own clothing. No other subject has been so subject to political interference in its agenda. It's partly to do with the name itself, of course; 'English' can mean a subject, a discipline, a culture or a people. And politicians have sought to impose their own definition of Englishness on the curriculum. Or to use the English curriculum in schools as a means of exercising control.

In the period following the First World War, a time of some social instability and unrest, the authors of the *Newbolt Report* of 1921 sought ways to create unity in a nation which they saw as fragmenting into class-based groups constantly in a state of conflict. The study of standard English and of a canon of English literature was a means by which the committee sought to develop social cohesion and a notion of Englishness. As George Sampson (1926), a member of the Committee, put it:

> Surely, if there is a unity called England there should be a unity called English. (p. 44)

What Sampson wanted was the use of standard spoken English taught at all stages in the education system as a way of breaking down class antagonisms.

Defining Standards

What are we to make of *Circular 10/97*, lacking as it does any overt glimpses into its thinking? The introduction to the document provides us with the nearest we get to any statement of intent and we are left in no doubt as to the key word. In the space of nine lines the word 'standards' is used five times, modified four times by the word 'raising' and once by 'higher'. Just as most of us had got used to talking and writing about 'competences' this word has, in an exercise worthy of Orwell's Ministry of Truth, now been all but obliterated from the record.

Standard(s) is an interesting word with all sorts of resonance. The CD-ROM version of the OED devotes something like 20 pages to definitions of it. The original, twelfth century, usage related to the notion of a physical standard or totem round which the king's supporters rallied to defend him, and the pennant at the top of the standard, to the death. This emblematic usage does appear as a major element in the thinking of the Labour Government. Education is undoubtedly the standard round which they want the country to unite in supporting the Government's policies. The most insistent rallying call during the election campaign of 1997 was: 'education, education, education'.

But the term has also assumed moral aspects on occasion. In one much-quoted comment on radio 4 in the 1980s Norman Tebbit (1985) managed in a couple of sentences to move from a discussion about standard English to a statement about the morals of the young:

> If you allow standards to slip to the stage where good English is no better than bad English, where people turn up filthy at school . . . all these things tend to cause people to have no standards at all, and once you have no standards then there's no imperative to stay out of crime.

Though we don't suppose either David Blunkett or Norman Tebbit would be flattered by being linked together we do see in the first period of the Labour Government something of the same reforming zeal that characterized most of Mrs Thatcher's term in office and this desire to lead a moral crusade is just one of several features the Thatcher and Blair Governments share.

These two meanings do appear to conflate in the introduction to *10/97*. However, perhaps of more relevance to our immediate concerns are two, rather more mundane, meanings of the word 'standard' between which there is an uneasy tension. A standard can be either the baseline, the norm, or it can mean the target to aim for. As used in *10/97* it seems clear that the standards represent targets which students have to achieve by the end of their training. But, as far as schools are concerned, the standards will represent a baseline for NQTs. This tension could, we believe, result in some lack of clarity within schools as to the value to be given to the standards as set out in *10/97*.

As far as the English standards in *Circular 10/97* are concerned providers will have to decide at which point in the course a student can be said to have achieved a standard or group of standards. If some are achieved at the start of the course, perhaps in knowledge about the grammar of English as set out in paragraph 12 of section C, will there be any need to revisit these standards? The problem with the standards as they are set out in *10/97* is that they seem to represent absolutes. There is no notion of progression; once a target has been reached the trainee has no further to go within the context of the Circular.

This tension between the notion of norms and targets also raises a further issue of concern to all providers of ITT courses and relates to the standard of English of entrants to courses. As *10/97* points out, providers have to ensure that entrants have to be able to communicate clearly in both written and spoken standard English.

How can providers monitor standards? One reliable way of checking should be provided by the achievement of the standards in public examinations such as GCSE. However, in something of a confession about standards at GCSE English, the authors of *10/97* confess that we cannot assume that students are: 'confident in those aspects of English which they have studied and which they are required to teach'. There is also an admission that the standards in GCSE cannot be assumed to have 'equivalence' across the whole country. This seems to us a damning indictment of the current examination system in English for 16-year-olds.

There is a double bind here. Providers have to ensure that the level of entrants' English is sufficient to ensure clear communication yet one important gatekeeping mechanism is judged unreliable. Some sort of gate keeping test must be in place to guarantee a minimum standard of English. Such a test, presumably carried out on an interview day must necessarily be sketchy, able to pick only surface aspects of the interviewee's use of English. A more detailed audit is obviously needed once a trainee is accepted on a course. Of course, once the trainee *is* accepted it becomes the responsibility of the provider to ensure that the standards of *10/97* are met.

Knowledge and Understanding of English

These general concerns provide us with a context for discussing more specific issues arising from *10/97* related to the provision of English ITT courses whether for a four-year QTS or a one-year PGCE. Specifically, we want to focus in detail on the challenges posed by section C of the English document 'Trainees' Knowledge and Understanding of English' before moving on to consider issues related to the audit and assessment of students' achievements in English.

The authors of *10/97* make it clear they have no intention of setting out how providers are to create a course or scheme of work from the 'full and detailed codification requirements' which the standards represent. Nor does the TTA intend that the standards represent everything that students need, though no indication is offered on what else might feature in an English course for a one-year PGCE, for example, which will at most consist of perhaps 70/80 hours of taught content.

How are providers to deal with the issue of knowledge about grammar and language in general which features very prominently in *10/97*? The content of section C of *10/97* seems to represent the model of grammar which the National Curriculum Council was calling for in the 1992 document *NC English: The Case for Revising the Order*: a very detailed list of discrete aspects mainly to do with the forms of English grammar, a 'naming of parts' (to use Bill Mittin's phrase) model with little reference to the application of such knowledge in investigating how it works in real texts, whether spoken or written, literary or non-literary.

Ten years ago, in presenting his Report of the Committee of Inquiry into the Teaching of English Language, Sir John Kingman (DES, 1988b) wrote:

> We argue that it is possible to give a sound and accessible description of the structure and uses of the English language. (p. iii)

The model of language that Kingman produced seems to us to be a far richer one than that in *10/97*, based as it was on a wider interpretation of the word 'grammar'. Thus, Kingman presented a model based on the following headings: the forms of English (traditional grammar); communication and comprehension; stages of language acquisition; and historical and geographical variation.

Kingman also intended his model to be used at all stages of the education process: in schools with both pupils and teachers and with students in ITE. Kingman did accept that his report carried with it serious implications for INSET and ITE and it was ultimately supported by a three-year training programme (LINC) which cost some £21m. At the last minute the Government of the day refused to publish the training materials. Tim Eggar, Minister for Education, claimed that teachers would misuse the materials in the classroom. Had the training in knowledge about language based on the Kingman model been fully carried through we feel it most unlikely that criticisms like the following by Professor John Honey (1997) would have still been valid 10 years after his report:

> Any project to restore the systematic teaching of English grammar would have to confront the limitations of knowledge of that 'lost generation' of teachers no longer confident about describing to children how English works. (p. 173)

On the other hand, it must be acknowledged that *10/97* will be far cheaper to implement. As the authors of the document point out in section C many aspects of it can be taught very quickly through the use of self-study materials. We agree that course providers should use any means at their disposal to deliver courses but we must be careful not to put too much reliance on self-study materials. Our experience of teaching under- and postgraduate students about grammar is that it is a topic which brings out many insecurities and students need support in coming to terms both with the terminology and its application in the classroom and elsewhere. New terminology affects us all. We are still trying to get used to the changes in discourse brought about by changes either in Government or Government policy. Instead of 'competences' we must now use 'standards' and 'students' became 'trainees' some time ago (though many of us still think of them by the former term). There is, of course, rich material here for discussion with students about language and how it changes to reflect a particular ideological view of the world.

We must also ensure in designing a course to meet the standards for grammar that we give students the opportunity to identify individual needs. Like other providers of courses in English, no doubt, we have found that large numbers of students cannot identify consistently the basic parts of speech (nouns, verbs etc) let alone discuss their function, while others (who have usually studied a modern foreign language) have the metalanguage off pat. What the latter group of students often can't do, though, is discuss the relevance of this knowledge in the real world; for example in talking about how the language of advertising or newspaper headlines works in particular ways to persuade or present a particular view of the world.

Crucial to the development of challenging and coherent courses to develop students' knowledge of grammar is a creative interpretation of key terms in *10/97*, one of which is clearly 'understand' or 'understanding.' Our experience over 10 years is that they can be introduced to a basic model of sentence structure reasonably quickly. However, what takes longer is the ability to apply knowledge of the model in a variety of textual contexts, whether written or spoken and we see this as a vital part of checking students' understanding and ability to apply their understanding. A range of children's writing can be used in order to discuss such issues as the development of skills in using a variety of sentence structures: simple, compound or complex. Other texts can be compared to discuss the main differences between spoken and written Standard and non-Standard English.

We are also concerned about lack of detail and oversimplifications at important parts of *10/97*. This is particularly apparent in section C where bland definitions, such as that of phonology as 'the sound system of language', indicate not just a partial meaning of technical terms but also a lack of insight into concepts underpinning the terminology. Such lack of understanding helps to explain the somewhat patronizing and simplistic advice that much of section 12 can be taught quickly through the use of self-study materials. Though we agree that self-study materials, whether printed or available in CD-ROM form, have an important role to play in the creation of courses about grammar, we do feel that the seminar discussion provides an appropriate forum in which we can develop students' understanding beyond the list of standards in *10/97*, particularly when the issue is over a word such as 'phonology' which has a range of meanings and concepts underlying it.

Auditing Subject Knowledge and Understanding

Many undergraduates are now entering institutions of higher education with English 'A' levels in language and have a good foundation for much of *10/97*. However, many graduates entering PGCE courses with English degrees whose main focus has been on the study of literature must worry about the value of their degree in the KS1 or KS2 classroom and we have heard graduate specialists express their feelings of inadequacy when faced with teaching a National Curriculum which they see as having a very strong language bias.

In the light of this any audit of the development of knowledge of grammar needs to reflect the notion that the students will have different needs at different parts of the course. We have carried out audits of students' knowledge of basic grammatical terms such as simple, compound and complex sentences as well as parts of speech after taught sessions on the sentence structure of standard English based on the model developed by David Crystal in *Rediscover Grammar*. We have also asked students to identify their own individual needs as well as distributed copies of a 'Repairkit Booklet' (see Appendix 1) to work through or use as a point of reference to check specific areas of uncertainty.

Specially designed grids (see Appendix 2) have been designed to audit students' knowledge and then used as evidence of the demonstration of subject knowledge which have then been filed in 'Professional Development Evidence Files'. Similar models have also been used in other areas of subject knowledge such as the teaching of reading.

Another area of concern relates to the role of the mentor in school in assessing student subject knowledge and the challenge of ensuring that both provider and mentor share a perception of the subject knowledge demonstrated by a student and whether such a demonstration is sufficient to have achieved a particular standard. In order to bridge any gap between provider and school there has obviously got to be a dialogue so that understandings and perceptions can be shared and developed. Subject departments must be involved in this. One training day in which we participated took the form of a moderation meeting. Representatives from schools, the subject departments of the HE provider as well as representatives from the Education Department took part. Video evidence from an English lesson was used and the mentors and college watched the video to assess subject knowledge being demonstrated by the teacher. A booklet containing a user-friendly set of grids, based on the word, sentence and text levels of reading outlined in *10/97*, designed by the English team, was used as an observation schedule and completed during the session. The format of the grid was changed slightly in the light of comments made by mentors and the whole exercise evaluated.

As far as the teaching of reading aspects of *10/97* are concerned it proved convenient to group the standards under the headings noted above which are, of course, the headings used in the structure of the literacy hour. Designing the grid gave us the opportunity to observe very clearly how loaded towards the 'word' aspects of reading the standards really are. There are far fewer standards under 'Text'. The model of reading presented in the document is very much that of a bottom-up model of reading in which the skills of decoding are regarded as the most important aspects of reading.

The booklet provided a common context within in which to discuss and note elements of subject knowledge which were being demonstrated on a moment by moment basis during a lesson and also provided mentors with evidence which could later be used in discussions with the students and subject or education tutors from the HE institution. This evidence could later form part of the student's evidence file and, if used over the course of a year, provided evidence of burgeoning expertise.

Mentors who piloted this document (see Appendix 3) commented that it gave them confidence that they were observing the same aspects of subject knowledge as a tutor from the HE institution.

Such a document could also provide evidence on which to base entries made in each student's 'Career Entry Profile' to support comments about achievement as well as noting areas for development during the first year of teaching. However, a note of caution should be entered here. How far can comments made under 'Areas for Development' be regarded as indicating weakness and therefore non-achievement of a particular standard? This once again revolves around the meaning of the word 'standard'. One member of the TTA commented in December 1997 that the standards represented a 'baseline' and therefore comments under areas for development could not be seen as failure to achieve a standard. As we have noted earlier there may well be another set of standards about which, at the time of writing, we have been given no information. Providers may well have to be wary of making any comment which could be taken to mean that a trainee has not achieved a standard. Not only would the trainee not receive QTS status, the provider would be seen as not complying with the mandate to ensure all students achieve all standards.

We believe that the success or failure of *10/97* as a document providing a blueprint for the future of ITE lies in the interpretation put on key words such as 'standards', 'demonstrate', and 'understanding'. There must be some kind of shared understanding about the meanings of these terms between the TTA, OFSTED, ITE providers and schools if the authors of the document mean it when they say there is no attempt to impose a methodology on providers. But the Cox National Curriculum was quickly replaced when powerful groups to the right of the political spectrum realized that it was not delivering the kind of curriculum they wanted. We think it highly significant that a curriculum, which was widely welcomed by teachers as enabling them to deliver both interesting and challenging work in English was taken away when it did not meet the targets set by a political agenda, to be replaced by what Brian Cox called 'basics without vision' (Cox, 1995).

If control of the ITE curriculum is not to be wrested totally from the control of providers we have to try to design courses in English which ensure students achieve the standards in courses which we would be proud to claim as ours. The alternative is to await the imposition of an ITE National Curriculum that is even more basic and with even less vision than the current schools' version.

References

BAKER, K. (1989) article in *The Sunday Express*.

Cox, B. (1991) *Cox on Cox: An English Curriculum for the 1990s*, London: Hodder and Stoughton.

Cox, B. (1995) *Cox on Cox: The Battle for the English Curriculum*, London: Hodder and Stoughton.

DES (1988a) *English for Ages 5 to 11*, London: DES.

DES (1988b) *Report of the Committee of Inquiry into the Teaching of English Language* ('The Kingman Report'), London: HMSO.

DES (1989) *English for Ages 5 to 16*, London: DES.

DfEE (1997) *Teaching: High Status, High Standards (Circular 10/97)*, London: DfEE.

HONEY, J. (1997) *Language is Power: The Story of Standard English and its Enemies*, London: Faber and Faber.

NCC (1992) *National Curriculum English: The Case for Revising the Order*, York: NCC.

SAMPSON, G. (1926) *English for the English*, Cambridge: Cambridge University Press.

TEBBIT, N. (1985) comment made during BBC radio 4 programme 'Any Questions'.

Appendix 1

FULLER DISCUSSION OF ASPECTS OF PUNCTUATION

APOSTROPHE

Catastrophes with apostrophes are everyday occurrences. A flower stall offers 'Lilie's, Anenone's and Mum's'; 'bargain T-shirt's and shell suit's' are advertised in the local freesheet. A notice at a school announced: 'This School and it's Playground will be Closed over Easter'. The confusion isn't helped, either, when a wordsmith of the stature of Tennyson leaves us with these immortal lines:

> Their's not to make reply,
> Their's not to reason why,
> Their's but to do and die: . . .

Their's? Their is? Their's is? Nobody has ever quite worked out what was on Tennyson's mind, but he certainly left us with a cute conundrum.

Actually, handling apostrophes is really a straightforward matter. But first, you must recognise that there are two kinds of apostrophes: one to indicate a *contraction* — that is, a word with some letters left out — and one to indicate *possession* of something:

> My God! Did you hear? London's burning!
> I hope London's fire services can cope!

In the first statement, the apostrophe is used to shorten the word 'is' in 'London is burning'; in the second, the apostrophe tells us that the fire services belong to London. Here are some examples:

possessive apostrophes:
Michael's mountain bike
the girl's tunic
the girls' gym
St James's Square

contraction apostrophes:
She'll be here soon (= she will)
It is six o'clock (= of the clock)
I won't do it (= will not)
It's not fair (= it is)

Appendix 2

GRAMMAR WORKSHOP

The aim of the workshop is to raise awareness of some of the terminology about grammar used in the current National Curriculum document.

1. How would you define the term *Grammar*?

2. What do you understand by the term *Standard English*?

3. *Sentence Structure*
   Define the following terms and give examples of each:

   - *simple sentence*

   - *compound sentence*

   - *complex sentence*

   - *subject*

- *verb*

- *object*

- *adverbial*

- *complement*

- *main clause*

- *subordinate clause*

Appendix 3

SECTION 2

KEY ASPECTS OF ENGLISH

[Please make brief comments under each heading, where appropriate, and put a letter in the box.]

N = *Not* attempted/   F = *Failed*   P = Making *Progress* towards
     not applicable   the standard
                    A = the standard has been *Achieved*

TEXT LEVEL

Assess the student's progress towards achieving the standards in

1   Fostering the progression of children's understanding of the text as a
    whole: [*e.g., developing explicit, implicit, deductive, evaluative and inferential understandings*];

☐

2   Developing children's ability to analyse aspects of a text: [*e.g., plot, setting, character, organisation*];

☐

3   Developing children's understanding of the relationship between spoken
    and written language:

☐

7 Mathematics — By Design With Confidence

Robin Foster

For no other subject other than mathematics would grown adults confess a lack of knowledge or a complete inability to cope. Yet very intelligent people will tell you without flinching that they hate mathematics and they happily admit that they cannot do it. When students come to teacher education many bring with them the same sorts of fear of mathematics displayed by the general population at large. Many of the students have had a bad experience of mathematics and as they want to be primary school teachers know that they will have to teach it but at the same time realize that it is not their strongest asset. Indeed many will have had very little difficulty in attaining the requisite non-mathematical paper qualifications to enter the course, but find the mathematics qualification a problem. In order to enter teacher education courses a student must attain qualifications an 'A' level or equivalent in certain subjects and in addition must attain GCSE in mathematics and English. The minimum requirement in mathematics needs to be attained by all entering training courses. To attain this some students will have spent a significant time concentrating on mathematics. Indeed some will have had a number of resits in mathematics. Many, feel a lack of confidence which is fed by the general feeling of society that mathematics is hard, but partially because repeated application to the subject has not brought them any real feelings of success.

Mathematics is, of course, one of the three core subjects of the National Curriculum and has been the subject of much speculation as to how a lack of mathematical knowledge can be addressed. Indeed when the National Curriculum was first introduced, the first documentation was related to mathematics. The 1988 documents for mathematics were soon followed by the documentation for English and science. They in turn were followed by the other subject documentation. The provision of a National Curriculum for Teacher Training would seen to be a logical extension of all of the documentation in schools to ensure a continuity of provision and some quality assurance. The publication of *Circular 10/97* underlines the need for aspiration to the highest possible standards (DfEE, 1997).

Circular 10/97 addresses the whole of the provision for teacher training in the present context. It provides a formidable list of qualities and standards to be attained by those entering the teaching profession. In the area of mathematics the list is large and students are required to demonstrate knowledge and competence over extensive areas of content and skills. For the purpose of this discussion, some of these areas will be explored generally and later in the chapter the issues of subject knowledge will be addressed more fully. The consideration of the material found in the Circular relating to mathematics rightly deserves a whole book rather than a chapter. In the subject matter of mathematics the Circular highlights several areas. Among these are the areas of subject knowledge, diagnosis of errors, classroom management, assessment and record keeping.

Subject Knowledge

It must appear self-evident that if one is to teach a subject, then knowledge is essential. The subject of mathematics has taxed the minds of many and has from time to time been the subject of much heated debate. The setting up of the Cockcroft Committee and its reporting in 1982 represented one of the recent ways in which this concern was expressed (Cockcroft, 1982). It was set up under a Labour Government and reported under a Conservative one. It is interesting to note that the concerns set in motion by a Labour Government were taken up by their Conservative successors and still are seen as a concern when the ruling party changed again.

The problem of knowledge seems an insoluble one. If knowledge is to be defined by content the answer would seem to be simple, for most agree on the content of the subject and also most agree that there is a problem. The fact that mathematics is seen as a single subject entity might actually cause some of the problems. Uniquely in mathematics there appears to be a gulf which separates those who can be described as successful and those who find it either not to their liking or too difficult. This aspect will be discussed more fully below.

Mental Mathematics

The Circular stresses the need for mental process. Indeed it is difficult to imagine doing any mathematics without some engagement of the mental faculties. Even the most routine processes rely on the recall of simpler mathematical facts. The application of multiplication of two multi-digit numbers requires one to use known facts based on single figure calculation. If these basic facts are ready and available it helps the smooth working out of more complicated ones. This mental knowledge is important. The acquisition of these number facts needs attention and the stress placed on it by the Circular is timely and important. Perhaps some caution needs to be addressed to the situation too. The essential need is for people who are able to *apply their knowledge in a meaningful way*, rather than being drilled by rote. Useful mathematical discussion, so emphasized by those following the Cockcroft recommendations in paragraph 243 is the basis for mental work as well as any other mathematics. Good understanding and efficient methods of recalling information is as true as it was in the past. Robert Recorde gives us a cautionary prompt. In an evocative passage he demonstrates that he is able to teach a learner how to work out a subtraction, but interestingly indicates that the real test of the learner is to learn something *beyond the confines of what has been taught*:

> *Master*   I wil propounde here ii examples to you whiche if you often doo prac-
> tice, you shall be rype and perfect to subtract any other summe lightly.
>
> *Scholar*   I thanke you, but I thynke I might the better doo it, if you did show me
> the working of it.
>
> *Master*   Yea but you muste prove yourselfe to do som thynges that you were
> never taught, or els you shall not be able to doo any more than you were
> taught, and were rather to learne by rote (as they cal it) than by reason.
> (Robert Recorde, 1543)

It has to be observed that some of the advice given in the Circular could be construed as encouraging a rote approach to mental arithmetic (DfEE, 1997, p. 32). In fairness however, if the advice is read in the sense of setting an environment where discussion is encouraged and inventiveness is applauded, then it is useful. Thus flexibility on the part of the student is required. This in turn requires a great confidence and knowledge.

Diagnosis of Errors

Related to this area of mental processes are the ways in which the wrong answer can indicate a great deal about the thinking which produced it. The Circular requires that '*trainees must be taught* to recognise children's errors' (ibid, p. 36). Included in *the trainees must be taught* section are words of warning about avoiding methods which contribute to or exacerbate pupils' errors. The section is laudable but it seems cursory. It brings to notice that there are important things to be considered, but in its brevity it sounds rather prescriptive and limiting. This important area needs to be linked with considerations of mental methods as well as to the assessment of children's progress. Experienced teachers tend to have an armoury of techniques to diagnose children's common errors. The development of this skill needs to be recognized as an important part of the training process.

Assessment and Record Keeping

The enormity of the task faced by students is compounded when the issues of assessment and record keeping are added to the specific requirements of mathematics. The central importance of mathematics is not in question. It is worth noting that considerations of assessment and record keeping are also concerns for other subjects in the core and foundation. By reflecting on the needs for assessing progress in mathematics one appreciates the measure of how multitalented any entrant to the teaching profession needs to be.

Classroom Management

The Circular also lists generic skills and how those pertaining to classroom management, like assessment, relate to the whole of the National Curriculum. The need for careful planning in mathematics is important as are considerations of management techniques specific for mathematics. The suggestion of a *numeracy hour* serves to stress the importance of mathematical activity in the National Curriculum but also to heighten the specific needs of helping students to cope with the complex demands of their future role.

In setting the scene we have treated the contents of the Circular in a very general sense. It could be argued that all are of equal importance. But it is to a limited focus of those listed that we now turn. This is not to diminish the importance of those we are not discussing further, but to indicate that if we dig deeper we begin to see that the issues are really very complex. If we consider the area of subject knowledge we might think we are addressing a single issue. Ensuring a better knowledge on the part of the teaching force might seem a simple solution to the problem of the teaching and learning of mathematics. The problematic nature of this apparently simple solution is central to our subsequent discussion.

The Search for a Reliable Standard

For entrants into teaching a basic knowledge in the subjects they are to teach is essential. Once this is established there is a difficulty in defining the standard which will define competence. This is particularly problematic for mathematics, as for many of the reasons already noted it is a subject area which causes problems for many adults, let alone those adults who are going to teach children. There is a compelling argument which notes that there is a cycle of decay encouraged if those teaching pass on their own fears and apparent lack of knowledge in the subject area. The guarantee offered by a GCSE pass at appropriate level would appear not to be sufficient. The concerns expressed by many is that even with the basic qualification there seems to be a lack of knowledge or competence in mathematics on the part of intending teachers. This shortfall, it is argued, should be addressed by the training courses. This sets a series of dilemmas not least ones relating to the time available on such courses. If the problem is so deep seated that some students will have had difficulties learning the appropriate mathematics in 11 years of compulsory schooling, what remediation will be really effective as a tiny proportion of a three of four-year course? This has to be set against the equally important task of helping students to teach children effectively in the area of mathematics and other subjects.

One route might be to increase the GCSE requirement, but this begs a question of how would courses be filled if this were to happen, for people with very high qualifications at 'A' level often only have the basic minimum in the area of mathematics. It needs also to be noted that degree entry qualifications for courses not leading to qualified teacher status do not call for GCSE mathematics, so students with good 'A' levels, without the GCSE mathematics, might be drawn to such courses.

Eraut (1994) looks at the wider issues of assessing and accounting for professional competence in a variety of professional situations. In the case of those preparing for teaching some definition of subject knowledge would need to be part of any measure of entrants' competence. He comments:

> Another problem is needlessly created when overenthusiastic proponents of standards try to invest them in an aura of perfectionism. Whichever purpose is being considered, one role of standards is to establish a reasonable level of agreement and common understanding, about the definition of competence. Well-defined standards will do this more effectively than poorly-defined standards; but there are still limits to what written statements can achieve on their own. The area of common understanding could be explained by additional conferences and workshops, and will improve still further when people continue to work together for a period of time, i.e., during the establishment of the verification process. But total uniformity of interpretation is an unattainable goal. Trying too hard to produce a foolproof system will only make intelligent people feel that they are being treated like fools. (p. 212)

This 'aura of perfectionism' seems particularly apposite in the case of mathematics. The cry on the part of the public and press about standards can so easily be amplified by the apparent ease with which individuals can be found who seem lacking in knowledge. Any arithmetical errors on the part of particular teachers are seen as being indicative that the whole profession is peopled with individuals who cannot do any computation successfully. The appeal to a previous golden age when teachers got everything right only emphasizes the difficulty of the present plight. In the rhetoric no one appears to ask how this golden age assessed competence on the part of those recipients of the crown of total accuracy in arithmetic, to say nothing of grammar and spelling! The sentiments are appealing and the search for that golden age where teachers were knowledgeable beyond reproof, would probably reveal that the politicians who ruled them were never the cause of concern for what is currently called 'sleaze'!

Standards by Content

To many mathematics is defined by content. In fact of all the subjects in the curriculum there seems to be a general agreement on the content. A stress on arithmetic is seen as the centre of any definition of the 'basics'. It would appear that if the content were clearly defined, success in the subject could be measured. This idea is not new. In various documents over the years this has been emphasized. In the 1912 *Regulation for the Training of Teachers* the syllabus included elementary mathematics up to, and including:

Geometry of lines, circles and simple solid bodies, but excluding conic sections.
Coordinate Geometry of lines and circles.
Algebra: Progressions. The Binomial Theorem for positive integers.
Logarithms and their use. Probabilities.
Plane Trigonometry. The solution of triangles.
Mechanics: Friction. Virtual work. Centre of gravity. Simple machines.
Motions of pendulums and projectiles. Motion in a circle. Impulsive forces acting
on elastic and inelastic particles. (Yoxall and Gray, 1912)

The content seems clear but the syllabus goes on to indicate two interesting points. First that training colleges were 'not required or advised to undertake the whole of the syllabus'. They were required to make the students sufficiently aware of the subject and have a thorough understanding of some of the content rather than the whole covered superficially. The second interesting point is that the documentation indicates:

Students taking this subject would probably derive more advantage from working simple problem papers than from attending formal lectures. (ibid)

Procedural Concerns

The apparently desirable paper qualification in mathematics might actually hide other problems. The way in which mathematics is performed by individuals has been the subject of much interest. In much of the recent work in mathematics education there has been a concern about the way in which children, in particular, perform calculations. The work of Hiebert and others (see Hiebert, 1986) have looked at theories of procedural and conceptual knowledge. The importance of this area of research cannot be underestimated as it relates both to the issues of what goes on in classrooms and to the knowledge base of individuals. The work of Gray and Tall (1991) has extended aspects of this and they put the issues even more clearly. They use the term *procept* to indicate a duality between process and concept. This duality is seen in a simple case of addition like:

$$3 + 4 =$$

To some learners this is a set of instructions which might be something like: *count three, count four, count seven and you have the answer.* To another learner the result seven is arrived at by no procedure at all, apparently they *just know it*. The first person's methods of solution for this type of question are dominated by a series of procedures or routines which have to be remembered, and each question elicits a prompting to start applying them. On the other hand the second learner is working conceptually and freed from the routines is able to manipulate and re-present the relationships to themselves with an astonishing degree of flexibility which demonstrates a thorough knowledge of arithmetic.

Extending this analysis to other areas of the mathematics curriculum, the person who is operating procedurally needs to remember a whole series of rules and techniques whereas the person operating conceptually with a confidence in the relationships is working on at least a different plane, if not another planet. When particular topics in the mathematics curriculum are considered, the procedural-conceptual divide is evident. The remembering of apparently unrelated rules worked for many people with arithmetic, but when algebra is encountered a rule-based approach is doomed to fail from the beginning. Rules like: *do the same to each side*; or *swap sides swap signs*, have only a limited application. To succeed with algebra a confidence in the area of manipulation of symbols is developed when these rules are replaced by a conceptual understanding of the basic structure of algebra itself.

Student Teachers

It is when these procedural and conceptual considerations are placed into the context of student teachers that the enormity of the task is fully revealed. In addressing this important learning issue we note that in the classroom some children operate conceptually and they seem to cope with the mathematics with no apparent difficulty, whereas others working procedurally need more time and often do not grasp the essential nature of the relationships which constitute mathematics. These children often rely on a rule-based series of routines to get the answers. It is precisely this group of children who may fail GCSEs and other tests. As we have noted some of the entrants to teacher education might fall into this second group. They will, of course, be performing very well in their selected 'A' level subjects but in mathematics may be working procedurally. The consequences for helping such students are vitally important.

First they need to be helped with their own mathematics. This to a large extent will probably be tackled by assisted self-study. Diagnosis might be achieved by a carefully planned, conveniently administered test. Once areas of difficulty have been identified, self-study with tutorial support of a drop in sort might be encouraged. Whatever teaching and support is given it needs to be realistic in terms of the very heavy load of other work undertaken as part of the rest of the course. This assisted diagnosis needs sensitive tutorial help but also relies heavily on the self-motivated commitment on the part of the students themselves. Additional diagnostic tests can be given in order to help assess progress.

Secondly they need to be helped to aid children. In particular they may need to be supported in ways which allow them to diagnose how children work on mathematics. A teacher who operates procedurally needs to be helped to appreciate that a 6-year-old who says, 'I know that five and six is 11, because five and five is 10 and one more is 11,' needs to be praised and encouraged to extend their ideas. Or the 8-year-old who says, 'I just know that 100 subtract 26 is 74', needs not to be directed to write it down in a vertical form and do a cross out, but encouraged to explain their thinking. For the student teacher who sees these and similar tasks as occasions to apply a procedure, it can be very difficult and threatening.

The Case of Subtraction

Historically there has been no lack of advice offered to teachers about the way in which mathematics needs to improve. Striving at improving standards in mathematics seems to have been the concern of many people over the years. Much of the advice has concentrated on the apparently laudable intention of assisting children to get the correct answer. This has led to rules to follow and to fashions in particular methods. To many the 'getting the correct answer' has been linked to applying a particular written algorithm. So the application of the written procedure is seen as the way to get the answer. This leads to legitimate concern which is expressed by the observations of Bierhof (1996) who observed that British children are more likely to resort to pencil and paper rather than mental methods. It might be worth noting that stressing *particular* mental methods procedurally might not really improve the situation. Rather, it is the ability to apply mental powers *in a flexible manner* which is required, rather than the overlaying of more procedures to be memorised. As we have noted some children are able to apply flexible thought without explicit instruction, others might be able to do this with careful instruction.

A lot of energy has been expended on pencil and paper methods with generations of school children and many pupils still labour under the yoke of showing their working and learning how to perform procedures, unthinkingly. Of all the arithmetical work in primary schools it is probably subtraction which causes the most difficulty for the learner. The particular method is often the cause of much debate. At parents' evenings on mathematics standard procedures often dominate, with questions like, 'Why do you do the sums differently from when we were at school?' Looking at some of the advice offered to teachers over the years is illuminating. There is much stress on applying a procedure.

Excursus

Subtraction Algorithms

An algorithm is simply a set procedure which can be applied reliably to a class of problems and if applied correctly will give the answer. The term derives from the name of an Arabic mathematician Al-Khwarizmi, who lived from about 780 to about 850 AD. Using an algorithm does not require an understanding of how it works; rather if the correct answer is what is needed it provides a simple convenient way of obtaining it.

There are various ways in which two numbers can be subtracted from each other. Two main algorithms are outlined here. (For some aspects of the history and origin of specific algorithms see for example Nelson, Joseph and Williams, 1993.)

The Equal Addition Algorithm

The success of the method relies on the mathematical fact that the difference between two numbers is the same if you add the same quantity to each. e.g. $9 - 5 = 4$. Adding two to the nine and two to the five produces $11 - 7$, which also give the difference four. The arrangement of the 10s and units means that 10 is added to the top number in the units and 10 is added, for convenience in the 10s in the lower number. The difference remains the same. When carrying out the procedure the child might record as indicated on the left, the expanded form on the right is an attempt to explain the logic of the process:

T	U	Expanded form	
6	^{1}3	$60 + 3$	$60 + 13$ (10 added to units)
-2_1	5	$20 + 5$	$30 + 5$ (10 added to tens)
			$30 + 8 = 38$

The Decomposition Algorithm

This method relies on the larger number being decomposed into two other numbers. Sixty-three can be written $60 + 3$, but also in many other ways including $50 + 13$. By decomposing the number to this more convenient form the subtraction can be carried out. When carrying out the procedure the child might record as indicated in below:

T	U	Expanded form	
^{5}6	^{1}3	$60 + 3 = 50 + 13$	
-2	5	$20 + 5 = 20 + 5$	
		$30 + 8 = 38$	

Ballard (1928) offered some strong advice. He seems to have formulated a novel definition of good and bad schools. It seems a good school is one where children are required to perform subtraction by using the equal addition algorithm, and a bad school is one which uses decomposition. If one were to survey schools today, Ballard's definition would indicate that most schools are bad. The following passage is from one of his books on the subject. A long section has been chosen to be included here for two reasons: first, to indicate the points he is making and secondly to give a flavour of the emotional side of the debate which he seemed to want to introduce.

> Just before the War I carried out extensive research into the ability of London children to perform the fundamental processes of adding, subtracting, multiplying and dividing. The tests consisted of simple mechanical sums to be worked on paper. When the results were examined, it was found that the schools fell into two distinct groups — those in which the subtraction was good and those in which the subtraction was bad. By 'good' or 'bad' I mean good or bad in comparison with the achievements of the same schools in the other three processes. On fully investigating the matter I found that where subtraction was good it was taught by the old–fashioned method of equal addition, and where it was bad by the new fashioned method of decomposition.

It was largely as a result of the vehemence of views like Ballard's that the standard algorithm of equal addition was virtually completely used in preference to the earlier favoured method of decomposition. The decomposition algorithm was dismissed by Ballard as a 'nursery method' and therefore to be avoided at all costs.

Work in the United States where equal addition was also used seemed to confirm the views of Ballard. The work of Brownell and Moser (1949) introduced a new element. They noted that all of the testing which had been done on children indicated that equal addition was the best method for getting answers. They reviewed several methods but focused clearly on *decomposition* and *equal addition*. They asked a different question. They wanted to include understanding. In their research they were asking a question about 'best' which included reference to how it was taught. Thus instead of having two groups they saw four groups. They investigated the methods taught *rationally* or *mechanically*. The four groups were decomposition taught rationally, decomposition taught mechanically, equal addition taught rationally and equal addition taught mechanically. By analysing this way they noted that the best method was *decomposition taught rationally*. Largely as a result of this research linked to the desire for children to understand the decomposition model was taught in preference to equal addition in many parts of the United States of America. Thus the fashion or pendulum swing is away from one method to another. However, in the work of Brownell and Moser, there was another side. In reporting on the mechanical teaching of the algorithms, the worst scenario was *decomposition taught mechanically*.

In reviewing the scene in Britain, there was a swing away from equal addition in the 1960s. I feel this was not directly as a result of the work of people like Brownell and Moser, but rather on the work of people like Dienes and Catengo (see for example, Dienes, 1971). It was fuelled by the desire to have children understand. The equal addition algorithm was seen as being employed mechanically and classroom materials which could model the process were advocated, so decomposition became the more preferred method. Brownell and Moser had noted the dangers of not teaching it rationally. The enthusiasm for teaching with understanding did not seem to allow for circumstances where understanding would not be generated or utilized.

Investigating the methods used by adults in working out subtractions revealed that most of those surveyed used decomposition (Foster, 1996). Two groups were interviewed. They were of particular interest as their academic achievement backgrounds were different, but members of both groups were training to work with children. The first group was from PGCE students specializing in early years and the second was a group of nursery nurse students. Decomposition was the main algorithm used. Further questioning revealed that additionally they used the algorithm mechanically. This might be considered to be rather worrying. This is not to say that this is an indication of declining standards, as I feel sure that the results reflect what might be found in any group of adults, for they represent a wide range of educational achievement. The reality is that to obtain answers many of the adults were operating procedurally by simply applying the rule. Even when invited to try to explain the process, they resorted to mechanical explanation. The real concern is how these people who are both in their various capacities intending to work with children in the classroom, can be helped to analyse their own understanding to help children develop their mathematical ideas.

Implications for Teacher Education Courses

The outcome of such observation is not to suggest which is the best method to carry out arithmetical manipulations, but how adults working with children can be encouraged to help children in their care. Whilst specific items of content are important, it is the learning which is even more important. If those presenting themselves to learn how to teach have in general a procedural approach there are some strong consequences for those planning for courses. Tackling this is a difficult and sensitive operation. For students who have struggled to obtain the GCSE qualification may very well have resorted to procedural methods to 'get through'. Courses need not only stress the importance on the part of the teacher to know how to do the mathematics, there is a deeper and potentially more difficult task: intending teachers need to be able to reflect on not only how they learnt but on how children learn. This in reality seems an impossible task, in the time given.

The function of any course of teacher education needs to address these learning issues. The practical outcome is that in looking at children's learning of the topics, the student teachers' ideas can be addressed at the same time. By talking about potential misunderstanding on the part of children, students' ideas can be clarified. This preparing for teaching of mathematics is central to college courses. It may mean that the student teacher has to begin to look afresh at some of the simplest of notions. It will also challenge them to think about how they think and how indeed some children might think in radically different ways. Central to this endeavour is student confidence.

The confidence needs to be of two sorts. First a confidence in being able to help children learn the mathematics. This is built on the second area of confidence, which is the teacher's own knowledge of the subject. There is an often quoted adage that you only really learn something when you have to teach it. This is particularly true with mathematics. The learning in the college situation is only a beginning which can only be furthered by work in the classroom and future in-service training needs. The 'aura of perfectionism' noted by Eraut (1994) needs to be seen in the context of the real needs of the teacher in the classroom and in the development of professionalism. Teachers who assess learning in the classroom and are able to react with knowledge to the needs of the development of mathematical thinking in the pupils in their charge are what our schools need. Initial courses can only be the start of this. The courses need to address both the knowledge base in mathematics and the importance of the way in which it has been acquired by the teacher and is to be acquired by children. This is a tall order and makes the role of the college course difficult. Repeated demands to ensure that teacher knowledge is content based may seem easy, but in reality this is the least of the problems to be addressed. The more intransigent problem is how to develop children's thinking without resorting solely to procedural methods, and the successful application of algorithms being counted as competence in arithmetic. In short how can college courses enable trainee teachers to help children think mathematically, rather than teaching them to do arithmetic?

References

BALLARD, P.B. (1928) *Teaching the Essentials of Arithmetic*, London: University of London Press.

BIERHOF, H. (1996) *Laying the Foundations of Numeracy*, London: National Institute of Economic and Social Research.

BROWNELL, W. and MOSER, H.E. (1949) *Meaningful versus Mechanical Learning*, Durham NC: Duke University Press.

COCKROFT, W. (1982) *Mathematics Counts*, London: HMSO.

DfEE (1997) *Teaching: High Status, High Standards (Circular 10/97)*, London: HMSO.

DIENES, Z.P. (1971) *Building up Mathematics*, London: Hutchinson.

ERAUT, M. (1994) *Developing Professional Knowledge and Competence*, London: Falmer Press.

FOSTER, R. (1996) *Subtraction Methods employed by Intending Early Years Professionals and the Consequences for Helping Children in the Infant Classroom. Learning for Life*, Coventry: Warwick International Early Years Conference.

GRAY, E. and TALL, D. (1991) *Success and Failure in Mathematics: Precept and Procedure — A Primary Perspective*, Coventry: Mathematics Education Research Centre, University of Warwick.

HIEBERT, J. (ed) (1986) *Conceptual and Procedural Knowledge: The Case of Mathematics*, Hillsdale, NJ: Lawrence Erlbaum Associates.

NELSON, D., JOSEPH, G. and WILLIAMS, J. (1993) *Multicultural Mathematics*, Oxford: OUP.

RECORDE, R. (1543) 'The Grounde of Artes', in HOWSON, A.G. (1982) *A History of Mathematics Education in England*, Cambridge: CUP.

YOXALL, J.H. and GRAY, E. (1912) *The Red Code*, London: Schoolmaster Publishing Company.

8   Beyond the Core: Raising Standards Across the Curriculum

Rob David, Kevin Hamel and Chris Rowley

The original intention of the National Curriculum was to give the foundation subjects a substantial role in the school curriculum. It was envisaged that they were to be part of the curriculum for all students from 5 to 16. Such an intent did not last long. The overcrowding of the curriculum was quickly recognized, and their status as individual subjects being taught for GCSE was soon eroded. The Dearing Review of the National Curriculum (1994) maintained their status at Key Stages One, Two and Three, but the slimming down of their content permitted many schools to reallocate time away from these subjects to the core subjects of English, mathematics and science.

Circular 14/93 from the Department for Education required teacher training institutions to teach all students a minimum of 150 hours in each of the three core subjects on primary education courses. The effect of this was to further crowd an overcrowded timetable, and one of the points of most give was perceived to be the time allocated to teaching non-specialists the foundation subjects. At the same time as the status of the foundation subjects was being reduced there was an expectation, at times a requirement, that they make a contribution to the delivery of further entitlements. These include IT and language, the development of spiritual, moral, personal, social and cultural qualities, as well as the five cross-curricular themes whose status, though currently ill-defined, dates back to the original National Curriculum.

With the Government increasingly voicing concern about the standards of literacy and numeracy among the nation's children, the foundation subjects have found themselves further threatened. These changes have been quickly reflected in new requirements for initial teacher training (ITT) (*Circular 10/97*).

The purpose of this chapter is to identify the problems now faced by the foundation subjects in the light of *Circular 10/97*, and to argue the case for a reconsideration of their place in the ITT curriculum. The publication of the National Curriculum for ITT (*Circular 10/97*) seems an appropriate moment to reflect on the present status and future prospects of three of the foundation subjects, namely geography, history and music, which together illustrate many of the problems confronting teacher trainers.

Current Assumptions

The current model for delivery of ITT courses tends to assume that generic issues will be addressed by education staff and that a large hourage is made available to the three core subjects. The few hours remaining, once school placements have been incorporated in the programme, are made available for the foundation subjects. Whilst appreciating the reasons for this shift in emphasis we are concerned that the model is based upon a number of assumptions and false premises.

The first of these is the assumption that the laudable attempt to raise standards in schools is dependent solely upon the quality of teaching and learning in the three core subjects. Given the minimal, and as has been shown, often reducing time allocation on ITT courses to the foundation subjects, the quality of teaching, and hence the quality of learning in a substantial part of the curriculum will not improve, and when contrasted with the anticipated improvements in the core subjects, will appear to decline. How long will it be before there is a hue and cry about falling standards in the wider curriculum? The current ITT model also assumes that the foundation subjects have little to contribute to basic numeracy, literacy and scientific enquiry, whilst at the same time there is an expectation that they will contribute to the extension of those same skills in the primary classroom.

Secondly *Circular 10/97* has created a new threat which is in danger of cancelling the gains made in primary ITT since *Circular 24/89*. The minimal reference to subject knowledge and the low level required to satisfy the standard — a derisory level 7 for each non-core, non-specialist subject, and only a GCE Advanced Level standard in a specialist subject, has given the green light for the re-emergence of curriculum unspecific generic education courses. We seem about to re-enter an era when primary teachers know all about planning, teaching and classroom management, the theory of assessment, recording and reporting, and the need for professionalism, but do not have enough subject knowledge either to teach effectively or to ensure high quality learning across the range of National Curriculum subjects. Such assumptions need to be challenged and the contribution of the foundation subjects, both to the enrichment of ITT courses and the primary school curriculum, needs to be forcefully restated. We believe that there is a need to rethink how the hourage is allocated so that students can receive a full entitlement to the foundation subjects in a way which recognizes the fundamental role of those subjects in the delivery of the whole primary curriculum.

Paradoxically, as the National Curriculum for ITT becomes established, the foundation subjects are those which future trainees will have had least access to since many will have ceased study of one or more of them at the end of Key Stage 3. By contrast the core subjects will have been studied at least until the end of Key Stage 4, and all students will have attained grade C or better at GCSE. In addition substantially more time will have been devoted to them throughout the years of compulsory education.

Level 7 Requirements

A new feature of the standards required of all primary trainees in the foundation subjects is the need to demonstrate a standard equivalent to level 7 of the National Curriculum by the end of their course. When the level statements were written, they were intended to act as a measure of attainment for children at the end of Key Stage 3 (at the age of 14). They have been inappropriately appropriated by the TTA as a base line standard for subject knowledge for future teachers. The terminology of the statements is an insult to adults (increasingly mature students entering the profession after other careers), and at times is plainly irrelevant.

In *music*, as in art, level 7 presents something of an enigma as expectations in both subjects are intended to be only broadly equivalent to numerical level descriptors. The revised National Curriculum orders for music indicate an expected standard of level 5/6 at Key Stage 3, with the addition of a further level descriptor for exceptional performance. Are we to assume that this provides an appropriate level 7 statement which we are able to apply to undergraduate students on completion of a 20 hour course? Consider this description from the National Curriculum with regard to performance alone:

> Pupils perform with confidence, control and an awareness of style, making expressive use of phrasing and subtle changes within the musical elements . . .

Obviously, there are real difficulties here. The clarity of the music orders are to be commended, and the description of exceptional attainment provides a useful guide within its intended context. However, the skills described require regular practise, consolidation and interaction within musical groupings, and it is doubtful whether the music working party would have seriously proposed that all QTS students could achieve such mastery of skills in performance, let alone in composing, appraising and listening, within the confines of at most 20 taught hours.

In *history* in order to meet the level 7 standard, trainees, strictly speaking, have to learn substantial amounts of content from the Key Stage 3 curriculum rather than from the primary history curriculum. This has to be learnt alongside key elements written specifically as a challenge for 14-year-olds rather than adults on a degree course. Any trainee who cannot show independence in following lines of enquiry, reach substantiated conclusions independently or select, organize and deploy relevant information to produce consistently well structured narratives, descriptions and explanations should not be on a course leading to an academic degree.

As it is virtually impossible in the time available, for specialist students to acquire the subject knowledge to teach the vast range of content, particularly in Key Stage 2 history (assuming that is what the standard requires), it is clearly unrealistic to expect non-specialists in the few course (or directed study hours) available to have a satisfactory competence.

In *geography* the level 7 descriptors, though skill rather than content related, are often as likely to have been achieved through other subjects, or from experience as from classroom practice. In order to prepare trainees for the primary curriculum every opportunity is needed to celebrate, develop and reflect upon the process of enquiry in geography. It is quite within our grasp to produce expectations for students in which the rigour with which they enquire into the subjects content reflects their present as well as their future role as teachers.

The level 7 requirement imposes constraints peculiar to the foundation subjects:

(i) In some subjects trainees are faced with a vast prescribed content knowledge.

(ii) In most of the subjects particular skills and knowledge appropriate to trainee teachers are not addressed by level 7, for example, level 7 does not necessarily offer the skills of critical inquiry which one would expect to be developing with an undergraduate who will shortly be making choices regarding resource purchase and teaching approaches in these subjects.

(iii) Non-specialist students in foundation subjects usually have less than 20 taught hours to develop their subject knowledge and to tackle pedagogical issues surrounding the subject. Whilst achieving level 7 will demonstrate that the students can complete the tasks and display their knowledge in certain limited contexts, that is very different to being able to create the contexts themselves, devise questions and with confidence assess pupils' responses.

(iv) There is a need to recognize a distinction between 'subject knowledge' and 'pedagogical subject knowledge' (Shulman, 1986). A trainee teacher who demonstrates pedagogical subject knowledge has an approach to learning which can, to some extent, transcend the subjects. Such a student would be able to demonstrate key research skills; an holistic approach to learning; an ability to tackle questions and show an awareness of what they do not know as well as what they do know.

The level 7 rubric in the Circular smacks of Teacher Training Agency (TTA) laziness with regard to defining adequately the pedagogical content knowledge associated with the foundation subjects. The standards required in English and mathematics reveal that the TTA does not consider that effective teaching and learning in those subjects in any way equates with level 7. Our first substantive proposal for enhancing the status of the foundation subjects is that the level 7 requirement for ITT be abandoned.

Enquiring Trainees

Our second suggestion builds on the new TTA vision for the teaching profession as one of lifelong learning and continuing professional development. In this context a major role of ITT must be to teach trainees how to study and learn on their own. Learning to learn must be founded in enquiry. At the end of 13 or 14 years study in a National Curriculum structured environment students often have lost the ability to ask questions, to recognize assumptions, and to judge the validity of points of view. A review of the hourage given to the foundation subjects is essential if standards in these subjects in schools are to be significantly raised.

This means that in *history* for example, given the hourage available, the emphasis of the non-specialist as well as the specialist courses should be on helping trainees study for themselves the content of units with which they are not familiar. Students, who will often be unfamiliar with the subject and its material, need to be taught to develop their own knowledge alongside a developing ability to reflect upon it. A key feature of this process, and a prime role of the ITT institution, is to make available the sources of information traditionally housed in libraries, and through structured learning help students use such resources critically and creatively. Adequate library holdings (which means investment in books and other sources of information) and supportive bibliographies which help students, who will often be unfamiliar with the subject and its material, to develop their own knowledge are a prerequisite. Any information booklets provided by tutors may be a bonus, but they will represent a disservice if students leave an institution unsure how to study once they do not have the support services of an ITT institution around them. Nettles have to be grasped. The administrative convenience which usually dictates that an early years non–specialist course in history is of the same length as an upper primary one, needs to be challenged. There is no doubt that in history there is a need to differentiate the time allocations between upper primary and early years courses. If upper primary teachers are insecure with the content of history, let alone the skills and concepts contained within the five key elements, they will inevitably fail to exploit the opportunities available.

Although the situation in *geography* is somewhat different, the need for increased course hourage is no less acute. As in history the potential content is vast, but with less prescribed content knowledge. What students require is the skill to view issues and interpret data in order to recognize questions that arise, and to know how to critically apply ideas to contexts. In geography trainees need challenge and dialogue, they need to read newspapers, argue a point, experience and respond to different views and contribute to group study. The ability to challenge assumptions and justify points of view are more important than any particular body of knowledge. However, successful geography teaching is dependent upon being able to select appropriate examples. Although the National Curriculum does not prescribe the content to the same extent as with history, students in some ways have a harder task because they have to find their own contexts, and need considerable time to become familiar with case studies that exemplify the issues that are required to be addressed. The time available to train the non-specialist students is not adequate to achieve this, and therefore, as in history, all that can be done is to show students how to study, without the opportunities to explore the issues raised by their investigations in group situations. The task facing the non-specialist student in both subjects is considerably harder than that of the specialist, and ultimately more children will be taught by non–specialists than by specialists.

It has already been suggested that confidence in *music* requires continuous opportunities for sustained practice. In addition if students are to develop children's skills and abilities in composition, they need to have experienced the decision-making process in music, and to be familiar and comfortable with the processes of appraisal. At present, opportunities to develop skills in composition are equally limited by time constraints.

Social, Moral, Spiritual and Cultural Elements of the Curriculum

If the basic knowledge and understandings associated with each of the foundation subjects cannot be secured in the time available, opportunities to contribute to the wider social, moral, spiritual and cultural elements of the curriculum (SMSC) will not be realized. Our third suggestion is to consider the foundation subjects' contribution to this new agenda as one of the means of enhancing their status, and increasing their time allocation. If anything more than lip service is to be paid to SMSC, the subjects that can develop ideas in these areas must be given some prominence in both schools and in the training of teachers. The foundation subjects are well placed to highlight the social, moral, spiritual and cultural aspects of the primary curriculum — better placed indeed than a core subject such as mathematics.

Spiritual issues such as the concepts of proof, truth and certainty are fundamental to the key elements of the *history* curriculum. The historical content provides opportunities for pupils to study religious beliefs, and to value the beliefs and works of individuals and communities. Opportunities to study moral issues in history, such as the nature of good and evil, abound, and pupils are constantly called upon to make moral judgments during their studies. The history curriculum has been devised to consider issues of nationality and culture in contexts as wide apart as the United Kingdom, Africa, America and Asia.

Geography offers other opportunities for SMSC, particularly if the subject is taught so as to develop a critical yet positive awareness of the nature of the world in which we live. Apart from the obvious moral issues surrounding our understanding of other cultures, aspects of the programme of study which deal with the environment offer a wealth of areas for which we have no known answers, and for which the teaching requires an approach which considers spiritual awareness of the environment, as well as an understanding of how we might tackle the ethical issues surrounding our relationship to plants and animals as well as other humans.

The NC orders for *music* emphasize both an awareness of the social and religious functions of music, and the need to view musical styles and traditions within their historical and cultural contexts. In addition, SCAA has recognized that music provides very specific contributions to, and perspectives on, spiritual, moral, social and cultural development, and has begun to seek advice on these. Clearly there are many opportunities here which will need timetabled time if they are to be exploited adequately.

Links Between Core and Foundation Subjects

A second means of enhancing the status, and thus the time allocation of the foundation subjects is to reconsider the relationship between core and foundation subjects. It is not without significance that the SCAA has highlighted the powerful and effective ways in which the foundation subjects may contribute to language through the unique experiences and the particular vocabulary that each subject offers.

Although the description of the curriculum as a 'seamless robe' suggesting interconnected strands of knowledge and shared approaches to learning is no longer tenable, the current model of teacher education which sees subjects in neat boxes which are distinct is equally flawed. There are clear links between core and foundation subjects, as well as links between the foundation subjects themselves, and those links are not always precisely what one would expect.

Take language as an example. It may seem that music and art share similar terms. Rhythm, pattern, texture, shape and form can be identified not only in music, but also, for example, in architecture. Nevertheless, although artists and musicians may talk of tone, line, colour, texture, rhythm, pattern, shape and form, they do not always mean the same thing. Each art form is unique, and the Gulbenkian Report (1982) indicates the need for caution in integrating the arts.

For the historian language is the means by which much of the evidence base has been communicated to subsequent generations. This could be in the form of oral traditions such as the Icelandic sagas which were eventually committed to writing; written documents or contemporary oral testimony with its links to speaking and listening. A specialized vocabulary emerges which will strengthen children's own grasp of language. In addition historians (and children's) interpretations will often be transmitted through the written word or spoken language, as well as in artists' reconstructions.

For the geographer language is embedded in perspectives on place. Developing a sense of place, in which both pattern and process is recognized, is considered an essential prerequisite to geography, and that sense comes both from experiencing different perspectives through language as well as from the perception of location which geography emphasizes.

We need to think holistically yet at the same time maintain the uniqueness of each 'way of seeing' which the subjects bring to the curriculum. The subject focus of the National Curriculum has driven the organization of ITT. Opportunities to consider the contribution that the foundations subjects can, and ought, to make to literacy and numeracy in particular have not been exploited. An acceptance that the foundation subjects should be making a contribution to the training of student teachers in the core subjects, (particularly English and mathematics), would not only help trainees reach the expected standards in these subjects, but would help them implement a more time-efficient primary curriculum.

The National Curriculum and subsequently published guidance explicitly states that the foundation subjects will make a significant contribution to the core curricula and IT. This is part of the entitlement of pupils. At present, however, the demands of adequate coverage of specific subject knowledge and skills, alongside the growing demands for foundation subjects to function in a cross curricular manner, and feed into the core, implicit in the National Curriculum for ITT, are unrealistic.

A solution is the radical rethink of the contexts in which the skills and range of knowledge within the core are taught. Some of the time for considering the teaching of speaking and listening, for example, might be made available to the foundation subjects. The requirement in *history* to consider oral testimony provides an excellent opportunity to develop speaking and listening skills, and the emphasis on communication in key element 5 encourages the use of a wide variety of approaches. Similar patterns of collaboration could take place both with other aspects of the English curriculum as well as with other core subjects. Much of the history curriculum relates to cultures where the evidence is largely archaeological. Children's fascination with archaeology provides an opportunity to dwell on the applications of science in this area. Historic buildings are one of the evidence sources that have to be studied, and the associated scientific and mathematical work that can be carried out in what is usually a safe environment has long been recognized. History key element 1 is concerned with the mathematical concept of sequencing, and the importance of story, particularly in Key Stage 1 history, provides further opportunities for children to develop their reading and listening skills. In *geography*, as in history, there is a rich heritage of story from around the world offering not only a context for developing reading skills but also an opportunity to think about other places, how they are similar to and different from our own.

The possibilities for the foundation subjects to reconnect to the core are therefore not limited to English. Science and mathematics can be enriched by a teacher trained to recognize the ways in which foundation subjects are a central part of children's experience of those subjects. Weathering of buildings offers evidence in history as well as a rich link to rocks, water and erosion in geography. Musical instruments are a natural link to sound in science, and mathematics is so often taught in the environment that it seems bizarre not to consider its applications in history and geography.

A Plea

We are now used to shallow analysis, woolly thinking and ill considered change from the Teacher Training Agency. The suggestion that foundation subjects be offered as 'taster courses' is likely to be yet another example of that lack of vision or rigour, and will legitimize their lowly status, with a corresponding impoverishment of the curriculum of both the trainee teachers and primary school pupils. It will also diminish the role, self-esteem and enthusiasm of the trainers, who even more than at present, may have to repetitively teach basic introductory courses. If by following a 'taster course', trainee teachers are not required to reach the minimum standards for the foundation subjects that have been written into *Circular 10/97*, an opportunity to improve the quality of teaching and learning across the primary school curriculum will have been missed. We do make a plea that the DFEE and TTA recognize the value that the foundation subjects will have in enriching the curriculum by giving more consideration to the appropriate standards to be reached by trainee teachers. This will then require ITT institutions to reconsider creatively how these may be achieved, without diminishing the quality of training given to students in the core subjects. ITT courses will therefore need some reconstruction to provide non–specialist students in the foundation subjects with the time to achieve the required standards. We hope that the discussion in this chapter will help inform what could be a lively, and overdue debate.

Rob David, Kevin Hamel and Chris Rowley

References

CALOUSTE GULBENKIAN FOUNDATION (1982) *The Arts in Schools: Principles, Practice and Provision*, London: Calouste Gulbenkian Foundation.

FLYNN, P. and PRATT, G. (1995) 'Developing an understanding of appraising music with practising primary teachers', in *British Journal of Music Education*, 12, pp. 127–58.

SHULMAN, L.S. (1986) 'Those who understand Knowledge Growth in Teaching', *Educational Researcher*, February 1986, pp. 4–14.

9   IT: Meeting The New Requirements*

Dave Murray and Jill Collison

At the time of writing there is a strong interest in issues associated with subject knowledge requirements for information technology (IT) in initial teacher education (ITE). The DfEE (1997) has set high standards for the award of qualified teacher status (QTS). A National Curriculum for IT in ITE will soon further raise the profile of IT in ITE. The thrust of the DfEE requirements and the National Curriculum proposals will have a major impact on ITE courses and the level of experience of IT within ITE courses of all kinds. School-based PGCE courses run by consortia of rural schools to the largest metropolitan providers of three and four-year BA and BSc (QTS) degrees together with their partner schools will all have to revise their courses to address subject knowledge and other requirements.

The changing nature of the partnership between traditional ITE providers and primary schools is a recurring theme in this book. Teachers in our partner schools often assume that even student teachers in early stages of training are more 'expert' than they are themselves in relation to computers. Williams (1996) offers widespread evidence of primary schools unable to support students and outdated hardware; over half the computers available in sample schools (133 placements across three LEAs) were BBCs. Lack of access to hardware and software was given as a dominant reason given for students' inability to complete IT tasks in school. Our more detailed discussion of school-based training which follows suggests however that there are broader perspectives and other factors which impact on students' experience of IT in schools.

The new requirements and the developing partnership with schools raise issues of course design for provider institutions. Currently, primary ITE courses have diverse models of provision for IT and time allocated to IT in training varies from course to course and from institution to institution. Whilst the proposed National Curriculum for IT in ITE is likely to define the skills and knowledge to be addressed, it is less likely to prescribe how the curriculum should be delivered. The length of time needed to deliver the curriculum and achieve the prescribed standards will probably be left to institutions to decide. These are not likely to be easy choices at a time when higher education generally is required to do more and more with less and less funding, particularly in a resource intensive area such as IT. The third section of this chapter will focus on the balance and potential roles of discrete IT components and cross-curricular delivery. The former tends to be expensive (needing specialist staff) but whilst the latter might be cheaper, evidence from secondary schools would suggest that it is a less effective method of developing high level IT skills.

---

* This chapter was written before the publication of the ITT Curriculum for the use of Information and Communications Technology in subject teaching.

There is a strong argument for recognizing the increasingly technological emphasis required in ITE and increasing funding accordingly. The TTA has recently provided additional funding to support the implementation of the National Curriculum for IT. Whilst additional monies are welcome, this ad hoc approach to funding developments in ITE does not help providers plan coherent medium-term strategies for ITE. A cynic might assume that rigorous inspection will continue to be the main 'encouragement' provided to ensure trainers somehow deliver the goods!

And, finally we intend to look briefly to the future. Knowing well the seventies predictions for IT in the nineties it is most likely that we will be underestimating the pace of development and change but it is also important to note that to date the development of IT in the majority of schools has not matched the pace of technological developments elsewhere. However, we are hopeful that the positive climate for change in the country as a whole and the exciting rhetoric of the Government's National Grid for Learning will lead to teachers reading this chapter in disbelief in less than ten years' time.

Subject Knowledge

The DfEE's (1997) most recent requirements for primary ITE place a strong emphasis on subject knowledge in IT. Most teachers would support the philosophy that all entrants to the teaching profession should not only be IT literate but also professionally competent with computers. However given the current level of IT literacy amongst student teachers this emphasis on subject knowledge is likely to be problematic for ITE providers.

An early study by Simmons and Wild (1989) reported 80 per cent of students to be unfamiliar with major applications of IT. Since then evidence from a range of ITE institutions has been of a slow rise in IT expertise of entrants to initial teacher training courses. At UCSM we involve all ITE students in self-assessment prior to selecting IT study skills packs. Data from recent years suggest our own primary ITE intake is broadly typical. Our students continue to show a lack of basic IT skills although as elsewhere we are aware of a widening of the differences between the least and most IT literate applicants. For 1996/97, of the 151 BA (QTS) and PGCE students responding, over 50 per cent claimed to be inexperienced with databases, spreadsheets and desktop publishing (DTP). Less than 20 per cent regarded themselves as experienced users in these aspects of IT. The size of the annual improvements over recent years suggests that for some years to come the majority of ITE entrants will not have a foundation of basic skills and knowledge on which to build teaching competence and a high level of personal IT skills.

Given the importance of applications such as databases, spreadsheets and DTP in the schools' IT curriculum ITE providers face the considerable challenge of delivering basic IT literacy for the majority of their intakes before they can begin to address the current level 8 standard set by the DfEE. This may be an area of particular concern for primary SCITT schemes where expertise to develop students' IT skills might not exist.

It is obvious that students who are not confident with the use of, for example, databases are not going to be able to deliver primary IT curriculum requirements or use such software to enhance pupils' opportunities for interpretation of historical data. However, any assumption that simply increasing the emphasis on IT subject knowledge in ITE will lead to improvements in students' use of IT in teaching needs consideration. Oliver (1994) cites a range of research indicating that, 'the development of teachers' personal IT skills has little bearing on teachers' instructional use of computers'.

Whilst our experiences of teaching IT show us that students are unable to concentrate on pedagogic issues whilst they lack personal IT skills we would argue that it is simplistic to assume that knowledge of IT alone is the key to successful teaching of or with IT. We believe that it is the interface between subject knowledge and pedagogy that is significant in determining teaching effectiveness. Student teachers need both professional competences and personal IT skills to utilize IT effectively in classrooms.

Disparities between entrants' subject knowledge and TTA career entry requirements mean that ITE providers will have to allocate more and more of the limited training period to developing students' personal skills with IT. This focus on the development of students' skills could result in an overemphasis on skills to the detriment of professional courses which focus on how to teach using IT. Students need a critical framework to evaluate the impact of IT on learning. They need to understand the nature of IT in the National Curriculum. Students also need models of good practice in teaching and classroom management. Only then will they be able to become professionals able to judge, develop and adapt IT to suit their individual circumstances and teaching styles.

One way to balance the content of IT components would be to set personal skills in relevant professional contexts. For example, at UCSM students learn to design database structures for work in science and they design and use concept keyboards or on-screen word-banks to support literacy development. In effect they are designing IT systems for particular purposes for others to use. This is exactly the type of undertaking that might be used to demonstrate level 8 IT capability but the professional context means the nature of the challenge places more emphasis on professional awareness and less emphasis on technical competence than might be found in typical Key Stage 3 or 4 level 8 work!

The emphasis on subject knowledge has increased dramatically in the last two years. Entrants to primary ITE are required to have qualifications at level 7 in core subjects to be considered for places. Raising students' subject knowledge from level 7 on entrance to level 8 on qualification is challenging but achievable for colleagues in English, Mathematics and Science, particularly with the specified training times of the immediate past. Perhaps the IT National Curriculum for ITE needs to specify a time allocation for IT until entry standards are raised by initiatives such as Dearing's proposed key skills curriculum for 16 to 18 year olds. It is interesting to note that the McKinsey report (1997) found that IT was typically allocated a total of 30 hours within ITE programmes but recommended a minimum of 60 hours. The DfEE could set entry requirements in IT bringing it in line with core subjects. This would certainly help ITE providers to achieve the standards required but the current lack of IT literate applicants for ITE would have a severe impact on recruitment which is already a cause for concern.

The proposed National Curriculum for IT in ITE will have a major influence; an influence that has the potential to either raise or depress teachers' abilities to use computers effectively in their teaching. The TTA's consultation version suggests a strong emphasis on the role of IT in the subjects but makes surprisingly little reference to IT subject knowledge. Could this result in teachers knowing how IT can enhance their teaching but leave teachers not having the personal IT capabilities to actually use IT to good effect? The TTA's draft proposals virtually ignore the need to teach pupils to use IT effectively as a precursor to pupils being able to make productive use of IT within subject contexts.

Students' Experiences in School

There is an interesting paradox within a rationale that requires more student time to be spent in school whilst OFSTED reports that standards of IT teaching in primary schools are poor. Goldstein (1997), drawing on OFSTED's evidence from almost 50,000 lessons, suggests that, 'teachers' command of the subject remained very weak'. Only half of primary schools were meeting the requirements of the National Curriculum in IT and there was a 'scarcity of work involving controlling and modelling'.

One assumption that can be made from OFSTED's evidence is that there is a lack of good role models in schools. Our own informal discussions with teachers in partner schools suggest that teachers generally do not feel able to participate fully in the training process as far as subject knowledge is concerned. Elsewhere, Loveless (1995) found teacher mentors expecting students to be able to help them with IT! In more extreme circumstances, Bell and Biott (1997) contend that teachers lacking confidence in their own use of IT avoid IT in the classroom and don't encourage students to use IT in their rooms either. Likewise we found that for about a third of the students the attitude of their class teacher to IT was a factor that restricted their use of IT in school (Murray and Collison, 1995).

Teachers' perception of their role as mentors of students, especially with regard to supporting the teaching of IT, are of considerable importance here. Our research (Collison and Murray, 1995; Murray and Collison, 1995) and evaluation of placement experiences shows that teachers do want to help students but that their focus tends to be on the mechanistic issues about running a piece of software or using the hardware rather than assisting students in gaining an understanding of the educational potential of IT or providing insights into how best to use IT to support learning. For example, the following was typical of the teachers' responses to a question seeking their views of their role in the support of students' computer use:

> Well, I'm happy to help them but they know more than I do. I'll try to make sure they have what they need but I can't help them if they don't know what to do.

Indeed it seemed that the teachers' lack of confidence with the technical aspects of computer usage prevented them from offering the sort of professional guidance that the students needed, and that the teachers were fully capable of giving. When prompted all the teachers interviewed agreed that they could offer guidance as to whether the students were planning a worthwhile activity that achieved its learning outcomes or advice as to how best to interact with the children or what questions to ask. We concluded then that the teachers were less able to act as mentors for IT work than for other subjects because of their own limited expertise with IT; two years on we have no new evidence to alter this view.

Bell and Biott (1997) suggest that if teachers could be more open and articulate their uncertainties with regard to IT then student and teacher might combine their individual expertise and work together. They could jointly explore the role of IT through cycles of planning, implementing and evaluating activities. This approach would result in even the less IT-confident teachers being able to support the development of trainees' professional competence through professional dialogue. We might even hope that in some classrooms the students would be change agents bringing about permanent improvements to the level of IT use.

As attention in ITE increasingly focuses on students' competence in specific subjects perhaps mentor training needs to focus increasingly on subject-specific concerns rather than the more generic support and teaching competences which have tended to feature strongly in our own model of primary mentor training to date. This year we hope to offer our partner schools mentor training which focuses on an already successful school-based information book making project. English department tutors, with a strong interest in mentoring, will collaborate with IT tutors to plan and deliver a training session for mentors which looks at this specific project. The training will examine how mentors can use their professional insights to raise students' awareness of professional considerations with regard to IT and English. The training will also include some practical IT activities to ensure that school partners feel more confident utilizing IT techniques such as basic DTP and searching CD ROM information sources effectively.

An Issue for HEIs: Discrete Versus Cross-curricular Models of Delivery of IT

In the world of ever decreasing time and funding for HEI-based elements of teacher training cross-curricular delivery of IT in ITE programmes might appear to be a good idea. It can even seem a good idea from a less pragmatic viewpoint. Oliver (1994) for example, argues:

> If IT is not a critical component of the instruction and teaching process that student teachers receive in their training, it will be difficult to create teachers who will place importance on IT in their own teaching. There is a need to integrate computer technologies into teacher education programmes rather than to include IT courses as discrete entities. (p. 141)

Whilst it is hard to argue against Oliver's first premise we should be aware of the difficulties of achieving integration. Indeed the findings of the Initial Teacher Education and New Technology Project (INTENT), urge caution; cross-curricular delivery of IT in HEI may not be a panacea. Project INTENT was an ambitious and nationally funded programme which set out to support the development of IT use in five UK ITE institutions. The project aimed to support the use of IT across subjects and was thus in keeping with Oliver's (1994) favoured approach. Somekh's case study (1996) describes one of the INTENT institutions where one-to-one support and team teaching were funded for one year yet at the end of the year these approaches were felt not to have had sufficient impact on some colleagues for them to be able to continue unsupported. The enduring impact of the project was felt to have been so small that once the funding period was over that it had not even 'left a shadow'. Clearly initiatives to integrate IT across all subjects in ITE are likely to be problematic. The IT National Curriculum for ITT will require all main subject areas to devote considerable attention to the role of IT within subject teaching. This will have major staff development and resource implications for many ITE providers.

The proposal outlined previously to work collaboratively with English tutors in mentor training may prove to be an effective means of moving towards a cross-curricular model. It has the potential to extend the English tutors' confidence with IT *and* their understanding of the professional issues surrounding the development of others' IT skills. Thus the lack of consideration for the development of IT skills that one sees in cross-curricular IT delivery in secondary schools might be avoided. However, even then it is hard to believe that English tutors would wish to take responsibility for developing the students' IT skills to levels required. Collaboration between IT tutors and their subject colleagues may be unarguably a good thing if it leads to a more fully integrated delivery of IT in a professional context but discrete IT sessions are likely to go on being necessary for some time to come to allow students to achieve the required level of personal IT knowledge.

Looking to the Future

Looking ahead there are reasons to be optimistic. It is reasonable to expect that sixth formers' key skills will improve as a result of the Dearing Review, so we might expect entrants to be better qualified in IT within the next two to three years. Also if HEIs find some way out of the 'chicken and egg' trap (the paradox of school-based ITE at a time when the majority of teachers are unable to provide good role models for IT use) that they currently find themselves in, then new entrants to the profession will be able to provide suitable school-based support for successive students. As suggested earlier it might be that one way out of this trap is to use current students as change agents to bring about developments in existing teachers which in itself would add to the pool of teachers willing and able to support students' school-based IT work.

Perhaps the most significant change in recent times is the new Labour Government's apparent commitment to drag education into the twenty-first century. There seems to be recognition of the fact that the increasingly technological emphasis required in ITE requires increased funding. Most notably there seems to be an understanding of the fact that this funding needs to redress the balance of spending on equipment and training in favour of *training*. The opening of the Virtual Teachers' Centre in the spring of 1998 is exciting, early evidence of this commitment in action. The Government's proposals to use funding from 'The People's Lottery' insist that the money can only be spent on the training of teachers, not used for equipment purchases. There is also a suggestion that this funding will be available via vouchers to ensure that the money reaches its intended destination. At last this should help schools escape the 'computers-in-the–cupboard' syndrome which has been an all too frequent outcome of spending funds on equipment without matching those monies with spending on staff training. The National Grid for Learning sets some ambitious targets; a key one being that by 2002 all teachers will be ICT (Information and Communications Technology) confident. It is hoped that lottery funding will be available for training of the 450,000 existing teachers from 1999 which allows just three years for the target to be reached. A tall order one might say but a very exciting prospect; perhaps readers of this chapter in just five years time will wonder at the need to discuss the issues we have set out.

References

BELL, M. and BIOTT, C. (1997) 'Using IT in classrooms experienced teachers and trainees as co-learners', in SOMEKH, B. and DAVIS, N. (eds) *Using Information Technology Effectively in Teaching and Learning Studies in Pre-service and In-service Teacher Education*, London: Routledge.

COLLISON, J. and MURRAY, D. (1995) 'What goes on in school-based ITT?', *Journal of Computer Assisted Learning*, **11**, 2, pp. 99–109.

DfEE (1997) *Requirements for Courses of Initial Teacher Training (Circular 10/97)*, London: DfEE.

GOLDSTEIN, G. (1997) *Information Technology in English Schools: A Commentary on Inspection Findings 1995–96*, London: OFSTED.

LOVELESS, A. (1995) 'IT's just another plate to spin: Primary school mentors' perceptions of supporting trainee experience of information technology in the classroom', *Journal of Information Technology for Teacher Education*, **4**, 1, pp. 39–50.

McKINSEY REPORT (1997) *Information and Communication Technology in UK Schools*. Independent Inquiry, ICT in School Commission. See also http://rubble.ultralab.anglia. ac.uk/stevenson/McKinsey.html.

MURRAY, D. and COLLISON, J. (1995) 'Student IT capability within a school-based primary ITT course', *Journal of Computer Assisted Learning*, **11**, 3, pp. 170–218.

OLIVER, R. (1994) 'Information technology courses in teacher education: The need for integration', *Journal of Information Technology for Teacher Education*, **3**, 2, pp. 135–46.

SIMMONS, C. and WILD, P. (1989) 'Trainee teachers learning to learn through information technology', *Educational Research*, **33**, 3, pp. 163–72.

SOMEKH, B. (1996) 'Value conflicts in the management of innovation: Supporting information technology innovation in initial teacher training in the United Kingdom', *Journal of Information Technology for Teacher Education*, **5**, 1+2, pp. 115–37.

WILLIAMS, P. (1996) 'Resourcing for the future? Information technology provision and competency questions for school-based initial teacher education', *Journal of Information Technology for Teacher Education*, **5**, 3, pp. 271–82.

10 Teacher Education and PSMSC — Implications of the New Requirements

Tony Ewens

A major characteristic of the transition from the requirements of *Circular 24/89* to those of *Circular 14/93* and subsequently to the 'Standards for the Award of Qualified Teacher Status' in *Circular 10/97* is a shift from a description of the constituent parts of a primary initial teacher education course to a statement of its intended outcomes. This change of emphasis, exemplifying as it does the 'proof of the pudding' maxim, intends the employers of a newly qualified teacher to be assured that their recruit can, among many other things:

> plan opportunities to contribute to pupils' personal, spiritual, moral, social and cultural development. (DfEE, 1997, B.2.d)

> use teaching methods which sustain the momentum of pupils' work and keep all pupils engaged through . . . exploiting opportunities to contribute to the quality of pupils' wider educational development, including their personal, spiritual, moral, social and cultural development. (ibid, B.2.k. xii)

Providers and assessors of primary initial teacher education (ITE) consequently need to have:

(i)   a clear view of the nature of pupils' personal, spiritual, moral, social and cultural development;
(ii) strategies for its incorporation in the education programme, and
(iii) valid and reliable methods for assessing candidates against the two standards cited above.

These three aspects will be considered in turn.

Towards a Clearer View

Definition

None of the five adjectives — personal, spiritual, moral, social, cultural (PSMSC) — is susceptible of tight definition. Unlike words such as blue, hard or wet, they lack an objective referent. Against Wittgenstein's test ('The meaning of a word is its use in the language', Wittgenstein, 1974, p. 20) each, especially 'spiritual', demonstrates a reluctance to be pinned down, since each is used with a variety of nuances in different circles. In other words, there is a lack of public consensus about their meaning. For this reason numerous attempts have been made to seek, through consultation, or to expound, through prescriptive or advisory documentation, definitions which can gain and hold the support of the education service and its users, and this process can be traced back to the mid-seventies.

More recently the National Curriculum Council (NCC) has produced a discussion document (NCC, 1993), on spiritual and moral development, The Office for Standards in Education (OFSTED) a consultation paper (OFSTED, 1994) on 'Spiritual, Moral, Social and Cultural Development' (SMSC), and the Schools' Curriculum and Assessment Authority (SCAA) a booklet on young people's spiritual and moral development, with the promise from its successor body, the Qualifications and Curriculum Authority (QCA), of detailed advice to schools on incorporating opportunities for SMSC in their curricula. This extensive list of official publications has promoted considerable discussion of the nature and purpose of the aspects of pupils' development under discussion, especially spiritual and moral, though they have largely shrunk from attempting to codify meanings.

No such reticence has characterized OFSTED's *Framework for the Inspection of Schools*, first published in its *Handbook for the Inspection of Schools* (OFSTED, 1993), which set out brief definitions of SMSC development and the observable outcomes by which they were to be judged. A document establishing tight definitions might understandably be welcomed by a pragmatist, especially if it indicated the focus of an inspection. The OFSTED handbook tends to lead schools to adopt policies and practices with measurable outcomes which will, they hope, demonstrate achievement against the public criteria by means of which they will be publicly judged.

Two questions linger. The first is about the extent to which current working definitions of personal, spiritual, moral, social and cultural development are valid and appropriate. Given the coverage of the topic in official consultations and publications in the last 20 years, it can reasonably be argued that a consensus has been achieved and that Wittgenstein's 'meaning as use' test has been passed.

The second question is wider reaching and, because of the prevailing habit of paying attention to the discrete elements in any whole, is one which seems to have evaded public discussion. It is this: How and why has this particular list of adjectives (personal, spiritual, moral, social and cultural) been adopted?

Historical Perspective

R.A. Butler's 1944 Education Act placed upon local education authorities (LEAs) the responsibility to promote the 'spiritual, moral, mental and physical development of the community' (DES, 1944, preamble). Priestley (1985) records a meeting with

Canon Hall, then a Chief Officer of the National Society, who was one of the major contributors to the 1944 legislation, representing the Anglican Church's involvement in the dual system of education in England and Wales. Hall's explanation of 'spiritual' was of something wider that the concept of religion, something which should permeate the whole educational process and something which would act as a unifying and cohering factor.

My own meeting with Hall, in the mid-eighties, provided an opportunity to question him about the selection of all four adjectives, and of their combination. Remarking that I clearly didn't know my Bible, he quoted St Mark's Gospel: 'Thou shalt love the Lord thy God will all thy heart and with all thy soul, with all thy mind and with all thy strength' (Mark 12:29). Hall's exegesis of this passage in relation to the 1944 Act was that just as a religious believer's relationship with God involves every facet of the person's being, so education should concern itself with all aspects of people's development, not just their mental and physical faculties.

For Hall, and for Parliament legislating on behalf of the public, the classical educational ideal of *mens sana in corpore sano* was inadequate, and needed to be complemented by attention to values and feelings. The words 'spiritual' and 'moral' were chosen because it was felt that they were best able to convey a notion of permeation. Hall was insistent that none of the four words should be considered discretely, always in combination.

The set of adjectives recurred in the 1988 Education Reform Act, with the addition of 'cultural', the Parliamentary draftsmen thus betraying ignorance of the root and significance of the original foursome. This Act requires schools to provide a curriculum which 'promotes the spiritual, moral, cultural, mental and physical development of the pupils at the school and of society' (DES, 1988). It is noteworthy that this requirement is now a function of a curriculum rather than an aim of education, a sign of a shift in public policy away from abstract ideals and towards measurable outcomes as a means of establishing accountability.

The 1992 Education Act (DFE, 1992), which set up the system of school inspections by OFSTED, pursues the quest for the measurable to its logical conclusion by severing the link between 'mental and physical' and the other adjectives. OFSTED's new foursome of 'spiritual, moral, social and cultural' are elements which do not produce results capable of numerical analysis and comparison, or evidence which can readily be judged against consistent criteria. Their consequent marginalisation is reflected in the very variable content and quality of school OFSTED reports on SMSC. Mental and physical growth, conducive to measurement, are detailed at length across the reports in their sections on the teaching of subjects.

A Clearer View

Any effective and worthwhile definition of SMSC, together with 'personal', which was peremptorily added to the list by *Circular 10/97*, will demonstrate that these aspects of pupils' development are integrally linked to their learning, whether through the formal curriculum or by means of their nurture within the climate of values and relationships espoused by the school, and this makes them both overt and public.

Some thought needs to be given to the words which have become added to the original 1944 set of adjectives. 'Cultural' appeared in 1988, 'social' in 1992 and 'personal' in 1997.

Personal and social development form two sides of the same coin and relate to the relationship of individual to group. As an aspect of school life they frequently proceed together as an issues-based area of the curriculum, drawing on English and drama as well as cross-curricular themes, especially health education, careers guidance and economic and industrial understanding. Their concern with feelings, emotions and values places them as a sub-set of spiritual and moral development, and in my view they can be regarded as a particular example of spiritual and moral development within aspects of the formal curriculum.

Cultural development, likewise, is a specific example of the manifestation of spiritual and moral development within the formal curriculum, in which pupils are encouraged to develop appropriate attitudes and insights into their own and others' cultures, experienced through geography, religious education and the whole of the arts and humanities curriculum.

Spiritual and moral development seem irreducible, though interrelated. There is a fair consensus that spiritual development encourages pupils to:

- reflect (providing a link with physical development through stillness);
- use imagination and curiosity (a link with mental development);
- engage in discussion and debate (a link with moral development).

Much of its focus is on the notion of transcendence, whether in the sense of a striving to exceed one's previous limitations or in the religious sense of 'the beyond'.

Moral development encourages pupils to:

- develop concepts of right and wrong;
- appreciate the purpose of rules in groups and societies;
- behave according to rules while learning to evaluate and, where appropriate, challenge them;
- formulate their own approaches to issues of right and wrong.

Both categories, spiritual and moral, can be fostered readily through the teaching and learning of the formal curriculum. They are, however, far more than optional modes of curriculum delivery. If education is about the formation of persons, as well as about their preparation for adult life, it is crucial that spiritual and moral development be seen, alongside mental and physical development, as aspects of a whole. In that respect the 1944 Act has the advantage over later statutes which reduce education to its constituent and measurable components.

Designing the Curriculum

Since it is a requirement that all students demonstrate achievement of all the standards listed in *Circular 10/97* before QTS can be awarded, it follows that providers of initial teacher education must address the issue of personal, spiritual, moral, social and cultural development through their programmes. *Circular 14/93* regarded SMSC as a matter for CPD rather than ITE, so it was not essential to deal with it. For some providers the new requirements will therefore necessitate significant changes to their courses.

The contention of this chapter is that spiritual and moral development, which incorporate personal, social and cultural development, are educational aims which cannot be separated from mental and physical development. A consequence of this interpretation is that all these matters must be incorporated within any programme of teacher education.

Circular 10/97, through the standards for the award of QTS and through the programmes of study for the core subjects, set out in the National Curriculum for Initial Teacher Training, emphasizes the importance of the teacher's own knowledge of the subjects which they are being prepared to teach. It is likewise important that students have the opportunity to further their own spiritual and moral development while enhancing their subject knowledge. The students' self-awareness of their experiences in these areas are essential prerequisites of their development as teachers able to foster such growth in their pupils.

The task of auditing the curriculum in a programme leading to a QTS award gives an opportunity to providers, whether school-based or in school-HEI partnerships, to review their own understanding of the categories under discussion and seek ways of ensuring that they foster the appropriate development in students as well as equipping them in turn to make suitable provision in school classrooms.

To undertake a full exercise in curricular mapping would occupy a book in its own right, so two examples must suffice to illustrate areas ripe for consideration. These are AT1 in mathematics and science, and collective worship.

AT1 in Mathematics and Science

OFSTED reports on schools frequently identify the work associated with these attainment targets as weaker than that in other areas of mathematics and science. Reasons for this may be classified under two headings, subject knowledge and pedagogy. The two are intimately related.

The investigative and experimental work implied by AT1 in these subjects possesses an open–ended character. It is impossible fully to predict what hypotheses, discoveries and questions children may arrive at during activities of this kind. The acid test of teachers' subject knowledge comes, not at the stage of lesson planning, but at times of unplanned interaction. These may take the form of a contingent intervention instigated by the teacher, in which case the teacher needs to make an instant diagnostic assessment of the pupil's understanding or misconception and act appropriately to explain, reteach or suggest a way forward. Alternatively the pupil may prompt the exchange with a question. In either event, the teacher is taking risks with his/her knowledge. This sort of interaction cannot be 'planned', if by planning we imply a mechanism by which the teacher selects and controls the subject knowledge to be covered in the lesson. It requires a more general sort of planning: the development of a secure subject knowledge, including a grasp of the subject's conceptual basis, its 'depth grammar' (Wittgenstein, 1974), coupled with a preparedness to engage in the teaching and learning process interactively.

The restricted pedagogy which frustrates the intentions of AT1 in mathematics and science has roots in classroom management, as well as subject knowledge and issues. Doyle has shown that many classroom tasks are chosen for their potential to control pupils rather than to promote learning, and this leads him to depict the teacher as a circus ringmaster. His analysis of the role of tasks in learning suggests that a balanced programme, in which some tasks exhibit characteristics of risk and/ or ambiguity, will best promote learning, while maintaining equilibrium.

The relevance of mathematics and science to the task of fostering pupils' spiritual and moral development is most readily seen in AT1 of each subject. As we have seen, spiritual development requires that pupils have opportunity to reflect, use their intellectual curiosity, practise discussion and debate and experience wonder and mystery. Such possibilities abound in tasks which involve exploration, observation, hypothesis and theorising. Since the pedagogical framework for this work is interactive and investigative, there are also ample opportunities to experience situations conducive to moral development. The pupil-teacher relationship is distinctly different in this context in comparison with a didactic session in which the emphasis is on the transmission of received knowledge.

The reluctance of many teachers to risk open-ended tasks is therefore a significant limitation of the potential of AT1 mathematics and science to promote pupils' SMSC development.

Another factor may be at work, in addition to those associated with subject knowledge and pedagogy. This relates to assessment. The trend of public policy is still towards an assessment strategy which relies on quantitative data about prescribed discrete outcomes. It is understandable that teachers concentrate upon those activities which generate measurable outcomes, and this may lead them to exclude other types of task, notably those which would most readily support AT1 in mathematics and science, and similar activities elsewhere in the curriculum. The false Cartesian division, noted above, in OFSTED's separation of SMSC from the teaching and learning of the subjects of the curriculum is illustrated in this tendency to marginalize the immeasurable.

The importance of processes, rather than pre-conceived products, is central to the aspects of spiritual and moral development described above, and it is clear that pupils' competence in processes is fundamental to their ability to apply knowledge. This points to need for a broader conceptualization of assessment and inspection than is currently the norm.

Ironically, it may prove to be the case that a broad education which seeks to develop the whole person is more effective than a narrowly focused attention on testable items in raising standards in the basic subjects judged on empirical outcomes. Recent claims that basic attainment is enhanced when pupils have access to a broad range of extra-curricular activities, and that pupils given extra music lessons performed better in mathematics than those who had extra mathematics lessons, are intriguing pointers in this direction. A key task for educational researchers is to find ways of evaluating pupils' SMSC development to produce evidence sufficiently robust to be considered valid and reliable when placed in correlation with quantitative data about pupils' attainment.

Providers of ITE have a responsibility to ensure that students have sufficient opportunity to demonstrate achievement of the standards about PSMSC set out in *Circular 10/97*. In relation to the example of AT1 in mathematics and science, the following conditions would need to be satisfied:

- a consensus among providing partners about the nature and scope of pupils' personal, spiritual, moral, social and cultural development;
- a shared vision of the potential of the formal curriculum to support the fostering of such development;
- sufficient knowledge and expertise among school staff and HE tutors to ensure that students could observe good practice in promoting these categories of development through tasks related to AT1;
- access for all students to classrooms in which they could observe, replicate, adapt and routinize good practice;
- opportunities for students to evaluate and discuss their work with experienced professionals; and, one ventures to suggest,
- an inspection regime for initial teacher education which gives attention to these matters rather than confining itself to atomised and easily measured components of whole programmes.

The modelling of good practice is not a simple issue. The influence on students of their own school education is an important factor and their understanding of the mathematics and science curriculum is strongly conditioned by their experiences as pupils. It takes far more than the observation of a few good lessons to produce a significant shift in a students' attitudes to a subject, particularly one which they did not enjoy or succeed in at school. This factor suggests that students need early opportunities to identify and evaluate their own prior knowledge, experiences and suppositions as an intrinsic element of their learning.

Collective Worship

Traditionally, preparation of teachers for the task of planning and leading collective worship has not featured in initial teacher education programmes, unless as a minor adjunct to an RE course.

Three major factors inhibit the preparation of students to foster PSMSC through collective worship. These are:

- the absence of a consensual view of collective worship as a prime means of promoting PSMSC development;
- the fact that few, if any, teachers in a given school will have received any preparation in planning and leading collective worship;
- the negative experiences of school collective worship which many students bring with them.

The inclusion in ITE provision of a component preparing would-be teachers for collective worship could be a most effective and efficient way of attending to the standards relating to PSMSC. The realisation of this aspiration would necessitate:

- opportunities for students to consider the nature and purpose of collective worship as an activity of educational worth;
- an examination of the potential of collective worship to contribute to pupils' PSMSC development;
- chances for students to reflect on their own experiences of collective worship;
- opportunities to plan, lead and evaluate collective worship in schools.

An increasingly school-based model of ITE is not particularly helpful in areas such as this, in which many schools would be grateful for leadership. However, HEI/school partnerships may offer a forum within which expertise in both schools and colleges, coupled with that from LEAs and, where appropriate, dioceses, could usefully be shared.

Assessing Students Against the Standards

What would count as evidence of achievement by students of the standards relating to pupils' PSMSC development? Here there are some welcome pointers in *Circular 10/97*, albeit not overt ones.

The Circular pays close attention to the student's own attainment. Can s/he, for instance, demonstrate knowledge and understanding in mathematics at the equivalent of more than level 8 of the National Curriculum? By analogy, the student will need to demonstrate characteristics and qualities which testify to his/her own development as a rounded human being. A formal presentation or written assignment might check the student's facility in the relevant public discourse (can s/he play the language-game?). Observation of the student's interaction with a group of pupils is likely to be a more fitting context to observe and judge his/her performance of understanding. Does the planning reveal insights into the potential of the lesson to foster PSMSC?

Does the style of teaching give pupils the chance to reflect, respond, discuss, disagree, relate to others, value and appreciate difference? Does the student demonstrate personal engagement with both the subject matter and the pupils? Can the student identify and manage unplanned opportunities which arise during teaching? Is the student able, when evaluating the lesson, to point to evidence that children are developing with respect to PSMSC? Can the student articulate his/her own insight into the relationship between the pupils' PSMSC development and the school's mission and ethos, its shared values and climate of relationships?

All this is possible. What it tells us is far more than a question of making judgments against a couple of discrete standards.

Conclusions

The inclusion in *Circular 10/97* of statements relating to the personal, spiritual, moral, social and cultural development of pupils which has been absent from *Circular 14/93*, is a development with a potentially profound significance. It can and should be taken, alongside the requirements about students' subject knowledge, as a sign of a move away from a narrow form of vocational training aimed at the acquisition of job related competences. The renewed emphasis given by *10/97* to the development of the whole person as an educational aspiration means that the teacher's role cannot be reduced to a checklist of competences. Eraut (1994) has outlined the characteristics of the knowledge and understanding that need to underpin professional competence in such a way as to show that 'competence' needs major redefinition if it is to be applied to the attributes needed by professionals, hence perhaps the use in *10/97* of the wider term, standards.

But a move away from a model of a narrow vocational training for teachers should not be interpreted as a shift back to a narrow academic one. The key merit of the standards approach to assessment should be its insistence on the performance of understandings. This is much broader than a demonstration of mechanical skills, and it requires assessors and examiners to demand evidence that students can translate into effective classroom practice those things that they know and understand.

The potential is here for the development of what Pring (1996) has called 'vocationalized education' which brings together 'the qualities and capacities, the skills and the understandings, which enable all (young) people to live valuable, useful and distinctively human lives'. This combines a grounding in the concepts and processes of selected subjects with attention to the personal qualities which enable people to 'make sense of the world and act responsibly and knowingly within it', as Pring puts it.

Pring's is a model which makes great sense as a basis for initial teacher education. It combines knowledge with skill, theory with practice. Its implication is that the teacher needs to be a developed, rounded human being if s/he is to promote the full development of the pupils.

The next step should be to eradicate the artificial division between personal and academic development. The 1944 Act's foursome, inextricably interwined, of spiritual, moral, mental and physical development is very hard to better.

References

BROWN, A. (1996) *Between a Rock and a Hard Place*, London: National Society.

DES (1994) *The Education Act: 1944*, London: HMSO.

DES (1977a) *The Curriculum from 11–16*, London: HMSO.

DES (1977b) *Supplement to Curriculum 11–16*, London: HMSO.

DES (1985) *The Curriculum from 5 to 16: Curriculum Matters Book 2*, London: HMSO.

DES (1988) *The Education Reform Act: 1988*, London: HMSO.

DES (1989a) *The Education Reform Act 1988: Religious Education and Collective Worship (Circular 3/89)* London: HMSO.

DES (1989b) *Initial Teacher Training: Approval of Courses (Circular 24/89)* London: HMSO.

DFE (1992) *The Education Act* (Circular 1992/92) London: HMSO.

DFE (1993) *The Initial Training of Primary School Teachers (Circular 14/93)* London: HMSO.

DFE (1994) *Religious Education and Collective Worship (Circular 1/94)* London: HMSO.

DfEE (1997) *Requirements for Courses of Initial Teacher Training (Circular 10/97)* London: DfEE.

ERAUT, M. (1994) *Professional Knowledge and Competence*, London: Falmer Press.

EWENS, A. and MIDWINTER, D. (1997) *Collective Worship in Primary Schools*, Lancaster: UCSM.

NCC (1993) *Spiritual and Moral Development: A Discussion Paper*, York: NCC.

OFSTED (1993) *Handbook for the Inspection of Schools*, London: OHMCI.

OFSTED (1994) *Spiritual, Moral, Social and Cultural Development*, London: OHMCI.

PRIESTLEY, J.G. (1985) 'The spiritual in the curriculum', in SOUPER, P. (ed) *The Spiritual Dimension of Education*, Southampton: University of Southampton, Department of Education.

PRING, R. (1996) 'Values and education policy', in HALSTEAD, J.M. and TAYLOR, M.J. (eds) *Values in Education and Education in Values*, London: Falmer Press.

SCAA (1996) *Education for Adult Life: The Spiritual and Moral Development of Young People*, London: SCAA.

WHITEHEAD, A.N. (1929) 'The aims of education', in WHITEHEAD, A.N. (ed) *The Aims of Education and Other Essays*, London: Williams and Norgate.

WITTGENSTEIN, L. (1974) *Philosophical Investigations* (3rd ed), Oxford: Blackwell.

Part 3

Pedagogy in Initial Teacher Education

11 Initial Teacher Education as the Acquisition of Technical Skills for Teaching: A Panacea for the Future?

Neil Simco

During the 1990s there has been a well documented shift in Government policy in initial teacher education (ITE). This has been towards the ever closer specification of competences (DFE, 1992, 1993) and eventually standards for the award of qualified teacher status (QTS) (DfEE, 1997). Underlying this shift is an assumption that the specification of precise actions which a student teacher needs to demonstrate before they are judged to be competent will lead to higher standards being attained by new teachers. It is assumed too that the atomization of the craft of teaching into minute elements will make it easy to judge whether or not an intending new teacher has the range of skills required. Can teaching be equated with technical skill or is it much more involved? This chapter argues that the complexity of the acquisition of technical skill is frequently underestimated in ITE and as such the achievement of the standards for QTS (ibid) should be seen as professionally challenging. It argues that a major focus on the acquisition of technical skills is not in itself to be equated with a model of teacher education which is intellectually superficial.

The Notion of Technical Skill

Before going further, it is necessary to define what is meant by 'technical skill'. There are many definitions but here it is seen in terms of the extent to which a student teacher can manage classroom activity in ways which are clear. This is seen as important. Activity is central to teaching and learning in classrooms. The standards required for qualified teacher status (ibid) implicitly emphasize the centrality of clarity in managing activity. This is particularly so for section B of the standards relating to 'Planning Teaching and Class Management'. Standard Bkv for example is concerned with 'clear instructions and demonstration and accurate well-paced explanation' (p. 10). The extent to which the activity is clear relates to the management of pupil behaviour and the extent to which the framework for learning is communicated. Clarity is central to effective communication and the creation of relationships for learning. The idea of clarity is developed in the work of Wragg (1993) and Wragg and Brown (1993) who define the characteristics of effective explanation. These characteristics can be readily modified so that they apply to students' management of classroom activity.

(i)   *Clear structure*
      This is the extent to which activities have clear identifiable points and a sense of sequence. It refers to the ways in which there are links between ideas in explanations which give the whole of explanation — or activity — a sense of coherence and shape.

(ii) *Clear pace*
      This is the extent to which activities have a level of pace which holds children's attention. Too fast a pace and children may be unclear as to the content of the activity; too slow a pace and the pupils could become inattentive.

(iii) *Clearly understood words and phrases*
      An activity is clear if the teacher uses words and phrases which are generally understood and is less clear if children do not understand the meaning of key words or phrases.

(iv) *Clear questions*
      This is concerned with the extent to which the questions teachers ask are complex and wordy. It asserts that one question is clearer than another if that question has a clear structure and purpose, uses accessible vocabulary and is straightforward in construction. A less clear question is one where there are multiple phrases, unfamiliar vocabulary and where there are complex subsidiary questions.

(v)   *Clear non-verbal communication*
      This final element relates to the quality of non-verbal communication and is concerned with the teachers' use of facial expression, hand gestures, eye contact and body position.

The Complexity of Classroom Processes

This list of technical skills relating to the idea of clarity is not exhaustive and may at first seem straightforward to achieve. The reality is different because these skills are developed within a profoundly complex context. To develop these skills in classrooms is far from straightforward. This contention can be elaborated with reference to two aspects of the literature which probe into the structure of and processes within the classroom. Both these aspects provide a detailed framework for the view that classrooms are intricate and individual. Different individuals have different perceptions of the classroom environment and these perceptions vary over time. The importance of fine-grain interactions between individual children and between teacher and children is seen as it is these which determine the detail of the ebb and flow of classroom life.

Pollard (1985, 1990) uses a fusion of symbolic interactionism and social constructivism to define the complexity of classroom interaction. He implies that it is the ongoing process of all classroom participants, children and teachers, interpreting and responding to each other's questions and explanations which define the classroom environment. For all classroom participants the 'me' is important because it refers to the social self, that is, to the notion of individuals' actions and reactions being determined by those of others. It is in this sense that learning to teach is intrinsically demanding. The student teacher not only has to understand the significance of a myriad of interactions minute by minute but also has to act in such a way to achieve the stated purposes of a particular activity. Children's and teachers' behaviour is hence determined by and also determines the characteristics of the classroom environment.

One consequence of this is that difficult behaviour is exhibited by different individuals in different environments and in the same environment at different times.

Why is all this important? It is important because it places emphasis on the individual and the relationship between the individual and the kind of classroom environment that is created. It states that each individual interaction has a role in shaping its characteristics. For a student teacher to manage the environment in such a way that the clarity is maintained for each individual is far from straightforward.

A second idea in the literature which can be used to underpin this notion of classrooms as complex is Doyle's concept of multidimensionality (1977, 1986). It refers to

> the large quantity of events and tasks in classrooms. A classroom is a crowded place in which many people use a restricted supply of resources to accomplish a broad range of social and personal objectives . . . In addition a single event can have multiple consequences: waiting a few extra moments for a (*pupil*) student to answer a question can affect that (*pupil's*) student's motivation to learn as well as the pace of the lesson and the attention of other (*pupils*) students in the class. Choices, therefore, are never 'simple'. (Doyle, 1986, p. 394) (my italics)

Multidemensionality can be used to describe complex classroom environments because it defines the individual detail of these. The concept has three elements (Simco, 1997). Firstly there is time. Classrooms change moment by moment and one individual interaction can affect the characteristics of the classroom in the next moment. Secondly there is context. The characteristics of the classroom may be different in whole class contexts, group contexts and in individual contexts. In whole class contexts a certain framework for the activity may be defined and stated which is then modified by children during group and individual activity. Thirdly the classroom is seen differently by different individual children. Referring back to the definition of technical skill some children may see the activity as well paced and appropriately structured, and hence clear whilst for others the structure is not understood or apparent.

The concept of multidimensionality adds further expression to the idea that the fine-grain social fabric of the classroom is its defining feature. The impact of individuals is seminal and the different actions and reactions of individuals at different times are crucial. It is the actions of individuals which make up the classroom environment. There are many studies which provide illustrations of this notion (Jackson, 1968; Desforges and Cockburn, 1987; and Pollard, 1996). One example is taken from Doyle and Carter (1984) who provide a detailed description of how individual children are successful in negotiating with teachers in order to modify classroom tasks.

Linking the theoretical concepts outlined with the available research it is clear that classrooms are unendingly complex. This is because of individual interactions between teachers and children and between children and children. Meaning is built in different ways by different individuals as children react to others' actions. These interactions are constant and of course at any one time multiple. One interaction can have profound influence on the whole of the classroom. Interactions are also simultaneous (Doyle, 1986) and their nature depends on the history of that class (ibid) and the relationships which have been created within it. Different individuals develop different understandings of what is going on in the classroom at any one moment.

Learning to Teach in Complex Classroom Environments

It is in this kind of environment that the student learns to teach. If it is the case that the nature of the classroom environment is as complex as the research suggests then it seems that the process of acquiring skills to manage classroom activity is far from straightforward. The technical skills outlined, including pace, structure, kind of questions and so forth appear now to be considerably more problematic than at first sight.

Take the pace, for example. During a teacher explanation it may be that for one child the 'rate of flow' matches his needs. He is able to understand what is being said and his interest is retained. For another the pace is too fast and he becomes restless and inattentive causing the student to intervene constantly. This then has implications for a third child who finds the pace of the explanation too slow and the structure disjointed. He also shows this in inappropriate behaviour as he disrupts another child causing him to become inattentive. The example is grossly oversimplified, but it shows this emphasis on the importance of the individual in having power to determine the characteristics of the classroom. For a student to acquire the skill of managing classroom activity so that it meets the needs of individuals and provides a well-ordered environment for teaching and learning is more problematic than is commonly acknowledged.

It is in this sense that the technical skill needed for effective management of classroom activity involves being able to understand the nature of that activity. If this understanding is apparent then the student teacher is more likely to manage the activity so it is clear to individual children. Yet to have this understanding is problematic because of the intricate nature of the environment.

This kind of technical skill is different in emphasis from that assumed in some quarters in early stages of teacher education reform. Here there was a tendency to see teacher education as apprenticeship, the implication being that the acquisition of skills to manage the classroom environment is unproblematic. This was part of a wider agenda aimed at divorcing initial teacher education from higher education (McCulloch and Fidler, 1994). Lawlor (1990) in Reid (1994) for example claims 'that teacher training in higher education institutions could be done away with since skills could be picked up from being in a classroom' (p. 8). Phillips (1996) in a scathing attack on education suggests that 'many teachers believe the only training that is of much use is provided by actually doing the job. But all the evidence suggests that the vast majority of teacher training institutions subscribe to a doctrinaire, often highly politicised approach which strips teachers of the authority they need to do the job' (p. 39).

Furlong and Maynard (1995) summarize the Government's view of learning to teach in the mid-1990s '. . . teaching is best learned simply through experience itself. All that is needed is the definition of a number of broad competency statements, sufficient to focus the attention of student and mentor alike' (p. 25). To put the argument in other words there was an assumption amongst some that the skills required for teaching can occur almost by osmosis through experience in classrooms and that there is no need for intellectualizing about teaching and learning. The assumption is open to challenge. It is not so much that intellectualizing about teaching and learning through using theoretical perspectives is inappropriate; it may well be in the initial stages of initial teacher education. It is, crucially, that the very nature of classrooms is misrepresented. The research shows them to be infinitely more complex than the assumptions behind the early reforms.

If classrooms are complex places in which technical skills for teaching are gradually acquired then there are at least three implications. The first of these relates to the rate of professional development. A number of authors, notably Calderhead (1991) and Calderhead and Shorrock (1997) provide evidence of the slow rate of professional development. Learning to teach demands the ability to rapidly interpret, create and respond to the constantly changing classroom environment. To acquire the skills of maintaining the clarity of activity within this environment is difficult.

If the rate of professional development is slow and the classroom environment is complex then it may well be appropriate to have an initial stage which focuses quite closely on the development of technical skill. This is not to deny the validity of engaging with theoretical views and perspectives about teaching and learning. It is to suggest that this engagement makes more sense when a student teacher is reasonably secure in his/her understanding of the nature of classrooms and how activity can be influenced to ensure its clarity. From a secure understanding of how classroom environments work, it is then possible to consider the 'large' questions pertaining to its organization; how much ownership should be given to children? Can there be effective interaction with individuals in whole class teaching? and so forth.

This initial emphasis on technical skills adds weight to those who wish to specify standards for QTS. It is of critical importance that students can manage clear activity in classrooms and it is right that this should be achieved before QTS is awarded. The extent of this achievement should, however, not be underestimated.

The straightforward language of the TTA standards is seductive in terms of the amount of expertise which each standard represents. Standard Bg states that trainees must demonstrate an ability to 'monitor and intervene when teaching to ensure sound learning and discipline' (DfEE, 1997, p. 10). This involves an unending series of judgments about when to intervene, with whom to intervene, and in what context, group, individual or whole class should such intervention occur. It demands that the student is clear about the purposes of such intervention and is able, through effective questioning or explanation, to challenge children's learning. It also assumes that the student is able to monitor the classroom by understanding the social complexity of that environment and discerning the appropriate point of intervention.

A second implication relates to the kind of reflection that is endorsed by the contention about slow development of technical skill in complex classroom environments. McIntyre (1993) builds on Van Manen's work to make explicit the growing consensus in the definition of levels of reflection. The first of these is technical reflection, involving a focus on basic classroom performance. The second is practical reflection and is about the relationship of classroom practice to underlying personal values and beliefs and the third is the critical or emancipatory level in which teachers look beyond practice to become actively aware of the role of institutional and societal forces impacting on their teaching. McIntyre (ibid) goes on to suggest that very few student teachers reach the third level; that is to say their professional growth is at a pace which does not readily provide opportunity for links to be made between their approach to teaching and their reaction to the societal context in which they are working. The reflective practitioner is not so much concerned with 'armchair philosophy' but rather with a focused consideration about the quality of technical aspects of teaching and the management of the classroom environment. Reflection in the initial stages of training could have a focus on the extent to which activity is clear because, as has been argued, this communicative aspect of teaching is central to the creation of effective activity.

Leading from this a third implication is concerned with the quality of interaction between a mentor and a student. Reflection is of most benefit if it is focused on specific classroom incidents and is undertaken in the context of dialogue based on this. Sixsmith and Simco (1997) have devised a model which describes this process of focused reflection on specific classroom incidents. The student and the mentor/classteacher/supervisor firstly negotiate an activity which the student is to subsequently teach. It is at this stage a focus for reflection is defined. This could be the extent to which explanations are used to structure the activity or the way in which problems are anticipated through initial instructions so facilitating pace. After the activity has been delivered both the student and the mentor reflect on the student's performance before there is a meeting between them to reflect together on the focus. The role of the mentor and the understanding that this person has of the classroom environment is central as they will act as reflective trigger in terms of the kind of questions, which are asked and the kinds of response to the student's questions which are offered.

From this dialogue a second experience is negotiated and there then follows a repeat of the evaluation process based on ensuing action from the first. It is in this way that the student crosses the zone of proximal development expressed in terms of their technical understanding of classroom environments.

Acknowledgment of classroom environments as complex provides intellectual and professional validity for the dominance of technical skill in the early stages of beginning to teach. Put simply the processes involved in understanding the nature of classrooms and how to manage them take considerable time to develop. Even then the process is not direct. There is probably no one way in which a student progresses from being unable to structure and pace classroom activity to a situation where they can. Individual children within classrooms impact on this process and individual classrooms in their diversity and 'history' provide a range of contexts which lead to the ebb and flow of professional development.

A Model of Initial Teacher Education

It is possible to speculate on the kind of model of initial teacher education which emerges. According to Reid (1994) the motivation for the increasing emphasis on competence and standards has its roots in Government distrust of colleges and universities peddling theories about exploratory learning and the wilder excesses of child-centredness. This sloganizing does not help move teacher education forward but the specification of standards does.

In essence the wrong argument may have been taking place. The debate of the early and mid-1990s was spurious because of the assumptions that were implicit within it. HEIs were angered about what they saw as the deintellectualism of teacher education through the advent of competences. The Government of the day saw that the so called 'trendy' theories of child-centredness led to liberal provision in ITE and low standards.

The major point has been missed. Because of the immense complexity of the classroom environment in which standards are worked on by student teachers, professional development in terms of the acquisition of technical skill is a painstakingly slow process. The quality of it is heavily dependent on the professional knowledge and understanding held by mentors in school and their ability to engage in focused dialogue with students. Far from being divorced from intellectual rigour the development of standards demands considerable engagement over a long period of time. Learning how to teach is problematic. HEIs can be assured that the inauguration of standards does not mark the demise of intellectual rigour; it merely changes its context from a focus on formal theory to a close analysis of classroom environments,

Desforges and Cockburn (1987) lend support to the validity of close analysis of teaching and learning in classrooms. In the conclusion to their study of mathematics in first schools they state

> put bluntly, we have found what teachers already know: teaching mathematics is very difficult. But we feel we have done more than that. We have shown that the job is more difficult than perhaps even teachers realize. We have demonstrated

in detail how several constraining classroom forces operate in concert and how teachers' necessary management strategies exacerbate the problems of developing children's thinking. (p. 155)

If the notion of standards can be enhanced by teacher education institutions — as it should be — then the next stage is to see the implications for the kind of teacher education that is needed. Leaving to one side, but by no means marginalizing, the acquisition of subject knowledge (dealt with elsewhere in this book), it seems that there are two clear phases. The first involves a period of focused practical work in schools with opportunities to engage in dialogue with mentors about specific classroom incidents. This has the aim of developing understanding of the nature of classroom environments and of developing teaching approaches which lead to clear activity. This focused practical work in classrooms needs to be contextualized by formal input of two kinds. It is important that students understand that the classroom is complex and reference would be made to the considerable number of studies which provide this framework. Additionally students would be introduced to the literature which considers issues related to the clarity of teaching, and again there is a considerable amount of research evidence here. Each element of the preparation, the practical and the theoretical, is important in the development of technical skill but the way in which trainees link the two is paramount.

Having acquired and consolidated technical skills the student is then in a good position to enter a second phase of learning to teach concerned with developing a view about appropriate pedagogy. This involves exploring the literature on learning theory, effective teaching and education policy. It also critically involves relearning technical skills in new contexts such as approaches to giving more ownership to children or in developing whole-class interactive teaching. It can be argued that this second phase is particularly worthwhile because the student has already acquired technical competence. It is apparent that present models which mix the two phases can lead to conceptual confusion or a perception that learning about pedagogy has little relevance to practical teaching.

The Sutherland Report (1997) speculates on possible models of ITE but comes to related but different conclusions. Sutherland argues that the existing PGCE route may have limitations because it is too short to lead to adequate levels of competence on entering the profession. He also suggests the existing BEd pathway has limitations in terms of preparation for subject teaching at the upper end of Key Stage 2. From this analysis Sutherland goes on to propose a model which links three years of teacher education and training (including one probationary year in a first post) with two initial years focusing on subject knowledge for teaching. This model would be aimed at trainees wishing to teach in Key Stage 2.

There is nothing in the proposal put forward in this chapter that is at variance with the Sutherland model, although concerns will arise in some quarters at the apparent separation of a Key Stage 1 route from a Key Stage 2 route. What this chapter does is to problematize the curriculum for the three years of teacher education and training. This may be significant in terms of the current intense scrutiny on the role of subject knowledge in effective teaching. Whilst it is true that the accurate representation of subject-specific concepts is at the heart of good teaching, it is important not to lose sight of the demands which are placed on student teachers when they work in highly complex classroom environments. The latter needs close systematic attention in the development of approaches to initial teacher education. It follows that the current focus on English and mathematics subject knowledge in the National Curriculum for ITT (DfEE, 1997) is a necessary but not sufficient condition for effective practice in ITE.

Although some of the ideas in this chapter are speculative, the broad approach to initial teacher education advocated here may have some currency. Teacher educators need to move forward from the debates in the early and mid-1990s which at their most simplistic saw the process of learning to teach either as intellectual rigour through a study of the philosophy, psychology and sociology of education or as a drive to higher levels of classroom performance through the specification of competence. Standards are clearly not separate from intellectual engagement if it is accepted that the social fabric of classrooms has unending complexity with which students can grapple.

References

CALDERHEAD, J. (1991) 'The nature and growth of knowledge in student teaching', *Teaching and Teacher Education*, **7**, 5/6, pp. 531–5.

CALDERHEAD, J. and SHORROCK, S.B. (1997) *Understanding Teacher Education*, London: Falmer Press.

DESFORGES, C. and COCKBURN, A. (1987) *Understanding the Mathematics Teacher, A Study of Practice in First Level Schools*, London: Falmer Press.

DFE (1992) *Initial Teacher Training: Secondary Phase (Circular 9/92)* London: DFE.

DFE (1993) *The Initial Training of Primary Teachers (Circular 14/93)* London: DFE.

DfEE (1997) *Teaching: High Status, High Standards: (Circular 10/97)*, London: DfEE.

DOYLE, W. (1977) 'Learning the classroom environment, an ecological analysis', *Journal of Teacher Education*, **28**, pp. 51–5.

DOYLE, W. (1986) 'Classroom organisation and management', in WITTROCK, M.C. (ed) *Handbook of Research on Teaching*, New York: Macmillan.

DOYLE, W. and CARTER, K. (1984) 'Academic tasks in classrooms', *Curriculum Inquiry*, **14**, 2, pp. 129–49.

FURLONG, J. and MAYNARD, T. (1995) *The Growth of Professional Knowledge: Mentoring Student Teachers*, London: Routledge.

JACKSON, P.W. (1968) *Life in Classrooms*, New York: Holt, Rinehart and Winston.

LAWLOR, S. (1990) quoted in REID, I., CONSTABLE, H. and GRIFFITHS, R. (1994) (eds) *Teacher Education Reform, Current Research*, London: Paul Chapman.

McCULLOCH, M. and FIDLER, B. (eds) (1994) *Improving Initial Teacher Training? New Roles for Teachers, Schools and Higher Education*, London: Longman.

McINTYRE, D. (1993) 'Theory, theorising and reflection in initial teacher education', in CALDERHEAD, J. and GATES, P. (ed) *Conceptualising Reflection in Teacher Development*, London: Falmer Press.

PHILLIPS, M. (1996) *All Must Have Prizes*, London: Little Brown.

POLLARD, A. (1985) *The Social World of the Primary School*: London, Cassell.

POLLARD, A. (1990) 'Towards a sociology of learning in primary schools', *British Journal of Sociology of Education*, **11**, 3, pp. 241–56.

POLLARD, A. (1996) *The Social World of Children's Learning, Case Studies of Pupils from Four to Seven*, London: Cassell.

REID, I. (1994) 'The reform: Change or transformation of initial teacher training?', in REID, I., CONSTABLE, H. and GRIFFITHS, R. (eds) *Teacher Education Reform, Current Research*, London: Paul Chapman.

SIMCO, N. (1997) 'An investigation into the classroom activity generated by pre-service teachers', unpublished PhD thesis.

SIXSMITH, S.C. and SIMCO, N. (1997) 'The role of formal and informal theory in the training of student teachers', *Mentoring and Tutoring*, **5**, 1, pp. 5–13.

SUTHERLAND, S. (1997) *Teacher Education and Training: A Study*, London: National Committee of Inquiry into Higher Education.

WRAGG, E.C. (1993) *Primary Teaching Skills*, London: Routledge.

WRAGG, E.C. and BROWN, G. (1993) *Explaining*, London: Routledge.

12   Towards Effective Communication

Kay Mills

Introduction

The interaction between teacher and learner has been the focus of many studies in education and beyond. The quality of the interaction is a key issue for everyone involved in teacher education and yet the ability to communicate effectively is often left to the individual and, to an extent, the 'hidden curriculum'. Interpersonal and communication skills, as such, are seldom overtly taught and yet these are fundamental skills to our profession. There is evidence from research that individuals experience limitations to their ability to communicate when they wish to address some difficulty which has arisen. I wish to explore this evidence and offer a number of models of dialogue which, I have found, greatly enhance the process to the advantage of everyone involved. These models come from the field of counselling, as it is within this arena that people explore difficulties with a view to changing perceptions and moving forward. I will argue that these models provide an opportunity to develop transferable skills, in that they are equally useful for teachers when interacting with children. If mentors can successfully model positive interventions with their student teachers, they are providing a very useful learning opportunity.

During a recent training session, with mentors from a variety of schools, it became apparent that the teachers were thoroughly enjoying their role, they said they were more reflective, self-aware and professionally stimulated by the process. They agreed that it added an extra dimension to their professional lives in school. However there was one very significant area which they found difficult and stressful; when they felt there was some difficulty, some aspect that they felt needed addressing, they were reluctant to challenge the student and intervene. There was a fear that in so doing they would discourage and upset the student, lower self-esteem, and create an impediment not only to the future relationship but also to the work in the classroom. They perceived working with adults as different from working with children though they acknowledged they felt skilled in managing these interventions with children.

Research

A number of writers have conducted research which gives insight into the mentor/student relationship and supports the findings within this group of teachers. The process of reflecting upon practice has been a major focus of Donald Schön (1983, 1987). In a variety of professional settings he has examined the interaction which takes place between, what he calls, the 'novice and coach'. In his research he identifies key issues regarding the dialogue which takes place and suggests that, 'Their dialogue has three essential features: it takes place in the context of the students' attempts . . . ; it makes use of actions as well as words; and it depends on reciprocal reflection-in-action' (Schön, 1987, p. 101). The context of the school and the nature of the job, teaching children, actually mirror the process in which both the 'novice and coach' are involved. It is therefore significant that the words and actions of both, with the children, and the reflection which both are encouraged to make upon that teaching, are key to the success of moving the novice onto the track towards gaining the expertise of the coach. This reciprocation suggests an honest sharing of thoughts, actions and feelings as the two explore what has occurred in the classroom, the learning outcomes for the children and possible improvements to the process of teaching and learning, which are essential for the development of professional expertise. In his examples of this interaction, Schön recognized that the dependence of the novice upon the expert, in the work place, can lead to a 'learning predicament', in that the development can only take place through the interaction. If either is unwilling to engage in this process then, he suggests, 'unsatisfactory outcomes are likely' as, 'essential elements are frozen in miscommunication' (ibid, p. 154). This seemed to describe the bind of which many of the teachers spoke, the bind which prevents the ongoing developmental process to continue due to a difficulty in reflecting upon the practice without causing one of the pair to disengage from the dialogue due to negative feelings. This miscommunication may also be due to a mismatch between what the teacher assumes the student needs at a given moment and what is actually required by the student. If the student is to gain insights from the experienced teacher, the student needs to have the skill to elicit that information, and the teacher needs to offer the student such opportunities.

Edwards and Collison (1996), following a three-year project of research into mentoring in primary schools, analysed the interactions which took place. They discovered that the majority of the interaction was supportive and encouraging. However there was evidence of 'mentors' reluctance to criticize students' practice for fear of discouraging' (p. 45). One might question the use of the word 'criticize' in this context, (it has a negative connotation) and ask if they know what it means to truly coach? Mentors were seen to be unwilling to explore difficult and sensitive issues as there was an assumption that it would lead to negative feelings. Once again there is evidence of 'frozen miscommunication'. In the avoidance of intervention by the teacher mentor, the student was allowed to continue and repeat strategies which were actually considered inappropriate. Allowing the student to thus proceed, not only established the strategy for the student, but also, by delaying or ignoring the intervention initially, made the issue more difficult to address in the future.

Another key aspect from this research involves the assessment of the student. When a qualification is at stake this dual role of the mentor and assessor can obviously create tensions. The student may not wish to be seen to be lacking in knowledge and understanding and therefore not ask any questions which might arise. There may be a tension at the end of the placement which prevents the professional dialogue from continuing. How does the mentor manage the duality? Is there a point when the developmental issues are put to one side as the assessment takes place? Having explored this issue, Edwards and Collison concluded that to be successful, 'sound formative assessment is also dependent upon the quality of the relationship that exists between mentors and students' (ibid, p. 110). Once again we see the relationship as being the key to successful learning and professional development in school.

Edwards (1997) recognized a situation where the mentor played 'host' and treated the student teacher as 'guest' in the classroom, 'guests who bear gifts'. This dynamic, she suggests, limits the potential development of skills and understanding and confirmed her earlier findings that student teachers present themselves as 'operators and not learners'. This focus on the task and its implementation, instead of the children and students as learners and the process of teaching, which she identified, allows both the teacher and the student to direct their discussions away from their own personal skills and understandings. This prevents the professional development which occurs through personal reflection and thus avoids the potentially more sensitive interpersonal perceptions involved when the process is aired. Once again there are examples here of students being left to either ignore their professional learning, or for it to be established inappropriately, through a defection in the communication away from themselves as novice learners through the teacher's unwillingness or lack of skill in accessing their expertise.

Field (1997) recognizes the diversity of the mentoring role, 'the role involving a combination of being a "friend", "counsellor", "supporter", "a shoulder to cry on", "assessor", "facilitator", "advisor", and "role model"' (p. 25). Understanding the different approaches required by these roles, the interpersonal and communication skills involved and an appreciation of the complexities of the school context in which the professional development takes place seem to be keys to successful mentoring.

The evidence from this research confirms the experience of the original group of teachers. There were inherent difficulties. Once we become an expert in the classroom, we become unconsciously competent, and often unaware of the implicit knowledge which ensures our success. The students, however, are initially often unconsciously incompetent, in that they do not have the understanding to know what they need to do or say. There seems therefore a need for the teachers to be conscious of their competence in order to make it explicit and therefore access the students to the skills, knowledge and understanding they posses thereby making them initially conscious of their incompetence. From that position the communication must take place around overt, explicit skills and understandings. The responsibilities put upon colleges of higher education to train teachers in partnership with schools necessitate that we address these key issues of interpersonal and communication skills in order that we meet the entitlement of students to an education and professional training of the highest quality.

Models

To gain insight into the dynamics of interpersonal communication I wish to draw, from the field of psychology and counselling, a number of models which I have found are successful in solving difficulties, changing perceptions and enhancing dialogue. In so doing I hope to enable the issues highlighted above to be avoided and to give teachers and students strategies for productive dialogue. Initially I wish to explore the work of Carl Rogers, well known for his writing and expertise in counselling and education. He proposed three core conditions as necessary for a helpful relationship: genuineness, acceptance and empathy. Genuineness is the willingness to be oneself, totally, to acknowledge one's own feelings and attitudes, and honestly express oneself without compromise. Teachers will say, 'the children will see through you', as they easily detect a lack of congruence, a lack of genuineness. In being genuine one will own one's feelings and thoughts and not project on to others blame and criticism. A 'genuine' person will say, 'I think that, I believe, I feel', and not accuse the other by saying, 'You are, you made me, you did or did not', all of which may be assumptions. The second condition, acceptance, means a warm regard for the other person, involving understanding. The third condition, empathy, involves a respect for the other's individuality, their behaviours, feelings and attitudes. Referring to education Rogers (1961) states, 'To the extent that the teacher creates such a relationship with his class, the student will become a self-initiated learner, more original, more self-disciplined, less anxious and other-directed,' (p. 37). Is this not what we want for our students? The research supports the views that when this rapport exists and the teachers offer honest open friendship, accept and acknowledge the point at which the student has reached in their professional development, and fully accept the students as equals in terms of respect and rights, there is a relationship which is more trusting and thus conducive to addressing issues which arise.

Research indicates that where teachers over protect, and 'look after' the student, the student often feels patronized or lapses into learned helplessness. Where the teacher dictates their requirements upon the student there is a tendency for them to rebel in an attempt to regain their self-control. On the other hand they might comply and become dependent on the teacher's direction. The Parent, Adult, Child (PAC) model developed by Eric Berne (1974), enables us to recognize what is going on in the above examples and allows us to objectively consider an alternative strategy. Berne identifies and names three modes of communication which he calls 'ego states'. He proposes that one could identify, in dialogue, a parent ego state which, like ordinary parental interaction with children, is either nurturing or controlling. For young children this is appropriate of course, but when individuals mature one might question the appropriateness of this way of communicating. This, I suggest is the guest/host dynamic identified by Edwards and Collison (1996): the teacher mentor acts as a nurturing parent to the student who as a guest complies in the child ego state. The second state is that of the child, which is either compliant or rebellious when it adapts and responds to the parent interaction or is free and spontaneous. Edwards' (1996) research draws attention to a common approach to the mentor which illustrates this, 'adapted child' state; 'Student teacher elicitation of mentor opinion was rarely direct but was usually evident in a statement offered for discussion with a degree of tentativeness' (p. 31). The student needs to appeal to the mentor, and feels unable to ask a direct question, as a child might appeal to a parent figure using such words as, 'if you like', and 'can I do.' The 'rebellious child' is evident in the stubborn or hostile response to a parent command. This is evident when we see a student refuse to follow the line of the teacher without a reasoned negotiation. There is, Berne suggests, a power struggle for superiority and a sense of blame and failure when either the rebellion or the compliance does not lead to the required outcome.

The third state which Berne recognized is the adult, the problem solving, information–giving state based on fact and evidence, where issues are addressed and negotiated with a win-win outcome for the two people involved. There is no blame, no dependence, no commands; the parent child interaction is put to one side. Yeomans and Sampson, in their recent research (1994) also recognize the 'important influence' of the relationship between mentor and student and draw attention to the dialogue and the relationship which fit precisely into the Berne model. 'Its personal and professional dimension was fused, and in spite of an apparent imbalance of power, it had some of the characteristics of a relationship of equals. Although participants sometimes used the analogy of "pupil-teacher", or even "child-parent", such assumptions presented some dangers. A more helpful characterisation was "friend" and "colleague", although the two were not inevitably linked,' (p. 120). This latter dynamic characterises the adult/adult dialogue, when each respects the other and negotiates from their own perspective based on information and evidence with a view to a positive outcome for both.

The drama triangle is developed by Stephen Karpman (1968), as he takes this model further. He considers the outcome when the dialogue between parent and child becomes tense and unsatisfactory for one of the participants. He proposes that when one person inappropriately either controls or nurtures another they place the other in a controlled victim position. The position may not be tolerated and this results in a switch as the 'victim' shakes off this control in rebellion. In schools this point can be recognised as the point of crisis, such as when people stop speaking to one another, and are not prepared to continue with the placement. Berne (1964), suggests that this switch is a dynamic of a psychological game which is entered into unconsciously. Returning to the mentors in training they all recognized the point, when they were fed up with helping, although they had been happy to be over helpful at the start of the placement, thus moving from over nurturing to controlling and demanding. Some felt they were too controlling and directive initially, and then the students simply did as they were directed, became compliant and dependent, (victim), and thus never regained their autonomy much to the teacher's annoyance. Sometimes the trainee switched to aggressively rejecting the direction or the assistance, moving from victim to controlling themselves.

Interactions

The understanding of the PAC model and the drama triangle allows us to reflect upon our interaction and consciously determine our position. Given the three core conditions, we need to avoid a situation where one dominates the other, or where one wins at the expense of the other. We need therefore to foster an adult-adult interaction, one where there are no blamers, no losers, and no failure only feedback. We wish to ensure professional development continues through two people identifying areas for improvement and sharing expertise.

This adult position is often achieved through the asking of open questions to prompt and provoke a response, thus promoting and facilitating dialogue. Possible examples which can be used in school following a teaching session might be:

'How can I help you?'

'Do you know what needs to be done?'

'To become a teacher you must achieve this standard, (fact) do you have any ideas. . . . ?'

'What did you think about . . . ?' 'How do you feel about . . . ?' 'What else do you need?'

'Can I make a suggestion here?' 'Would you like to know what I have done . . . ?'

'Can you imagine what might ease this situation?'

'From what I can see (fact), you might like to . . .' 'What can we do about this?'

'Where could we make changes . . . ? The use of 'we', acknowledges the joint responsibility for the development and the fact that the two, mentor and student teacher, are in partnership.

'There seems to be something you have not understood yet?' The word 'yet' implying that it is an incremental process and it is possible in the future.

'Would you like to see how I manage that?' Observation allows modelling to take place.

Through active listening to questions and responses, the teacher/mentor allows the student teacher to articulate their needs and gain information free from the assumptions of the teacher. This process gives a basis for identifying where changes are required. This respectful position promotes trust, and builds rapport through adopting the core conditions. The two work together to promote learning, skills, knowledge and understanding, and find solutions to difficulties which arise.

Owning an opinion keeps the dialogue in adult and avoids the expression of sweeping generalizations of the parent ego state; it also builds rapport through respect for the other person. Here are some examples taken from reviewing a lesson; instead of saying,

'There is a problem with . . . — 'I think we have a problem, . . .

'You are not . . . — 'From my position I don't think, . . .

'You must . . . — 'I think it might work if you . . .

'You have to . . . — 'I have found . . . and you might like to try . . .

'That's dreadful . . . — 'I don't like it when . . .

'You should . . . — 'In my experience, I . . .

'It is chaotic . . . — 'I feel you need to reorganise . . .

Either asking or answering questions, and expressing opinions based on evidence, keeps the dynamic free from the 'oughts', 'shoulds', 'musts', right and wrong critical statements of the parent.

The next question to be asked is, 'How do we deal with the difficulties?'. Again it is useful to examine a strategy from the 'helping' professions. The three-stage model of helping has been developed by Egan (1982) and used very widely by a variety of professionals involved with people. Together the two individuals, novice and coach, teacher/mentor and student teacher, initially 'explore' what is sensed to be a difficulty, what needs to be achieved or where the knowledge and skill is lacking. This is achieved through observation, actively listening to what is being said and questioning to gain clarity in order to define a specific target or desired outcome from the dialogue. The second stage is to gain 'new understanding' by looking at the issue from different perspectives and identifying the strengths available and alternative resources which can be utilized. Finally an option is selected and the decision is made to take 'action'. Why and how this option is selected becomes a key learning point for the student, the rationale for future reference. What do we have to do, when will we do it, how will we do it, what do we need and how will we know we have succeeded? The reflective practitioner will then review that process, evaluate the effectiveness in terms of learning and then move on to the next issue to be considered.

Many teachers spend time considering how they might address a student teacher about an issue. They say they often run through in their heads possible sentences they might use, they do not however think about testing their sentences out from other perspectives. It is often useful to consider three basic positions. The first position is from one's own point of view, how will saying this be for me, how will I feel? The second position is to think about the situation or the sentence from the recipient's point of view. For example: if I was in their shoes and heard that, how would I respond, how would I feel, what would I think, what might I do? What would the impact be, as that person, hearing a teacher/mentor say these words, in that manner and in that context? This is the position of empathy identified by Rogers (1961). The third position is to look at the dialogue from the position of an observer and usefully a film producer. From this position one can consider both the speaker and the recipient and rearrange what is said, how it is said and where the conversation takes place in order that the outcome of the dialogue might be positive.

In an exercise one teacher spoke of a major issue which was concerning her. She knew what she wanted to say, she could empathize with how that might be received and she suspected there would be a crisis and upset feelings and therefore had avoided the intervention. From the third position she realized that to speak across a table or face to face would make it very stressful for her; she then visualized a number of alternatives. She decided to suggest a short stroll round the block. Walking side by side she would hopefully be able to address the issue, without any tension and a strategy could soon be found to solve the difficulty. The following week she confirmed that in fact not only did she address her issue, but also another major concern had been fully aired. Both teachers agreed that they had recognized a significant improvement in their relationship as a result of this conversation. This 'reciprocal reflection' had been possible due to attention being given to the context in which it took place.

Within this chapter I have briefly explored the 'core conditions' of genuineness, acceptance and empathy, which build rapport and create a positive working climate; the parent, adult, child model and the 'drama triangle', which indicate appropriate equal adult stances from which productive dialogue can take place; the three stages of helping which facilitate difficulties being addressed and ways forward being found; and finally the 'three positions' from which we can consider any intervention. Returning to the mentors in training they confirmed the usefulness of this new awareness. There was subsequent evidence that they had found the models useful both in their management of children and students in school. They had found the use of the PAC model of particular use, through avoiding the parent ego state. One teacher reported that, 'situations are no longer escalating and ways forward are being found without loss of face or any bad feeling on either side'.

Standards

'Communication has been viewed as a key component of classroom life and therefore has an important influence on the learning which might take place' (Pollard, 1997, p. 270). One might therefore expect that it would be included in the Standards for the Award of Qualified Teacher Status, (*Circular 10/97*). Although many of the standards require communication skills the only overt reference for all teachers is in Standard B,k,viii, 'listening carefully to pupils, analysing their responses and responding constructively in order to take pupil's learning forward'. This chapter is aimed at meeting this standard. Teachers need to be able to model good practice to students in order that this skill is developed and achieved. In the final section, 'Other professional requirements' we might have expected to see further awareness of this dynamic and the need for overt interpersonal skills being included in the standards. However the skills are only alluded to in phrases such as 'effective working relationships' (Db), 'professional responsibilities' (Df), and 'need to liaise effectively' (Dg). As communication skills and interpersonal skills are central to teaching and learning in schools and part of the National Curriculum for children, it seems essential that everyone involved in preparing teachers have the necessary skills and understanding to communicate effectively and thus ensure the management of difficult issues is effective and productive while maintaining confidence and self esteem.

References

BERNE, E. (1964) *Games People Play*, London, Andre Deutch.
BERNE, E. (1974) *What Do You Say After You Say Hello?*', London: Corgi.
DfEE (1997) *Teaching: High Status, High Standards*, London: DfEE.
EDWARDS, A. (1997) 'Guests bearing gifts: The position of student teachers in primary school classrooms', *British Educational Research Journal*, **23**, 1.

EDWARDS, A. and COLLISON, J. (1996) *Mentoring and Developing Practice in Primary Schools*, Buckingham: Open University Press.

EGAN, G. (1982) *The Skilled Helper*, California; Brook/Cole.

FIELD, K. (1997) 'You and your mentor', *Mentoring and Tutoring*, **4**, 3.

KARPMAN, S. (1968) 'Fairy tales and script drama analysis', *Transactional Analysis Journal*, **26**, pp. 39–43.

POLLARD, A. (1997) *Reflective Teaching in the Primary School*, London: Cassell.

ROGERS, C. (1961) *On Becoming a Person*, London: Constable.

SCHÖN, D.A. (1983) *The Reflective Practitioner*, London: Arena.

SCHÖN, D.A. (1987) *Educating the Reflective Practitioner*, San Francisco, CA: Jossey–Bass.

STEWART, I. and JOINES, V. (1987) *TA Today*, Nottingham: Lifespace.

YEOMANS, R. and SAMPSON, J. (1994) *Mentoring in the Primary School*, London: Falmer Press.

13 Drama as a Way to Teach Teachers about Teaching

Nigel Toye and Francis Prendiville

Our purpose in this chapter is to show how trainee teachers can be taught, using educational drama methodology, to reflect on the nature of teaching and therefore helped to achieve the required standards.

How Does Drama Illuminate the Teaching Standards?

The Department for Education and Employment in annexe A of *Circular 10/97* has listed standards for the award of Qualified Teacher Status and it is clear that these standards can be applied to the teaching of all subjects, they are not subject content specific. The good drama teacher will therefore display the successful application of the QTS standards in the same way as the good history teacher. However we would claim that the methodology of teaching about drama confronts the trainee with a multiplicity of teaching issues that are as pertinent to the teaching of mathematics as they are to the teaching of history as they are to drama. There are two reasons for this. Firstly much of the pedagogical content knowledge of drama in education is related to teaching strategies, organization and classroom management and secondly the single distinctive feature of drama, the use of 'teacher role play' and the setting up of fictional contexts means the training situation is a replication of the classroom with the active involvement of the trainees at their own level. In order to learn successfully about drama, trainees are required to engage at two discrete levels, one as an active participant engaged with the drama and at another level as a teacher percipient, making sense of the teacher strategies, purposes and possible teaching and learning opportunities. What makes this dialogue distinctive is that it is possible to engage *at an adult level* with a drama about *Goldilocks* that has been planned for 3 to 5-year-olds. This is because issues of badly behaved children, parents not able to cope and needing help, can be interesting for 3-year-olds and 23-year-olds.

When trainees are learning about drama they are put into an actual teaching and learning situation which replicates teaching and learning for children. Unlike the lecture and seminar where there is a great deal of talking about teaching, with all the incumbent theorizing and hypothesizing, the training of drama teachers opens up a debate about the very nature of teaching and learning through the active participation of the trainees in a replication of the classroom.

Effective Teaching

Let us return to the standards to be demonstrated by trainees for the award of QTS and link these to training in drama methodology. Consider what would underlie the demand on trainees to 'demonstrate' that they:

> ensure effective teaching of whole classes, and of groups and individuals within the whole-class setting, so that teaching objectives are met and best use is made of available teaching time. DfEE

What is 'effective teaching'? How does drama exemplify it? Paulo Freire (1990) maintains that for there 'To be an act of knowing, learning demands among teachers and students a relationship of authentic dialogue'.

Drama creates a paradigm for 'authentic dialogue'; it constructs a learning environment with the teacher at the centre in a unique way. Dorothy Heathcote (1984), one of the most important educators of this century, highlighted the need for authenticity in teaching, particularly stressing the need for the authentic teacher. Looking at teaching from the pupil's point of view she sees the problem as 'the dead knowledge which is still being taught . . .'. She expands upon this idea when she refers to 'the ways in which . . . collected and useful knowledge is still being served up as if we'd only got books and writing to learn from . . .' and worse still there is 'teacher telling talk'. The amalgam of 'dead knowledge' and 'teacher telling talk' makes school seem 'inauthentic as soon as children stop being given "play" environments'.

What do we mean by 'authentic' here? How is the teacher speaking and listening? One pupil, when reflecting on the failings of normal classroom talk with teachers, seems to identify with Dorothy Heathcote when she picks out a problem of language:

> Sometimes I think children have a different language to adults and adults have a different language to children, because sometimes they don't understand. When they don't understand they just think we're talking a lot of rubbish, so they just leave us.

To avoid this problem we need a genuine interchange where both adult and child (or trainer and trainee) find a common language. That is the only way we can genuinely 'use teaching approaches and activities which develop pupils' language and provide foundations for literacy'. (DfEE, 1997)

Drama for Understanding

What does drama offer the trainee to exemplify more potent communication? We are not meaning drama as 'theatre' or performance here but 'drama for understanding' (Bolton, 1979). This, in its simplest form, involves a role play with both children and teacher taking part. What does this give the pupil?

First of all it offers a fictional context for learning which is happening as the children experience it and which requires children to talk and listen, and the teacher to do the same. Secondly the teacher takes part not always as teacher, but taking a role within the fiction alongside the children. This enables a breaking through of the 'teacher' language that blocks the authentic dialogue. For example in the *Goldilocks* drama the trainer goes into role as a child who is in trouble with his/her parents and is seeking help from the children who might be in role as an agency that helps children in difficulties. While engaging in the same drama the trainees can consider how they help children with parental problems just as easily as the children can. At the same time they see dialogue at the centre of the learning and can reflect on the nature of that dialogue.

Play and Learning

Dorothy Heathcote (1984) draws a link between authenticity and 'play environments' and it is important to be clear about what kind of play she is talking about. The roots of drama in education are embedded in children's ability to use social role play in order to make sense of their new and sometimes confusing social world. Pretending to be someone else or pretending to be somewhere enables a child to rehearse or re-enact particular situations and in so doing possibly learn about how to deal with them. Shifting the pupil into a fictional 'play' world also enables the teacher to:

> assess and record each pupil's progress systematically, including through focused observation, questioning, testing and marking, and use these records to . . . monitor strengths and weaknesses and use the information gained as a basis for purposeful intervention in pupils' learning. (C ii, *Monitoring, Assessment, Recording, Reporting and Accountability*)

This intervention and subsequent dialogue can of course be from within a role, in other words, the teacher is also operating from within the 'play'. The implication of this is that the heightened stimulation to talk that teacher in role often produces from children, will generate further evidence upon which assessment of children's knowledge skills and understandings can be based. If the role taken on by the teacher is the role of someone 'who doesn't know' and if the teacher from within the role seeks the help and guidance of the pupils, who take the role of those 'who can help', then we have created an unusual teacher/pupil relationship, one that challenges the status quo of teacher who knows.

Trainees who see this change of relationship operating and attempt it themselves can learn a great deal about questioning in teaching, by 'not knowing' all the answers they have a chance to shift into a wondering mode of questioning, one that we believe is far more productive than the 'have you got the right answer' or more usually, 'have you got the answer that is in my head' type of questioning. Children have the status to feel confident to offer more.

As children go through the school system the use of 'play' as a way to learn becomes more and more redundant. It becomes in conflict with 'proper' learning, to be left behind in the nursery or reception class. However, this is a great loss and it is possible to structure some of the features of social role play into a wide variety of teaching and learning situations and maintain the interest and commitment of the learners no matter what age they are. It is necessary for the teacher to negotiate the context with the group and to demonstrate authenticity and demand it from the learners.

Here the drama method connects to the demand on trainees to

> demonstrate that they: ... set appropriate and demanding expectations for pupils' learning, motivation and presentation of work. (a iii, *Planning, teaching and class management*)

In practice this means an agreement about the rules of the game and a demand that the work should be taken seriously. This latter demand has to be demonstrated by the teacher who must be on the inside of the work with the learners, usually through the use of teacher role play. The teacher does not stand on the outside telling the learners what 'to do' but operates from the inside as a leader of the learning process, challenging, reflecting and drawing together the ideas of the group. The teacher can use her social role play skills and in so doing signal to the group the high status and responsibility of being a learner. This can lead to 'play' which is serious, highly sophisticated and a very powerful promoter of learning, because it is exploratory and interactive.

We have found that this kind of teacher behaviour meets and illuminates for trainees the *10/97* standard that they:

> ... use teaching methods which sustain the momentum of pupils' work and keep all pupils engaged through:
> (i) stimulating intellectual curiosity, communicating enthusiasm for the subject being taught, fostering pupils' enthusiasm and maintaining their motivation. (k i, *Teaching and Class Management*)

How does drama, based as it is on fiction and play, help us understand the way a teacher needs to

> ... establish a safe environment which supports learning and in which pupils feel secure and confident? (j, *Teaching and Class Management*)

Fiction and Learning

Let us consider what the usual classroom situation entails for the pupil. The task that is set is artificial. Most of what happens in school is *practice* for real events rather than real events themselves. Sometimes 'real' events happen (trips out, a visitor from outside) but they are the exception and cannot be organized all of the time. This is where the 'play' element in drama symbolizes the nature of schooling.

Just as young children by pretending 'play' seriously to learn about the events that happen to them, to revisit them, make sense of them, understand them or practise for them, so tasks and lessons in school should be seen as ways of coming to terms with the process of life outside school. If we recognize that practice and artificiality are the nature of the teaching situation, why not take the logical consequence and use that fact most positively: start from where everyone agrees to accept the artificiality and together create a fiction as the context for the learning. This is the 'play' concept, a major step in thinking about teaching ... to see it as serious practice and not to try to pretend that it is real to ourselves or to the children.

Using the fiction positively, we can utilise and build on the advantages of practice as opposed to real events. Firstly it brings *protection* for the participants:

- we can experiment and see what we learn;
- mistakes are part of the learning process — when we experiment we try to get it right but it is also acceptable to get it wrong;
- there are no 'real' consequences and we can reflect on what making the mistakes teaches us and what the consequences would be if it were for real.

The second advantage of moving trainee teachers (and the children) inside a fiction relies on what Augusto Boal (1979) calls 'metaxis', acting in the fictional world and at the same time knowing that it is not real, thus being able to reflect on it, to think about it. We can stop and step out of the fiction to discuss the implications, the consequences of actions and the concepts embodied in it. It is the acme of a reflective mode. Gavin Bolton (1979) sums up the relationship:

> Drama is a metaphor. Its meaning lies not in the actual context nor in the fictitious one, but in the dialectic set up between the two.

This dialectic makes the 'pretending' very powerful because it is the opposite of escapism; it is about relating the possible to the real and so understanding more about each as a result. So we move the learning teacher towards being clear that school is practice, is not 'for real'. That helps the teacher make all his/her intentions/objectives more explicit that the teacher and learner are moving forward together with the teacher clearly leading:

> setting clear targets for pupils' learning, building on prior attainment, and ensuring that pupils are aware of the substance and purpose of what they are asked to do. (a. iv, *Planning*)

What drama offers is a pretend situation, agreed to by all the participants, which then has a greater possibility of authenticity because we all contract into making it work. These conditions are what drama can achieve that all teaching should aspire to. Drama's mode of operation fits the five criteria which Applebee (1990) uses to help define when true learning takes place:

'Ownership' resting with the learners, and there is 'appropriateness of the activities, structure, collaboration' and 'transfer of control' in the creation of meaning.

In picking up on the need for ownership for the learners and for the shift of control towards collaboration, drama offers the possibility of reshaping the way we conceive of the relationship of the teacher and learner. This is where we need to look at the way new teachers learn how to operate, how to intervene. As the ITT standards given by the TTA conceive of it for early years' pupils we must have:

planned adult intervention, which offer opportunities for first-hand experience and co-operation and which use play and talk. (g, *Additional standards relating to early years*)

Teacher Intervention

The standards as a whole ask trainees when assessed, demonstrate that they:

. . . monitor and intervene when teaching to ensure sound learning and discipline. (g, *Teaching and Class Management*)

This could be applied to all teaching as exemplified by drama. What kind of intervention is best for the pupils?

At this point readers might see us as subscribing to the spectre of a 60s 'progressive' tenet for drama as free expression for the children. Far from it; we are advocating something far more teacher-structured. Teachers must not see teaching polarized only as *either* teacher dictated *or* children dictated. As John Dewey (1938) recognized, this is a false polarity. He rejected an approach to teaching which he called the 'Traditional scheme' and which he saw as:

one of imposition from above and from outside. It imposes adult standards, subject matter and methods upon those who are only growing slowly toward maturity. The gap is so great that the required subject-matter, the methods of learning and behaving are foreign to the existing capacities of the young.

However, he also identified how some of his so-called followers misinterpreted his rejection of teacher spoon-feeding as an advocacy of licence for the children. He saw that in rejecting the 'traditional' they were casting aside proper teaching, the idea of the teacher shaping learning as a whole. He was aware of how such a reduction of the teacher's authority was a caricature of his ideas. As such he attacked the looseness and lack of educational rigour of 'the progressive movement' in 1938. He advocated the need for recognition of the most effective way for teachers to influence the learning:

When external control is rejected the problem becomes that of finding factors of control that are inherent within experience . . . it does not follow that the knowledge and skill of the mature person (here the teacher) has no directive value for the experience of the immature. On the contrary, basing education upon personal experience may mean more multiplied and more intimate contacts between the mature and the immature than ever existed in the traditional school, and consequently more rather than less, guidance by others. The problem then is: how these contacts can be established without violating the principle of learning through personal experience.

Here Dewey identifies facilitating as proper guidance, proper teaching, not the abnegation of responsibility. If we accept the burden of his description we then have the responsibility of finding the teaching strategies and structures that will provide these 'contacts'.

The demand on the teacher is to intervene productively. Buber identified the delicacy of intervention, warning 'that intervention/interference is inappropriate for successful learning. He does not deny that it is teacher responsibility to use the authority, knowledge and experience of their adulthood but it must be used as a hidden influence proceeding from integrity' (Morgan and Saxton, 1993).

The 'hidden influence' means that the pupil can initiate and not feel that the teacher is always the arbiter. Then we have the possibility of pupils learning first hand. Drama can illustrate the subtle intervention. An example of such a situation in drama happened when a year 4 class had become a mountain community and taken in a fugitive girl with her baby (derived from work based on Brecht's *The Caucasian Chalk Circle*). Some 'villagers' were suspicious of her and when she was asleep one suggested searching her bag. As he reached to do that another said, 'No, she is our guest. How can we take her in and then search her belongings? They are private to her.' The teacher then intervened to make the children think through the dilemma. The group of 9-year-olds involved in this drama spent 20 minutes discussing the issue of the morality of the act. They went on afterwards (out of role) to look at the concepts of privacy, guest and host etc.

In addition, the subject matter of this example drama is showing the trainee teacher how to

> plan opportunities to contribute to pupils' personal, spiritual, moral, social and cultural development. (d, *Planning*)

This is a subject raised elsewhere in the standards where trainees must be capable of:

> exploiting opportunities to contribute to the quality of pupils' wider educational development, including their personal, spiritual, moral, social and cultural development. (K xii, *Teaching and Class Management*)

The dynamic nature of the learning process illustrated in this example is defined by Paulo Freire (1990):

> The act of knowing involves a dialectical movement that goes from action to reflection and from reflection upon action to a new action.

Action and Reflection

Drama can reinforce the trainee teacher's understanding of this dynamic because of its combination of thought and external action as the above example illustrates.

The element of reflection and its centrality to learning is very graphically illustrated in the drama process. The teacher can be in role, as the father of the naughty girl (see *Goldilocks* example mentioned earlier) and be talking to the pupils about her in an angry voice. Then she can shift out of role to ask, 'Why does he feel like that about his daughter?'

The very action of shifting out of role is a tangible symbol of moving to reflection about the activity, more obvious than reflection in a normal teaching situation, for example, a teacher stopping a science experiment to discuss what is happening is not obviously taking a different stance from teacher carrying out the experiment. The teacher coming out of role in drama *is* someone else and talks about their role in the drama from a reflective point outside that role. If we can move new teachers to giving active opportunities such as the *Chalk Circle* one above, with plenty of reflective deliberation then we will have a very potent teaching force.

Such a teacher can learn:

- not to be afraid to share responsibility;
- not to be afraid to be wrong;
- not to be afraid to express feelings;
- not to be afraid to take risks;
- not to be afraid to take themselves less seriously;
- not to be afraid to value a multiplicity of intelligences;
- not to be afraid of students' superior knowledge;
- not to be afraid of joyful delight for it is the aesthetic indicator of powerful learning. (Morgan and Saxton, 1993)

If we can get trainee teachers to this point then they will avoid the deadly perception of themselves as having to be infallible, having to be all-knowing, having to be perfect, having to be *the* authority. It is the demands of this self-perception that threatens the inexperienced teacher immediately they face their first class and can lead to instant and counterproductive confrontation with pupils as the first step in asserting authority, very often the most inappropriate step. For effective teaching lies in leading well, a role where acknowledging the abilities and knowledge of the led is important. Does this not undermine discipline?

Drama and Control

Let us consider how drama opens up the issue of discipline and control.

The standards define the need to

. . . establish and maintain a purposeful working atmosphere; . . . set high expectations for pupils' behaviour, establishing and maintaining a good standard of discipline through well focused teaching and through positive and productive relationships. (h and i, *Teaching and Class Management*)

So the basis is clearly *positive and productive relationships*. We need to help the new teacher see how achievement of these relationships is dependent on making the right decisions about how to structure for learning and how to act when carrying out the work.

Drama can help us make explicit the nature of these relationships. Because the teacher who adopts drama deliberately shifts the usual relationship of pupil and teacher to a fictional one we are also confronted with examining what the usual relationship entails and can examine those features of the teacher/pupil relationship. For example, in the drama about the naughty girl, *Goldilocks*, the pupils will need to know that in spite of the fact the teacher is going to pretend to be Goldilocks' anxious father (inside the fiction), she is not going to leave her responsibility for being in charge of the class (outside the fiction). One of the conventions the teacher will negotiate with the class is that she may at anytime return to being teacher out of role, to reflect upon what is happening in the drama or to deal with the responses of the class to the drama.

listening carefully to pupils, analysing their responses and responding constructively in order to take pupils' learning forward. (k viii, *Teaching and Class Management*)

As well as managing the class by dropping out of role, she can make explicit her teacher demands through the role itself. She may use her role, as Goldilocks' father, as a control strategy by telling the children, if they are shouting out or not listening to the role, that 'I will have to leave because everyone is speaking at the same time and they don't seem interested in my problems. I thought you were going to help me.'

This highlights to trainees how teachers choose particular strategies to manage behaviour and in this way enable the learning to take place.

By raising the question of how this control strategy from inside the role play is different from, for example, the teacher as teacher saying to the class, 'Nobody is listening to me and therefore I will stop the lesson until everybody is paying attention', trainees become aware of the nature of teacher behaviour. By examining the nature of the 'drama game' we can make explicit features of teaching that trainees may take for granted or adopt inappropriately, without thinking, because they are in common usage.

Planning and Assessing

The issues of planning and assessing pupils' work are central in attaining authentic and effective teaching.

The standards require that trainees when assessed, demonstrate that they:

> plan their teaching to achieve progression in pupils' learning through:
> identifying clear teaching objectives and content, appropriate to the subject matter
> and the pupils being taught, and specifying how these will be taught and assessed.
> (a i, *Planning*)

As with all planning trainees must make explicit their learning intentions and in doing this they need to look at the sticky question of what do we actually hope the pupils will learn? One strategy we get trainees in drama to look at is hard and soft objectives. For example in the drama *Goldilocks* the objectives might be:

> Objective a (soft): to get the children to work cooperatively
> Objective b (hard): to get the children to deal with a father who is very upset,
> using appropriate language (verbal and non-verbal).

The reason for getting trainees to make the distinction between hard and soft objectives is to undermine the tendency they have to describe only soft objectives, those objectives which could be applied to all dramas. For example 'to work co-operatively', 'to listen to each other', 'to negotiate ideas', 'to accept others' ideas even if they are not their own', etc.; these can all be found in most dramas. While these are laudable objectives we primarily need some that are more focused and specific to the learning areas the particular drama offers.

Because drama, like PE, requires activity in a space without the supportive organizing factor of desks or seats, its planning highlights the need for detailed structure and therefore makes more apparent the standard to

> provide clear structures for lessons, and for sequences of lessons, in the short,
> medium and longer term, which maintain pace, motivation and challenge for
> pupils. (b, *Planning*)

As for assessment, the currency of the drama lesson is language and trainees must be able to apply the level descriptions described in the National Curriculum documents to each individual in the class. Trainees must reach a standard where they:

> are familiar with the statutory assessment and reporting requirements . . . and where
> applicable, understand the expected demands of pupils in relation to each relevant
> level description or end of key stage description. (d & e, *Monitoring, Assessment,*
> *Recording, Reporting and Accountability*)

It helps trainees to have the descriptions broken down into component parts, so that a profile can be drawn up. In diagnosing where particular pupils are in relation to these levels we recommend that in any drama only a small group of pupils is focused upon to make the task more manageable.

Having learnt how to assess, trainees are then in a position to demonstrate progression. Using a profile based upon the level descriptions, trainees can monitor for any *gains* in knowledge, skills and understanding and in this way demonstrate progression, i.e. progress made in relation to prior attainment.

Trainees must reach a standard where they can demonstrate their ability to:

plan their teaching to achieve progression in pupils' learning through: . . . setting clear targets for pupils' learning, building on prior attainment . . . (a ii, *Planning*)

Trainees should be able to demonstrate that they can:

recognise the level at which a pupil is achieving, and assess pupils consistently against attainment targets, where applicable, if necessary with guidance from an experienced teacher. (g, *Monitoring, Assessment Recording, Reporting and Accountability*)

The nature of drama gives them opportunities to do this, in particular in relation to English AT1 and, where drama is cross–curricular in content, it gives them the opportunity to apply level descriptions from more than one subject.

Finally we will return to the issue of classroom management raised earlier. In planning drama trainees are confronted with issues of classroom management, and in particular, issues of discipline, in a way that is different from planning for other subjects but at the same time raises several generic points. Firstly, unlike most lessons, desks and tables have been pushed back or the teacher is working in a large space in a hall. This change in physical environment can feel threatening to both teacher and pupils[1]. Secondly, the use of teacher in role means that the nature of the relationship between teacher and pupil is going to be different and the idea of negotiating the teaching and learning situation emerges. Trainees must demonstrate that they can:

. . . monitor and intervene when teaching to ensure sound learning and discipline (g, *Teaching and Class Management*)

From this list of the principles for successful drama lessons we can see that they have a generic relationship with all teaching.

- The negotiation of what is going to happen is the starting point.
- Making clear what are teacher decisions as distinct from the decisions the children can make, i.e. clarifying the negotiable and the non-negotiable.
- Making clear what is going to happen in the drama and what you expect from the pupils.
- Making clear what will happen if there is a breakdown of the drama.
- Stopping the drama to talk about it, to check out the understanding at that point.
- Stopping the drama if someone's behaviour is inappropriate and is getting in the way of others' learning.
- The consequences of behaviour is made explicit. Teachers will look for any opportunity to praise valid and constructive ideas and actions.

If we look closely at these ingredients they are very similar to good advice for all teaching:

- Clear expectations — making explicit the rules and conventions of the teaching and learning situation.
- Explicit consequences of behaviour.
- Teacher valuing of pupils' contributions.
- Teacher commitment expressed in the seriousness in which they take the work — this will be mirrored by the pupils.

The culture nurtured by the teacher using drama is one of the learner having high status — learning is seen to be a venue in which the learner can not only make a contribution but just as importantly can fail safely, and this includes the teacher's attempts to make it work. Trainees' examination of drama as a methodology enables a debate to begin about values, teacher values and pupil values. Trainees can understand that because language is the currency of the drama lesson and language is value-laden, therefore they cannot avoid the spiritual, moral, social and cultural aspects of what they teach.

Thinking about their own values confronts training teachers with themselves and the decisions and responses they make in lessons. They see that they cannot divorce their own value system from the teaching they engage in. The decisions they make about what to teach and how to teach it are wrapped up in their own perception of the world. Because drama enables teachers to step outside the usual teacher pupil relationship through the use of 'teacher in role', the decisions a teacher makes in setting up that role reflects his/her own values and the kind of values he/she want the pupils to examine.

When trainees were asked to list the qualities they perceived that drama offered them they came up with the following list:

Drama heightens confidence, breaks down barriers, frees relevant speech and thought, improves listening, helps share experiences, deepens feelings, provides protection for the individual, ensures team work, is practical, works through detached reality, creates experiential learning, explores feelings and prejudices, evokes empathy, differentiates by ability, broadens the ability to communicate and trains in social skills.

These are qualities we would wish to see in all trainees, many of which go beyond the DfEE's standards.

Note

1 Of course, the same thing happens in PE or a dance lesson. However, it is usually accompanied by a change of clothing and consequently expectations are usually clearer. The tradition in PE and dance is also more universal and therefore the experience of the pupils in this situation is likely to be greater than in the drama lesson.

References

APPLEBEE, A. (1990) 'The enterprise we are part of: learning to teach', in MURPHY, P. and MOON, B. (eds) *Developments in Learning and Assessment*, Milton Keynes: Open University Press.

BOAL, A. (1979) *Theatre of the Oppressed*, London: Pluto Press.

BOLTON, G. (1979) *Towards a Theory of Drama in Education*, London: Longman.

BOLTON, G. (1986) 'Philosophical perspectives on drama and the curriculum', in DAVIS, D. and LAWRENCE, C. (eds) *Gavin Bolton: Selected Writings on Drama in Education*, London: Longman.

CANTER, L. and CANTER, M. (1992) *Assertive Discipline*, New York: Lee Carter and Associates.

DEWEY, J. (1938) *Experience and Education*, New York: Macmillan.

DfEE (1997) *Teaching: High Status, High Standards (Circular 10/97)*, annex A ('Standards for the Award of Qualified Teacher Status'), London: DfEE.

FREIRE, P. (1990) 'The politics of education', in MURPHY, P. and MOON, B. (eds) *Developments in Learning and Assessment*, Milton Keynes: Open University Press.

HEATHCOTE, D. (1984) 'The authentic teacher and the future', in O'NEILL, C. and JOHNSON, L. (eds) *Dorothy Heathcote: Collected Writings on Education and Drama*, London: Hutchinson.

MORGAN, N. and SAXTON, J. (1993) 'Dorothy Heathcote: Educating the intuition', unpublished paper given at the University of Lancaster conference 'The Work and Influence of Dorothy Heathcote'.

14   The Trouble With English: The Challenge of Developing Subject Knowledge in School

Sam Twiselton and David Webb

English (and particularly the teaching of literacy) seems to many to be a worry, the most prominent unlanced boil on the flanks of education, for ever causing concern. This is not for lack of offers of medication. Barely a day goes by without politicians, the Chief Inspector, or Melanie Phillips in *The Observer* offering healing counsel, despite the lack of any incontrovertible evidence that standards of literacy have declined, and no evidence at all that, if they have, teaching methods are implicated. English teacher educators, like their maths colleagues, have the privilege of their own copious National Curriculum for Initial Teacher 'Training' (1997) from the TTA and OFSTED, astonishingly explicit about the knowledge and skills which children need to become literate, presumably because its authors were fearful that 'trendy educationalists' would eschew any teaching of literacy skills at all.

Behind all this advice one can detect an ignorance of, and a contempt for, educational research and a connected obliviousness as to what is happening in real schools and in teacher education now. 'Theory' is seen as a narcissistic irrelevance indulged in by teacher educators leading very sheltered lives in their ivory towers. If the practices in school and in university teacher education of which these critics disapprove were ever widespread, those days are long gone. Furthermore, details of pedagogy are invisible in these exhortations. There is nothing about how to get pupils and student teachers to use effectively the skills and knowledge which are felt to be needed.

Yet all this ignorant public criticism renders literacy teaching more difficult. It makes for edgy teachers, suspicious parents, defensive teacher educators, and very jumpy students indeed. Even without this criticism, teacher educators, whether based in school or university, and the edgy class teachers face intrinsically difficult problems now teacher education is more devolved out to schools. As Edwards and Collison (1996) show, research into school-based teacher training has highlighted understandable shortcomings in the dialogues between student teachers and the members of school staffs who deal with them. They found that most dialogues were low level, and concerned with classroom practicalities. 'Theory' tended not to come up. Another problem was the pressure on students to 'perform', to address the whole class, and many were discouraged from practising the small-scale interventions of the kind advocated below as crucial for literacy teaching. ('You do a story with the class, and I'll hear some readers.') The *Literacy Log* discussed below began its life as an attempt by a colleague, Lorna Crossman, to ensure that students get appropriate experiences in school and was developed further by one of the authors in an attempt to direct student teachers to analyse their teaching in this way.

Edwards and Collison (1996) have used the notions of *'situated cognition'* and *'peripheral participation'*, drawing on the work of Jean Lave and her associates in the USA, to illuminate the pressure to perform and other related problems faced by learner teachers in classrooms (see as examples Lave and Wenger, 1991; and Chaiklin and Lave, 1993). *'Situated cognition'* emphasizes the view that knowledge cannot be fully separated from the context which helps to define it. Knowledge is not seen as a commodity which can be transferred directly from one situation to another. So a key part of education for teaching has to happen in the classroom, but the problem is that there seems to be no non-participatory role for students in busy classrooms to focus on their own learning. Lave and Wenger argue that students need a position in the classroom which makes possible *'legitimate peripheral participation'*, a licence to be involved in classroom activity but primarily focused on their own learning, and certainly not in charge of some activity. The *Literacy Log*, discussed below, has, as one of its functions, to stake a claim for just such a licence.

Furthermore, if *'situated cognition'* means that knowledge cannot be transferred unproblematically from one situation to another, the *Literacy Log* can help generate a 'generality of knowing'. It enables the details of experiences in the classroom to be recorded and reflected upon. The student's understandings can then be extended and deepened by discussion of the log in school with teachers and mentors, and can be further analysed and generalized in discussion away from the original context in the college or university. It is the bridge between particular moments in particular classrooms and the understandings of them generated there and the more generalized 'theory' which can be applied in many classrooms and which can be informed by the discourse of educational research.

There is another difficulty in the way of effective classroom student learning. The students we described as jumpy are troubled about theory as are the teachers. Understandably they are desperate for quick easy ideas for practical activities, and to them, compared with other subjects, English seems overtheoretical. The transmission model which students perceive as operating in other curriculum areas is strikingly inappropriate for most language and literacy teaching. Yet literacy teaching needs what may seem like fuller and more detailed theorizing than other parts of the curriculum. It can never be a series of good lessons containing new content which can be taught to students who then teach it to children. Effective literacy teaching cannot be captured simply by ideas for activities. Learning to be literate is more like learning to drive. For the pupil it does not usually involve learning to do new things but rather doing the same things repeatedly with increasing insight and skill. Furthermore, activities which can be used by the skilled teacher to teach literacy are going on in the classroom all the time.

Focusing on Teacher Interventions

What will make an activity effective in the promotion of literacy is very often the way the teacher responsively *scaffolds* the learner through it, by making what

Wood (1988) describes as *contingent interventions*. Successful contingent interventions depend on the teacher's ability to identify and respond appropriately to an individual learner's needs, and that depends on 'theory'. The teacher must draw both on an understanding of the concepts being developed and knowledge of the learner. 'Contingent teaching' is one of the key factors which will define a teacher's effectiveness, particularly in literacy teaching where so many literacy teaching/learning opportunities arise as pupils tackle the range of the primary school curriculum.

Effective adult assistance will be constantly tuned to the needs of the individual, defined by his/her level of performance. Wood (ibid) identifies 'contingent teaching' as a major factor in young children's' learning, involving pacing the amount of help children are given on the basis of their moment to moment understanding. Particularly clear instances of this type of help occur in literacy teaching when an expert teacher scaffolds a young learner through a reading or writing experience, drawing on what he/she already knows and taking it a little further. For example, sharing a book with a child and noticing which strategies are being used to decode unknown text and modelling or discussing alternative possibilities, or gathering of a small group of children who are at a stage in the composition of their own stories where it will be useful to have a discussion linking their own characterization with the way it is done in the class story. In both cases the teacher is responding to a learning need by bringing together a range of knowledge about the children and the subject into an intense contingent teaching intervention.

This ability to draw on a range of understanding in order to meet the precise requirements of the moment as it arises (often unforeseen, or at least not directly related to the planned desired learning outcomes) is a key factor in becoming an effective literacy teacher. In considering this, the notion of 'time epistemologies'. provides a useful model for describing the way successful contingent interventions occur. (The term 'epistemology' comes from philosophy, and can be defined in this context as a way of knowing and organizing thinking.) Edwards and Hodgson (1996), drawing on Tochon and Munby's (1993) identification of significant differences in 'time epistemologies' between novice and expert teachers, categorize a study group of teachers into two distinct types, using the terms 'synchronic' and 'diachronic'. (Readers are most likely to be familiar with these terms from linguistics. Diachronic or historical linguistics deals with changes in language through time whereas synchronic linguistics is concerned with the varieties of language, dialect, accent and register, for instance, which exist at the same moment.) The teachers in group A are described as having a mainly synchronic notion of teacher time. They focus responsively on the many opportunities which crop up unpredictably and almost simultaneously in the classroom, and seize on particular ones to make an effective contingent interventions. Group B contains a group of teachers who have a mainly diachronic view of time. This is an essentially linear approach to time with a strong emphasis on planned use of curriculum time as a sequence.

Tochon and Munby make a distinction between didactics and pedagogy. The former is defined as the organization of subject-matter knowledge either before of after the teaching action has occurred. Pedagogy is seen as stemming from the interactive management of time around and within the teaching act. Didactics deals with the subject content within a sequential processing and has a central role in the codifying and formalizing of time within the planned curriculum. It is a diachronic anticipation of the content to be taught or a diachronic representation of the content that *was* taught. In contrast pedagogy is seen as the immediate image of the teaching situation, which is essentially interactive and drawing on a range of factors synchronically.

Tochon and Munby claim expert teachers operate with a synchronic epistemology and link novice teachers with a greater reliance on diachronic ways of working. Novices tend to anticipate and sequence their teaching actions in advance, whereas experts often adapt entire semantic or propositional mappings to a particular event; restructuring their actions in the light of an unanticipated response from an individual or group.

To illustrate this further it is useful to examine three short extracts of teaching, taken from an experienced teacher, a student teacher near the beginning of her training and a student teacher in the third year of a four-year course. The extracts are approximately 10 minutes long and are taken from roughly equivalent stages of the whole session where the children are on task, either individually or in pairs, having being started off previously.

The observations have been annotated according to the strategies demonstrated and the knowledge they were based on. Specific literacy concepts are noted, using the National Curriculum and SCAA Desirable Outcomes as a framework for headings. Specific teaching strategies have been categorized into a series of headings developed from Tharp and Gallimore's (1988) categorization of ways of assisting performance. These are explained below.

CLASSIFICATION OF TEACHING STRATEGIES

TEACHING STRATEGY	DEFINITION AND EXAMPLES
COGNITIVE STRUCTURING	Providing explicit information in order to develop conceptual understanding *That's the same sound as the end of your name*
COGNITIVE SUPPORT INSTRUCTING	Implicitly reinforcing conceptual understanding *Pointing to words as the pupil tries to read them* Directing pupils in specific ways *Explaining that they are going to write a story today*
DIAGNOSTIC QUESTIONING ELICITATION QUESTIONING MOTIVATIONAL SUPPORT MODELLING	Questions specifically aimed at assessment *Where should I put the full-stop?* Questions designed to prompt thoughts or ideas in the pupil *What are you going to write?* Encouraging and promoting self-esteem *That's a lovely piece of writing!* Demonstrating actions and thought processes *Scribing and explaining*
TASK MANAGEMENT	Keeping order *Making sure they are doing what they are supposed to be doing*

Sam Twiselton and David Webb

AN EXPERIENCED NURSERY TEACHER ANALYSED

Teacher Commentary: C1 *is just beginning to make the links between sounds and some of the letters she knows how to write. We have to build on that. The difficulty lies in developing her awareness, without making her inhibited so that she will only write if she knows the right letter or word.*

All the children need constant reinforcement of left to right orientation. For C2 it is a particular problem as he always starts on the right.

All the time I am concerned that all the children should retain ownership of their work, and see the purpose of it. Within that framework I try and develop the specific skills and understanding they need to progress.

LITERACY CONCEPTS	OBSERVATION NOTES	TEACHING STRATEGIES
WORDS CARRY MEANING **PURPOSES OF WRITING**	9.23 X is talking to child (C1) about her picture of a ladybird: 'Do you want to do some writing to tell everyone about this?' (C1 nods)	**COGNITIVE STRUCTURING**
	'What shall we write?'	**COGNITIVE STRUCTURING**
LEFT TO RIGHT	C1: 'The ladybird is sitting on a leaf' X: 'Excellent. Which side shall we start?'	**MOTIVATIONAL SUPPORT** **DIAGNOSTIC QUESTIONING** **COGNITIVE STRUCTURING**
	C1 'Over here' 9.25 X: 'You go ahead and write it and show me in a minute' X is explaining the spider's web pattern to a child (C2)	**INSTRUCTING**
LEFT TO RIGHT	9.27 X 'Can you make the lines go all along the web? It's very important you start at the left and finish on the right because we are practising for writing. Where's the left? Where will you start?' (C2 shows her; she observes closely as C2 starts the web.)	**ELICITATION QUESTIONING** **COGNITIVE STRUCTURING** **DIAGNOSTIC QUESTIONING**
	X: 'Lovely, don't forget to keep your pencil on the line. Nice and slow.'	**MOTIVATIONAL SUPPORT** **COGNITIVE SUPPORT**
PHONIC KNOWLEDGE **NAME RECOGNITION**	9.30 X: 'What a lot of lovely writing. I can see some of the letters of your name. Where's the "m"?' C1: 'Here and here'	**MOTIVATIONAL SUPPORT** **COGNITIVE STRUCTURING** **DIAGNOSTIC QUESTIONING** **ELICITATION QUESTIONING**
WORDS CARRY MEANING	X: 'You've done those beautifully. Can you read me your writing now?'	**MOTIVATIONAL SUPPORT**
	C1 'The ladybird is sitting on the leaf. She has lots of children and they like flying.'	**COGNITIVE SUPPORT**

LITERACY CONCEPTS	OBSERVATION NOTES	TEACHING STRATEGIES
PHONIC KNOWLEDGE	9.32 X: 'Wow! You've added more to it! You told me earlier on that there was a "l" at the beginning of ladybird. Where might the "l" have gone here?' (C1 points randomly and vaguely)	MOTIVATIONAL SUPPORT COGNITIVE STRUCTURING DIAGNOSTIC QUESTIONING
ASSOCIATE SOUNDS WITH WORDS (ONE TO ONE CORRESPOND-ENCE)	X: 'Can you read it again and point to the words at the same time?' (C1 moves her finger along the line from left to right, but there is no attempt to match up the writing with what she is saying.)	DIAGNOSTIC QUESTIONING COGNITIVE SUPPORT
LEFT TO RIGHT LEFT TO RIGHT	9.34 X: 'Now I'll write my writing. Where shall I start?' (C1 shows her, X writes the words and reads them as she does so)	MODELLING DIAGNOSTIC QUESTIONING ELICITATION QUESTIONING COGNITIVE STRUCTURING
ONE TO ONE CORRESPOND-ENCE	X: 'Let's read it again together.' They read it, X gently holds C1's finger and helps her to point to the words as they read.	MODELLING COGNITIVE SUPPORT

It can be seen immediately that the experienced teacher demonstrates a wide range of strategies which could be explained in terms of her having a very broad area of knowledge, including knowledge of the learner, the context, the subject and pedagogy. The number of different strategies which are used in a relatively short period of time is particularly notable. Three strategies warrant special examination: the constant use of cognitive structuring, cognitive support and diagnostic questioning. The teaching is directed by a system of frequent checks and is strongly underpinned by a range of literacy concepts. These are kept to the fore and the teaching actively promotes them at every opportunity. The concepts themselves are covered in a fairly balanced way; a small number of interrelated concepts are revisited regularly, and they are directed by the assessments the teacher is constantly making. The teacher is visibly drawing on her knowledge of individual children to direct both her assessments and actions.

When interviewed about her teaching this teacher was able to place her actions within a well-articulated understanding of the subject as well as being grounded in knowledge of the context. She demonstrated a 'connectionist' orientation, in which beliefs are based on both valuing pupils' methods and using teaching strategies with an emphasis on establishing connections within literacy. So, for example, phonic knowledge is viewed and promoted in relation to graphic knowledge and an awareness and recognition of how patterns of letters and sounds tend to cluster together.

The second example is from a first year student teacher who is not an English specialist.

Sam Twiselton and David Webb

A NON-SPECIALIST FIRST YEAR STUDENT ON BLOCK PLACEMENT WITH RECEPTION ANALYSED

STUDENT TEACHER COMMENTARY

I was helping the children to play a word matching game I had made myself. Each child had a board with four pictures of items of food on it, with labels underneath. They had to take it turns to turn over a card from a pile of single pictures and labels and see if they could match it with their board.

My main focus was word recognition — matching pictures to words of common foods that are in their cafe at the moment. I tried to make them read them as I was going along. My role was organization — make sure they went in turns — went clockwise. Give encouragement. It's just helping them with their reading really. Trying to get them looking at the word rather just the picture.

I kept the group small so they wouldn't have to wait long for their turn. It was very important to keep them motivated. Especially that because it was a competition. They thought it was a race and I kept trying to reassure them that it wasn't, that the next person was also going to finish.

LITERACY CONCEPTS	OBSERVATION NOTES	TEACHING STRATEGIES
LEFT TO RIGHT **WORDS CARRY** **MEANING** **PHONIC** **KNOWLEDGE**	10.10 TT to C1: What does that say? (points from left to right over the label) No answer from C1 TT: What does it start with? C1: It's a drink	**ELICITATION** **QUESTIONING** **COGNITIVE SUPPORT** **ELICITATION** **QUESTIONING** **COGNITIVE SUPPORT**
TASK **MANAGEMENT**	TT: Yes, but what does it start with? C1: Don't know TT: It's milk! 10.12 TT to the whole group: Take it in turns to choose a card — see if you can match it.	**TASK MANAGEMENT** **TASK MANAGEMENT**
WORDS CARRY **MEANING**	C2 takes a card TT: What does that say? (C2 is looking at the picture) C2: Chocolate TT: Good girl! Put it in the right place.	**ELICITATION** **QUESTIONING** **MOTIVATIONAL** **SUPPORT**
WORDS CARRY **MEANING**	10.14 C3 takes a card with a sandwich label TT: What does that say? Have you got that? C3: It says pizza	**ELICITATION** **QUESTIONING**
WORDS CARRY **MEANING**	TT: It's not pizza. What does it say? It says sandwich!	**ELICITATION** **QUESTIONING** **TASK MANAGEMENT**
PHONIC **KNOWLEDGE**	10.17 C1 takes a card TT: What does that card say? (no answer) TT: W. . . . C1 Watermelon TT: Brilliant!	**ELICITATION** **QUESTIONING** **COGNITIVE SUPPORT** **MOTIVATIONAL** **SUPPORT**
	10.19 C2 takes a card TT: What does it say? C2: Ice-cream TT: Have you got ice-cream? (TT points to game card) C2: No 10.20 TT: Well done!	**ELICITATION** **QUESTIONING** **COGNITIVE SUPPORT** **MOTIVATIONAL** **SUPPORT**

The contrast is marked, both in this extract and the transcript of the subsequent interview. In the extract there is no explicit assessment and the student teacher is restricting herself to a narrow range of both strategies and literacy concepts. The concepts themselves are covered in a much more tentative way, with no cognitive structuring and a high frequency of elicitation questioning. The student teacher appears to have a much less confident grasp of the literacy concepts the pupils need and is happier to prompt in a general, undirected way. In her discussion of the literacy concepts in the interview she demonstrated a restricted view of the strategies and conceptual understanding required in learning to read, which was, in practical terms, confined to the phonic sounding out loud of each letter. Managing the task and ensuring things run smoothly in a general way are high on her list of priorities. This is borne out by the interview in which she talks about her role purely in terms of management and makes no reference to the subject or to pupil learning.

A THIRD YEAR SPECIALIST ENGLISH STUDENT TEACHER ON SERIAL ATTACHMENT WITH YEAR 2

STUDENT TEACHER COMMENTARY

I began the session by reading aloud a letter from the publisher asking the children to produce the information for a blank information book. I showed them how to select important words in a piece of text by underlining on a prepared sheet and then I gave each child a passage of text to underline.

My main focus was to help the children with their reading for information: to refine the skills of skimming and scanning and picking out essential information. I think the teacher demonstration worked well to show them what to do. As long as it isn't just something that's just left and we think 'Oh well they've done it now'. They need to consolidate and apply it to their own writing and see how the process works, backwards and forwards. How you can work both ways. Building on things and then just picking things out — I don't think they can apply that as well to their own writing.

I would have liked to have more knowledge of what their reading for information skills were and also writing information because sometimes you realize when you get down to it they've done writing out great chunks of text but they don't know how to make information their own, to convey what they know and what they've learned to other people.

Because it was out of context it was a lot harder to get them to use their reading skills. There was no picture so all of it was grapho-phonic and the whole thing was on their word recognition or phonic recognition. It made me realize personally how hard it is without pictures. I think they worked really well in picking out the words that were important from when I was doing it . . . That can be built upon.

LITERACY CONCEPTS	OBSERVATION NOTES	TEACHING STRATEGIES
SCANNING	11.08 TT to the whole group: I want you to underline the most important words. Do you all know what to do?	**INSTRUCTING DIAGNOSTIC QUESTIONING**
SKIMMING **READING STRATEGIES**	TT: Do you remember the first thing I did was to read through it all? Do that now. C1: I need some pictures. TT: Think about what else you do apart from look at the pictures. 11.10 TT moves around the group watching them work 11.12 TT to C2: Are you having problems reading this? Read it to me and I'll help you.	**COGNITIVE STRUCTURING COGNITIVE SUPPORT** **TASK MANAGEMENT**

LITERACY CONCEPTS	OBSERVATION NOTES	TEACHING STRATEGIES
PHONIC KNOWLEDGE CONTEXTUAL KNOWLEDGE WORD RECOGNITION CONTEXTUAL KNOWLEDGE	C2 reads hesitantly and sticks at a word. TT reads it for him. TT: What's the sound on the end? C2 's' TT: ..sorts of . . . ? (No answer) 11.14 TT reads the whole sentence: That's a hard word — 'receives'. Can you read me the sentence now? C2 reads it.	**MODELLING** **ELICITATION QUESTIONING COGNITIVE SUPPORT** **MODELLING COGNITIVE STRUCTURING DIAGNOSTIC QUESTIONING**
SCANNING **SCANNING**	11.17 TT: What are the most important words? C2: I don't know. C3 brings TT a finished passage. TT: Very good. You've got all the important words there. 11.19 C4 brings TT a sheet. TT: Have you read it all? C4: No	**ELICITATION QUESTIONING MOTIVATIONAL SUPPORT COGNITIVE SUPPORT** **DIAGNOSTIC QUESTIONING**
CONTEXTUAL KNOWLEDGE SCANNING	11.20 TT asks C4 to read it aloud. C4 reads it. TT: Have you underlined all the important words? What about 'warms the earth' — that's important isn't it?	**ELICITING QUESTIONING COGNITIVE STRUCTURING**

This student teacher is much closer to the experienced teacher in both the extract and the interview. She is using a broader range of strategies, and perhaps even more importantly is using cognitive structuring quite frequently. Her understanding of the tasks and its learning outcomes is placed firmly within the framework of the subject. There is a notable difference between this student teacher and the experienced teacher and that is that she uses relatively less diagnostic assessment. However, she was aware of this in the interview and commented on the difficulties of trying to do so many things at once.

What we can see clearly is that both the experienced teacher and the more experienced specialist student teacher demonstrate in their teaching a range of strategies which are linked closely to the learning of the subject. The major difference between the experienced teacher and the student teachers in this group is in the amount of assessing they do. A direct consequence of this, which is not clearly demonstrated in a 10 minute extract but is more obvious in the whole teaching session, is that the student teachers are not so effectively responding to the needs of the pupils *as they arise*. They are acting according to their stated desired learning outcomes which are usually thoroughly thought through in terms of the subject, but they often miss opportunities or fail to respond to needs. The experienced teacher is constantly checking and is subsequently responding to the moment. This strongly supports Tochon and Munby's claims in relation to the diachronic epistemology of novice teachers and the synchronic epistemology of experts.

There does appear to be some correlation between stage of training, specialism and strategies used and discussed, but perhaps not so strong as might be expected. In recent research (Twiselton, 1997) from which this data is taken an alarming number of student teachers still operated within a very restricted framework towards the end of their training. All student teachers tended to define the problems they had with English teaching in terms of the need for 'ideas' to deliver in the classroom and did not find it easy to analyse their teaching in terms of ways of developing the children's' conceptual understanding in English.

The skills required for the kind of contingent teaching associated with a synchronic epistemology are very complex and difficult to develop in higher education settings which are distanced from the contextual characteristics (i.e. knowledge of the learner and the learning environment) that help to define them. In addition, traditional methods of school supervision (for example, lesson observations, scrutiny of plans, records etc.) are essentially diachronic in their emphasis. While these are undoubtedly important for the development of student teacher expertise they fail to capture the more intensive, contingent teaching skills requiring a synchronic epistemology.

The data that has already been discussed suggests that although they had a fairly clear idea of what their role should be at the planning stage, when actually interacting with the children many student teachers were failing to adequately synchronize the planned teaching with a more moment by moment assessment of the needs of individuals in comparison with more experienced teachers. The main difference between the student teachers and the experienced teachers lay not so much in their identification of the strategies but in their ability to bring them into use effectively as an immediate response to an event which has been rapidly perceived as a suitable trigger for intervention, drawing knowledge of learner, learning environment, subject and pedagogy *in combination with* knowledge of the planned curriculum in so doing.

The Use of a Literacy Log

A way of encouraging student teachers to analyse their teaching in this more synchronic way seems crucial. One attempt to do this is through the development of a *Literacy Log*. This is drawn up using a combination of National Curriculum Programmes of Study and the competences indicated by OFSTED for the inspection of student teachers in ITE. In this a series of strategies are identified (6 for speaking and listening, 6 for writing and 8 for reading), each of which forms the heading for a section of the *Literacy Log* (see sample below). Student teachers are asked to complete the boxes regularly when they have experienced or observed the use of the relevant strategy in school. They are expected to analyse the strategy in terms of the situation leading to its use, the specific literacy learning it was

EXAMPLE SHEET FROM LITERACY LOG

1(W) Promote independence, confidence and a sense of purpose in pupils' writing

DATE
WHAT did the child (or children) do? **WHY** did you respond the way you did? **DID** it work?

DATE
WHAT did the child (or children) do? **WHY** did you respond the way you did? **DID** it work?

DATE
WHAT did the child (or children) do? **WHY** did you respond the way you did? **DID** it work?

TEACHER COMMENT

supposed to develop and how effective it was likely to be (and how this would be assessed). Student teachers are initially given case-studies in college to discuss and use as examples for filling in the log. Subsequently, after they have begun to relate it to their school experience, they are asked to share examples of their own in college sessions.

Too many systems devised to catch the 'competence' of student teachers in the classroom merely capture the student teacher's ability to plan and evaluate planning and record coverage of adequate and relevant experience in the classroom in a general sense. It is easier in these systems for mentors, or indeed supervisors, to be sure of a student teacher's class management skills than her/his subject and pedagogical knowledge. We wanted to find a way of helping the student teacher (and mentors in their conversations with them) to go beyond general, didactic procedures to particular, focused and conceptually underpinned analysis.

The strategies have been chosen so that they require students to analyse the situation giving rise to the strategy synchronically, and supposedly cannot be demonstrated simply by listing activities. Although in some cases the activities may play an important role, student teachers are required to relate the activities to the strategies used to make them effective and to analyse the pupil learning they should develop. This is being re-enforced by the discussions and use of case-studies centring around the *Literacy Log* in college sessions.

The format of the *Literacy Log* was deliberately left fairly open so that it would require student teachers to think for themselves, rather than simply answering questions or ticking boxes. This can lead to a failure to apply any analysis at all. The difficulty is finding a balance between directing student teachers enough so that they can see the value of what they are being asked to do, without either overrestricting them, or trivializing the process.

The need to use the *Literacy Log* to direct learning in both discussion and writing is both central and difficult. It requires time and attention in a programme that is already overloaded. When a group of second year student teachers were asked after block placement to identify the kind of help they needed most in their English teaching many said they needed advice about how to promote the literacy experiences of particular children, or within a particular situation. This is the kind of help college tutors cannot give effectively at a distance from the school situation. Ideally the *Literacy Log* will provide a bridge between school and HE by becoming the focus of both mentoring and college discussions. Student teachers will benefit from both the expertise of those with first-hand knowledge of the context and those with knowledge of the subject. However, we acknowledge this will be difficult to achieve. Arguably teachers do not yet perceive themselves to have the right or need to fulfil a proactive mentoring function. Data presented by Edwards and Collison (1996) suggest that teachers rarely overtly model for or support student teachers while the student teachers are considering or engaging in the contingent support of pupil learning.

Conclusion

The skills required for contingent teaching within a synchronic epistemology are very complex and difficult to develop in higher education settings which are distanced from the contextual characteristics (i.e. knowledge of the learner and the learning environment) that help to define them. In addition, traditional methods of school supervision (for example, lesson observations, scrutiny of plans, records etc.) are essentially diachronic in their emphasis. While these are undoubtedly important for the development of student teacher expertise they fail to capture the more intensive, contingent teaching skills requiring a synchronic epistemology. It seem clear that initial teacher training needs to find a way of encouraging student teachers to develop their teaching in this more synchronic way.

Early indications are that the *Literacy Log* is one way forward and it does help capture a type of teaching not easily caught elsewhere, and that the students do find some value in analysing their teaching in this way. However, there are factors which will crucially determine the extent of its success:

- To be really effective, the focusing and development of these strategies needs to take place in school as well as college. This means discussions must be carried out in both places, so that students are able to draw on both the contextual expertise of mentors and subject expertise of tutors. This is yet another demand on time in a programme already overloaded in both situations.
- To be really effective, both for assessment and development, student teachers need to be observed with the strategies being specifically focused. Again, this is not easy for mentors, or college tutors, because there are so many other aspects of the student teacher's performance demanding attention, many of which are more readily accessed.
- Mentors need to be secure in their own English subject knowledge in order to do this effectively; this indicates the need for subject specific mentor training.
- Student teachers need to have sufficient structure to provide focus while still allowing the scope for independent thinking and analysis. This is a difficult balance to achieve, particularly when coupled with the need for these demands to be manageable without becoming trivialized, so that student teachers see them as valuable without being unreasonably burdensome.

References

COLLISON, J. and EDWARDS, A. (1994) 'How teachers support student teacher learning in classrooms', in REID, I., CONSTABLE, H. and GRIFFITHS, R. (eds) *Teacher Education Reform: Current Evidence*, London: Paul Chapman.

EDWARDS, A. and COLLISON, J. (1996) *Mentoring and Developing Practice in Primary Schools*, Buckingham: Open University Press.

EDWARDS, A. and HODGSON, J. (1996) 'Managing pupil learning: Teachers' self-images, knowledge and action', paper presented at the ECER conference, Seville.

DFE (1993) '*The Initial Training of Primary School Teachers* (Circular 14/93) London: DFE.

LAVE, J. (1993) 'The practice of learning', in CHAIKLIN, S. and LAVE, J. (eds) *Understanding Practice: Perspectives on Activity and Context*, Cambridge: CUP.

LAVE, J. and WENGER, E. (1991) *Situated Learning: Legitimate Peripheral Participation*, Cambridge: CUP.

TOCHON, F. and MUNBY, H. (1993) 'Novice and expert teachers' time epistemology: A wave function from didactic to pedagogy', *Teacher and Teacher Education*, **9**, 2, pp. 205–18.

TWISELTON, S. (1997) 'Contingent Literacy Teaching: A Comparison between Novice and Experienced Teachers'. Paper presented at British Educational Research Association Conference, York University.

VYGOTSKY, L. (1978) *Mind in Society*, Cambridge, MA: Harvard University Press.

WOOD, D. (1988) *How Children Think and Learn*, Oxford: Blackwell.

Part 4

Emerging Issues in Mentoring

15 Mentoring: Possible Developments and Constraints

Hilary Cooper and Charles Batteson

Since partnership arrangements between schools and teacher training institutions became statutory mentors have had increased responsibility for the management and assessment of trainee teachers' school-based work. This has created a potentially dynamic situation in which new roles can be defined and developed which could be mutually beneficial for both mentors in schools and for college tutors. A new climate could emerge which would enhance the status of teachers and strengthen their professionalism. It is important to recognize and grasp this opportunity. For faced with attempts by the Government to blame schools for economic failure and cultural confusion the profession's best defence is to strengthen the knowledge base from which it works and to make this explicit in order to articulate it to others. Professional development through mentoring could be a catalyst for this process.

The Need for Effective Development and Funding for Mentors

There are multiple meanings of mentoring but there is a general consensus that mentorship uses observation and feedback to encourage reflection and trigger improvements and changes in practice. The Standards for the Award of Qualified Teacher Status (despite their limitations) could provide a basic framework of criteria for professional dialogue between mentors, trainees and other teachers. Such dialogue would enable them to analyse the complex interactions between theory, pedagogical skills and personal understandings, which underpin good teaching. This would encourage professional self-development and diminish the need for centralized, prescriptive and sanction-ridden forms of teacher appraisal and surveillance which discourage teachers from questioning the circumstances in which they work.

However this ideal of professional self-development through mentoring requires time and adequate funding. Otherwise there is a danger that the standards framework could be used simplistically and reduce teaching to a list of component parts, which underestimates the complexity of teaching. The development of mentors needs to go far beyond brief introductory sessions on 'how to observe, conduct tutorials and provide written feedback'. Effective setting of targets requires mentors to be firstly skilled in analysis of their own practice in order to identify their own strengths and weaknesses and to feel secure in making changes. It also requires skills in the analysis of the practice of others and in negotiating changes, and an understanding of the strategies available in supporting and mentoring trainees in each area of professional competence. Such systematic reflection about teaching and belief systems requires time and funding for ongoing high quality education and support. For example, in order to analyse what is required to 'develop effective questioning which matches pace and direction of the lesson and ensures that pupils take part' (Standard B K2 vi), mentors might spend time out of school with other mentors and college tutors to develop collaborative concept maps on 'questioning', drawn from their rich personal experiences and giving rise to debate and discussion. This process of making complex intuitive knowledge explicit, and the evaluation of the resulting maps against theoretical models of questioning, would value mentors' professional knowledge, enhance self-esteem and make it clear that theory is generated by practice and teachers are an essential part of the process. Theory cannot be created externally and imposed by either professional researchers or by politicians. Such theorizing could become an intellectual process rather than the body of established knowledge of 'accepted authority' on which teachers are becoming increasingly dependent and through which they are in danger of becoming deskilled. To value and support this process would require imaginative changes in political strategies for improving standards in education.

Partnership Between Mentors and Trainees

Supporting trainees in school requires a complex role for the mentor, who is counsellor, observer, giver of feedback, instructor and assessor. However, having analysed and evaluated the broad areas of their own practice in depth and in detail, in open collaboration with others, mentors would be in a position to develop a partnership relationship with trainees, which could extend the practice of both. By having their own practice observed by trainees using focused criteria, by analysing, evaluating and discussing the trainees' practice and defining targets for development, and by collaborative planning, teaching and evaluation trainees and mentors could share in the process of generating practical knowledge and make what they do an explicitly theoretical activity, in the sense of understanding more clearly both the nature of the practice and how it might be improved. This would require time; time for planning, observation and feedback.

If such time were made available the mentor and trainee together could assess the trainee's starting point in each area of professional competence at the beginning of a block placement, then identify key factors in development during the placement. This detailed analysis and monitoring might involve, for example, analysing ways in which concepts in mathematics can be broken down and translated into tasks at different levels for a particular group of pupils; devising organizational strategies for the management of their formative assessment; and judging the moment to help the trainee to transfer successful strategies to other subject areas. Progression planned for a particular trainee might move from:

- 'use of subject specialism to create something extra for the class' to 'extending subject knowledge to enhance the learning of staff and produce extra ideas for the school';
- 'the ability to recognize if something wasn't working and to cope with the situation' to 'having a contingency plan to recognize and avoid potential disaster', and finally to 'the ability to recognize and exploit useful teaching points';
- 'maintaining a stimulating environment which values children's work' to 'using the classroom environment as a tool for learning . . .';
- developing good relations with teaching staff, external agencies and parents' to 'using them to support the delivery of the curriculum'.

In a partnership relationship trainees can come to realize that they can contribute to the work of experienced teachers, as well as learn from them. As one mentor said:

> all students have elements of experience which are different from our own, from which we can learn. I also need feedback from students about how they learn to teach in order to evaluate my own role.

The creation of such a confident climate of self-development is a defence against centralized, prescriptive and authoritarian forms of teacher appraisal.

However, it takes time and trust to create a secure school environment in which existing practices can be challenged as a natural and systematic part of professional development and school organization, even amongst experienced colleagues. Mentoring alone cannot create such an ethos, but it can contribute to it. Indeed it could be argued that such a climate is a prerequisite for successful mentoring.

Whole School Development Through Mentoring

Yet a mentoring process which enhances the personal professional knowledge of both mentor and trainee could be a catalyst for whole-school development. It could help to develop a philosophy, climate and organization in which individual members, including parents and governors, are encouraged to continuously learn and develop. Collaborative teaching approaches, shared observation and feedback sessions could be extended from mentor and trainee to pairs or groups of experienced colleagues.

Mentors have claimed that mentoring specific skills have enhanced their self-esteem and their performance in giving feedback to not only colleagues but also to parents and children. The potential for whole school development through the transference of mentoring skills is illustrated by one school where 'two members of staff with mentoring experience supported each other with regular reciprocal observations, encouraging positive feedback and structured self-analysis. This resulted in several minor changes in classroom layout, and grouping. After seeing the success of these management changes the observations were extended to other classes and parts of the school. The whole school approach resulted in a major upgrading of the behaviour policy and on improvements in its implementation throughout the school'. The mentor concluded that 'this sort of school development', could usefully be incorporated into whole-school appraisal programmes and staff development plans.

Trainees' work in school, both block placements and two or three-day periods of school-based work linked to taught courses, could be planned for as an integral part of both the school timetable, and of long and medium-term development planning. Foci on particular subjects could coincide with specialist block placements or with residential visits. Responsibility for managing and coordinating the work of trainees in this way would be recognized to be a substantial staff and school development role.

Cluster Group Development Through Mentoring

Mentoring could provide the impetus for developing expertise and the cross-fertilization of ideas between groups of schools. There could be cluster groups of schools around the training institution where mentors, college tutors and trainees meet to plan school based work which reflects the locality and specific needs of the schools and which is also integrally linked to college courses; to share expertise of teachers and tutors in areas of strength and in response to the specific needs of these schools; to share experiences of school-based work through seminars during a block placement.

Alternatively a cluster group of schools may be at a distance from the training institution in a contrasting community and could become the focus of residential visits built into taught courses. Mentors with specialist experience in, for example, the field of literacy for bilingual pupils could plan focused work in their schools with trainees which contextualized and explored theoretical perspectives introduced then revisited in taught courses. In this way specialist mentoring qualifications could be developed.

Mentoring expertise and qualifications in subject specialisms could be developed through similar cluster groups where groups of subject specialist teachers meet with trainees in college to plan, and later share, evaluate and assess intensive work in school which is closely integrated with a taught course. This could provide intensive learning experiences for everyone involved, from their different perspectives. Pupils could work through sequences of activities normally spread over weeks, with greatly extended specialist adult support; this could be one way of reintroducing coherence and depth into a fragmented curriculum. Mentors would have the opportunity to work with colleagues in their specialist areas, and try out new ideas. Schools could benefit from the resources prepared by the trainees as part of their assessment.

Such sessions could be linked to action research in which tutors, trainees and teachers play a part, and disseminated through professional and academic journals. It may be funded research initiated by the training institution or groups of institutions, or it may be research linked to MA courses and other professional development courses for mentors.

The mentoring process could provide the rationale for a continuum of professional development. It could strengthen coherence between training institutions and schools through initial teacher training courses, professional qualifications, Master's courses and research degrees. It could be a vehicle for teachers' self-development and school development. It could contribute to a climate in which teacher's professional expertise is made explicit and valued, and in which a General Teaching Council becomes a genuinely independent body. It could . . .

Reservations

However there is nothing inevitable in achieving these progressive and exciting possibilities. Speculation within the 'it coulds' of mentoring needs to address prevailing political and ideological assumptions.

Future levels of involvement of the HE sector in primary teacher preparation are fluid and negotiable. In current SCITT programmes the role of HE is reinvented and may soon be entirely circumvented. The character of any national bodies or regional federations which assume roles hitherto performed by HE will have a major impact upon the orientation and nature of evolving mentoring systems. There is no certainty that the recent context or indeed the same players will continue to offer shape and colour to future provision. The post 1997 Labour Government, in the same spirit as its Conservative predecessor, has shown a disinclination towards favouring an 'educational establishment'. Traditional teacher training provision has become firmly identified as one cause of a malaise in English schooling. A political response has been vigilantly to police and monitor the sector. Central Government and its various agencies speaks and acts with a moral authority that hinges on the need to upgrade teaching standards and reflect firm images of what constitutes real and proper teaching. The future crafting of ways to prepare new teachers will be developed against a critical and even sceptical backcloth.

The optimistic scenario sketched earlier in this chapter is reliant upon five contingencies each of which may be subject to limitations or deficiencies.

(i)   *The necessity for effective and properly funded training for mentors*
Whilst this has been a common characteristic in pilot projects and at development stages it may not prove to be sustainable. It may be that the precursor Rolls Royce models get supplanted by cheaper, mass production alternatives. Evidence from the erosion in quality and effectiveness of teacher appraisal schemes since the early 1990s points to difficulties and dangers in sustaining new initiatives once they become routine and taken for granted.

(ii)   *The nature of mentor/trainee interaction and dialogue*
There is a certain irony in the fact that teachers have been variously demonized by media and political voices and simultaneously have been sanctified as mentors and role models for beginner teachers. How will OFSTED's subject-knowledge–deficient classroom performers instantaneously reincarnate as splendid moderators of trainee competence in the same areas? There is a need to alleviate the role crowding which teachers experience and to which mentoring conceivably contributes. Much debate about an extended role for teachers and schools in ITT has been abstracted from any consideration of prevailing working conditions which primary teachers experience.

(iii)   *There may be problems over the whole school and staff development outcomes of mentoring*
This is an area with considerable elasticity. Staff age-profiles, school size, geographical location and micropolitical terrains are amongst the variables that operate. In other words, alongside 'the coulds' we have to recognize some of the 'how things are'. A headteacher's comment: 'I know mentoring works in this school. I've already had the cheque' might tow our thinking back into a critical domain.

(iv)   *The alluring potential of cluster groups supporting new teacher moderation*
This item conjures up professional collectivisim and shared purpose which may have been denuded in the atomization of the education service and advocacy of interschool competitiveness which has been implanted particularly since 1988. On a practical level we will have to come up with some guarantees in providing time and money if cluster group involvement is to be real.

(v)   *Academic participants in new training processes might be excited by the fifth proposition — the endemic opportunities which arise for 'action research'*
There is considerable need to rescue the concept of research from an educational index expurgatorious. Current TTA moves to develop educational research models which are relevant, targeted and collaborative could be seen as exemplars. Alternatively they could serve to avoid or discredit any focus on broader dilemmas and could see research absorbed within a prescriptive and narrow field of vision.

Speculation within a pursuit of what might be some futures of mentoring has to engage with problematical as well as idealised prospects. There is merit in considering how mentoring fits into overall conceptions of teacher professionalism — the extent to which it enskills or deskills, empowers or imposes upon and constrains new and in-post teachers. One strand of on-the-job-training offers to enhance practical, routine and real-life competence. Another derides virtually everything which is not absorbed within the here and now. Mentoring could be one way of bridging the fabled divide in ITT between theory and practice. Equally it could produce happy and uncritical classroom technicians far removed from any notion of developing informed and reflective practitioners.

Acknowledgments

The authors are grateful to the many committed, energetic and idealistic mentors who have so generously shared their skills, experience and enthusiasm in working with college tutors and with their students, as over recent years partnership arrangements have developed. They are especially indebted to Liz Elliott, Margaret Foots, Ian Johnson and Anita Yearsley for many insights, suggestions and examples of practice quoted in this chapter.

16 Mentoring: Realising the True Potential of School-based ITE

Jill Collison

Introduction: The Rise and Rise of Mentoring

Ten years ago only a few of those involved in the education and initial training of teachers would have heard of mentoring. It was the introduction of school-based initial teacher education (ITE) as directed by Government circulars *9/92* and *14/93* which brought about its rapid development. These circulars did not make explicit reference to mentoring. But they did signal a significant change in the role of the school in ITE:

> Time in schools is particularly valuable for the acquisition of practical teaching skills, and allows students to apply their subject knowledge in the classroom. But the increased time spent in schools should not simply be an extension of traditional classroom experience; it forms an integral part of the course and may contribute in a variety of ways to the objectives of training. (DFE, 1993, para. 19)

Wilkin (1992), writing about a slightly earlier document (DES, 1989) noted the consequence of such statements:

> For schools to take some direct responsibility for training (*mentoring*) is very different from *supervising* students who are placed in schools in order to put into practice what they have learned in the training institution. (p. 17)

It is difficult to pinpoint the first usage of the term 'mentor' in the context of ITE in the UK but the Oxford Internship Scheme (Benton, 1990) was certainly one of the earliest documented ITE programmes to use mentors and the term was being used within licensed teacher schemes at a similar time. Since then mentoring has become widely understood to be the means by which student teachers' learning in schools is mediated.

Confusion does exist though as to what is meant by mentoring. School staff enquire at mentor training sessions if they now have to do the tutor's job of supervision — and sometimes mentor trainers have been known to reply 'Yes, that is pretty much what is meant', thus restricting the mentors' understanding of their role to one of observer and constructive critic of students' teaching. The idea that mentoring is an opportunity for a richer, more effective use of school experiences is lost in a programme of mentor training that focuses on the completion of 'crit' sheets. It is not accidental that the term teaching practice is no longer used to describe students' time in school. Practice implies that the students are in school to practice *how* to do what they have learnt *about* elsewhere. In the new way of things the students are in school to learn about teaching as well as to try out how to do it. This transformation offers the chance for teachers to play a much richer and more important role in the education of student teachers.

So What Exactly is Mentoring?

An all-encompassing definition of mentoring might be 'the interactions between a novice (the student teacher) and an expert (the teacher) which contribute to the novice's learning'. More specifically, mentoring is commonly understood as taking the form of observation, both of, and by, the teacher, and feedback to the student on his/her teaching, with talking about teaching highlighted as a particularly important mentor skill. What becomes evident though from a survey of the literature is that a single coherent definition of the term does not exist. My own conception of mentoring which I intend to describe here grew out of my experiences as research-evaluator for a pilot school-based programme of ITE that the University College of St. Martin initiated in 1992.

It is significant that this primary age phase pilot scheme was initiated in 1992, i.e. prior to the publication of *Circular 14/93*. It would be wrong to suggest that the initiative was not motivated, in part, by crystal ball gazing to the predictable future. However, it would also be wrong to imply that this was the only motive for the development. The team of teachers and college tutors who developed the programme held the shared belief that it was *right* to move towards a more school-based form of teacher education. It is perhaps because of this belief, and the fact that it was held jointly by college and school staff, that one of the outcomes of the project is a picture of how school-based teacher education can be effective, with positive advantages for all involved.

At the outset of the project no-one quite knew what school-based experiences student teachers should have or how their learning in school would be supported; indeed the overarching research question asked by the evaluating team was 'What does good school-based teacher education look like?'. The main body of the data collected in the research project has been published elsewhere (for example, Edwards and Collison, 1996). What is relevant here is the picture we built up, from numerous jigsaw pieces, of effective school-based teacher education. Amongst these jigsaw pieces it was clear that the quality of the interactions that the student teachers had with the class teacher in whose class they were placed were paramount.

The views of two class teachers who jointly produced a comprehensive account of their ideas about class teachers' involvement in the training of teachers illustrate the potential richness of this relationship (Collison, 1993). They listed that it was their responsibility to:

- provide a secure and happy environment for student teachers;
- enable and guide students to integrate with the whole staff team;
- ensure that the students function efficiently and effectively as classroom teachers, NOT as non-teaching assistants;
- discuss progress and performance in non-threatening ways with the students;
- give guidance, support, advice, enthusiasm for improvements to the students' teaching as part of the evaluation of lessons;
- listen to students' problems sympathetically and support them to overcome the problems;
- be open to new ideas and allow the students to experiment and to see the school as a 'workshop', to try out strategies and thus learn from experience;
- be flexible and open to absorb new strategies, present a willingness to learn from the students;
- welcome the opportunity for teachers to evaluate their own teaching;
- enjoy having the students;
- and, above all view their work with student teachers as a dialogue between professionals.

This listing is particularly powerful because it originated in the teachers' work with student teachers; it is not something that was imposed on them. The overlap between this spontaneous listing and key characteristics of 'ideal helpers' (equivalent to mentors) that Tough (1979, p. 183) identified from his extensive work with adult learners is, fascinatingly, almost total:

- They are warm, loving, caring, and accepting of the learners.
- They have a high regard for the learners' self-planning competencies and do not wish to trespass on these.
- They view themselves as participating in a dialogue between equals with learners.
- They are open to change and new experiences and seek to learn from their helping activities.

The teachers' listing is helpful in outlining the *manner* in which teachers can interact productively with their students (an aspect of mentoring that is explored further in Chapter 14). It is less useful, however, in demonstrating mentoring in action; we still don't know what mentoring *is*. Observations of one of these teachers (see 'Cathy' below), though, not only confirm that the list was what was actually practised (i.e. not simply rhetoric) but also provide us with a clear view of the full potential of mentoring as something richer and more valuable to learning to teach than supervision, something more than the collection of mentoring actions offered earlier as a commonly understood definition of mentoring.

Active Mentoring

There is a legitimate and understandable fear amongst teachers that accepting responsibility for the education and training of teachers will cause them to neglect their 'real' job of teaching children. However this need not be so. Paradoxically the key to ensuring that the pupils' education is not impaired, yet also attending to the student teachers' learning needs appears to be for all involved to allow that the student teachers are *learners* in the classroom, and to devise appropriate 'active mentoring' strategies. By active mentoring I mean responses offered by the mentor to the student teacher's teaching whilst that teaching is ongoing. Whilst more obvious mentor strategies that take place outside of the classroom, such as joint lesson planning or feedback and discussion after a lesson are vitally important, it is active mentoring that allows student teachers to learn how to see in classrooms and how to respond to what they see. The following extract of a lesson observation gives an indication of how one teacher actively mentored her students:

> *Cathy with student teachers Rachel and Ann. Setting: Reception Class*
> Rachel is working with six children testing the effect of gold and silver crayons on different coloured paper. Ann has five children with her who are talking about and sorting autumn leaves. Cathy is working with a group of children on a writing task. She also has an eye on small groups of children who are constructing models with Mobilo or playing in the home corner. She glances occasionally at Rachel and Ann. Rachel is coping fairly well but Ann's group has drifted away from sorting the leaves into making collage faces with the leaves.
>
> Cathy goes to Ann's group and suggests that they could sort the leaves into light and dark and spends a few minutes talking to the children about the leaves. She judges that two of the children have spent long enough at this activity and directs them to the free choice activities.
>
> Cathy now visits Rachel's group. She talks to the children about their choices and encourages them to express reasons for their preferred combination of colours. Cathy checks on Ann's group, discusses in which group to put a leaf that is dark on one side and light on the other.
>
> Cathy returns to the writing table. Ann and Rachel continue with their groups, Ann is now using some of the questions that Cathy has just modelled. Cathy initiates tidying the classroom for break and requests that the light and dark leaves be kept so that she can show them to the whole class. (Edwards and Collison, 1996, pp. 56–57)

Cathy's regard for her students as learners allowed her to be aware of their leaning needs but even more important is the fact that she provided contingent interventions. That is, the teacher behaviours she modelled matched the students' *immediate* needs. As we see in the example above when Ann began to use some of the questions that Cathy modelled, the timeliness of such interventions makes them easily assimilated into the student's repertoire of teacher actions. It is also important to note Cathy's skill at intervening in her students' teaching without adversely affecting their authority in the eyes of the children. In another lesson Cathy's interventions quietly established a completely different range of activities that allowed the students' activities to remain central whilst providing a much more effective structure of classroom management than they had planned for. She negotiated permission to do so by asking 'Is it alright if we work together?' and worked unobtrusively to leave the control of the class with the students.

It may be though that Cathy's actions were a little too subtle; unlike the first example, in this second situation there is no evidence that the students fully understood the shortcomings of their own arrangements. Contingent mentoring alone thus may not be wholly effective; perhaps what was needed here was discussion after the session to explore what may have happened without Cathy's intervention and to highlight her actions.

Active mentoring can also include simply being aware of the student teachers' work and offering immediate, well-focused feedback. For example:

> *Sue with student teachers Rachel and Hilary. Setting: Year One Class*
> At the start of the session Rachel and Hilary are working with a group of six children each. The groups are mixed ability and the work is to contribute to mathematics assignments that have been set for the students by the university. Rachel's group is playing games with coins that necessitate exchange and decomposition. Hilary's group is comparing candles, judging the biggest and smallest, ordering them in size, and measuring them with blocks. Hilary has differentiated the task on which she is working with the children into three levels and the children work in pairs on the related but graded elements of the task. Rachel's work is differentiated by the amount of support she gives to each child. Sue is preparing for a painting activity and monitoring the whole class as the children work.
>
> Rachel is experiencing difficulties with Jack, one of the pupils in her group, mainly because the task is too difficult. The other children are coping very well but when Rachel suggests that Jack should just colour in the work sheet they are using rather than continue the mathematics activity, the other children declare that this is what they want to do too. The break-time bell intervenes.
>
> During break time Sue initiates discussion with Hilary about the mathematics work. They look at the children's work together and talk about their abilities and progress. Sue then talks to Rachel. Rachel raises the problems with Jack which they discuss. Sue praises the way in which Rachel is stretching the most able and suggests that she needs to plan specifically, not just through outcome, for the less able children in her group. (extract from Edwards and Collison, 1996, pp. 60–61)

Collison (1994) noted a tendency for class teachers to treat student teachers as they would other adult helpers in the classroom; that is, not giving them more than a glance to check that 'everything looked alright'. The outcome being that many student teachers did not receive appropriate feedback on their teaching. If the children appear to be occupied the assumption seemed to be that they were learning. It was also apparently assumed that if the student was teaching that he/she must be learning about teaching, but as this observation demonstrates these assumptions need not be valid:

> *Student teacher Clare working with six reception pupils*
> Clare settles the children around the table and hands out two torches. She asks the children to try to make the torches work. One does not work and she asks them to try to find out why it is not working. The children discover that it has no batteries. Clare provides batteries. She stops the exploration when one child asks if she may

take the bulb out. Clare removes the torches; gives out bulbs, wires and batteries (sufficient for one set between two) and tells the children they now have all they need to make their own lights.

Two of the pairs are surprised that putting both wires on one end of the battery does not produce a lighted bulb. Clare allows them to experiment for about three minutes then tells them how to make a circuit. All the children make a circuit.

Clare then removes the equipment and gives out a work sheet with the title 'electricity in our homes'. She also hands out pages from catalogues. She explains that the children have to cut out objects that use electricity and stick them on the work sheet in the right room in the house that is drawn on the work sheet. She supplies scissors and glue. This activity lasts for about 20 minutes. (extract from Edwards and Collison, 1996, p. 85)

Clare's teacher had glanced at what she was doing from time-to-time but as the children had appeared to be occupied had not taken notice of what Clare was doing in any greater detail. However closer observation would have shown him what we can see: Clare clearly would have benefited from some guidance on how to maintain an authentic science activity. Her lack of expertise may have had many explanations. It may be that Clare did not understand that her restrictive approach to the exploration of the torches/circuit making was inappropriate; or that she did but felt uneasy allowing free exploration so needed to curtail it for her own comfort; or she may genuinely have thought that the cut-and-paste activity carried her science learning objectives. It may even have been that her own science knowledge was lacking which raises an interesting issue. What level of responsibility should mentors be expected to have with regard to students' subject knowledge development? A recent Government directive on ITE (DfEE, 1997) has particularly strong demands with regard to student teachers' subject knowledge and their ability to transform it into appropriate teaching. The role that mentors can or should play in this is discussed elsewhere within this book (for example, see Twiselton and Webb, Chapter 14, and Murray and Collison, Chapter 9 in this volume).

The issue of subject knowledge aside, the point that is being made here is that Clare could not receive appropriate guidance because her class teacher was not paying sufficiently close attention to what was happening with Clare's teaching. Most class teachers, however, would probably agree that the short, purposeful interactions with their student teachers that Cathy and Sue demonstrated could easily be incorporated into existing classroom routines. That effective mentoring includes such actions might though, be a novel idea for many mentors.

I would suggest that one reason why it is rare to find class teachers behaving (Collison, 1994) in this way is that they are currently working from a restricted model of mentoring. In this restricted model mentoring is equated with supervision and the richer, more significant role that class teachers can play in the education of student teachers is not acknowledged. Using a supervision model the student can only be given feedback if the teaching has been formally observed; incidental, contingent mentoring is not even considered as a mode of operation. We should not be surprised that teachers are using the only model of supporting students in schools they have to inform their mentor practice. The challenge to alter this rests primarily with mentor trainers. There is a strong case for mentor training which allows teachers to rehearse the full range of mentor actions not just those which replace tutors' supervision visits. The full potential of the transformation to ITE promised by *Circular 14/93* and required by *Circular 10/97* will not be realised without a suitable transformation in teachers' perception of their role as mentors. In my view of mentoring (which mirrors Donald Schön's ideas [Schön, 1987]) this transformation would include that effective mentoring:

(i)   takes place in the context of the teaching (i.e. it has to be classroom-based and includes both the student's teaching and that of his/her mentor);

(ii)   makes use of actions as well as words, especially when the mentor can model appropriate teaching strategies which match the student's current learning needs;

(iii) depends on a form of co-enquiry where the mentor and student teacher jointly discuss and explore each other's teaching and its learning outcomes.

The Role of the Student Teacher in the Mentoring Relationship

Altering teachers' perceptions of their role to take account of my suggestions may not though bring complete success. I would suggest that there is a need also for mentee training which prepares student teachers for their role as learners in the classroom. It is not always easy to persuade the students of the position as learners in the classroom. They do of course face a dilemma in that they need to present themselves as teachers in the eyes of the children but need to behave as learners in their relationship with the class teacher. However students often feel that they should be able to present themselves as teachers to the teacher also (Edwards, 1997). This was strongly illustrated to me by a pair of students in the second term of their four-year training who declined their teacher's offer to demonstrate how to manage a science lesson with her year 2 class because 'they thought they should be able to do it themselves'. When questioned further they acknowledged that they would have learnt from the opportunity to observe their teacher taking the lesson but that they felt that such observation was not a legitimate use of their time in school. We could perhaps usefully take note of the ideas of Lave and Wenger (1991) on legitimate peripheral practice. Edwards and Collison (1996) suggest that:

> Peripheral participation can be seen as an important stage in the induction of learners into confident and competent practice. Gradually learners move towards full participation. (p. 25)

Mentee training (undertaken either by the university or by mentors themselves) would prepare the student teachers for their role as peripheral participants. It would also inform the students of the full range of ways in which their mentors will support their learning. Defining mentor actions explicitly for student teachers should help them to have a better understanding of their role as learners and how to realise the potential of being in school to learn about teaching, not simply to practise it.

References

BENTON, P. (1990) *The Oxford Internship Scheme*, London: Calouste Gulbenkian Foundation.

COLLISON, J. (1993) 'The introduction of school-based teacher training in the primary sector: An evaluator's perspective', paper presented at the annual meeting of the British Educational Research, Association, Liverpool.

COLLISON, J. (1994) 'The impact of primary school practices on the student experience of mentoring', paper presented at the annual meeting of the British Educational Research Association, Oxford.

DES (1989) *Initial Teacher Training: Approval of Courses (Circular 24/89)* London: DES.

DFE (1992) *Initial Teacher Training (Secondary Phase) (Circular 9/92)* London: DFE.

DFE (1993) *The Initial Training of Primary School Teachers: New Criteria for Courses (Circular 14/93)* London: DFE.

DfEE (1997) *Teaching: High Status, High Standards (Circular 10/97)* London: DfEE.

EDWARDS, A. (1997) 'Guests bearing gifts: The position of student teachers in primary school classrooms', *British Educational Research Journal*, **23**, 1, pp. 27–37.

EDWARDS, A. and COLLISON, J. (1996) *Mentoring and Developing Practice in Primary Schools*, Buckingham: Open University Press.

LAVE, J. and WENGER, E. (1991) *Situated Learning: Legitimate Peripheral Participation*, London: Kogan Page.

SCHÖN, D. (1987) *Educating the Reflective Practitioner*, San Francisco, CA: Jossey-Bass.

TOUGH, A.M. (1979) *The Adult's Learning Projects: A Fresh Approach to Theory and Practice in Adult Learning*, Toronto ON: Ontario Institute for Studies in Education.

WILKIN, M. (1992) *Mentoring in Schools*, London: Kogan Page.

17 Mentor Assessment of Trainee Competence — The Introduction of Grading

Chris Sixsmith

Over the last two decades there has been a slow but significant change in the assessment of the classroom performance of student teachers. This process of change, as with many aspects of teacher education, has gained increasing impetus over the last two or three years. As an aspect of this, there has also been a shift towards the process of change being increasingly driven by centralized agencies. In general this change has focused on three main areas; what is assessed, who assesses it and how it is assessed. The actual speed and direction of change have differed between different institutions but the overall effects and outcomes have been very similar. In order to identify and examine the issues raised by this process the experience of one college, specializing in primary teacher education, will be explored in some detail.

The Historical Context

In the mid-1980s the reductionist legacy of the Behaviourist tradition still had a significant influence on the thinking in college. The debate about appropriate approaches to planning and assessment centred around the distinction between the use of behavioural objectives or the adoption of a connoisseurship approach. The behavioural objectives approach focused on the outcomes of teaching, defining these in terms of observable behaviour. Learning was inferred from the performance of the learner. This approach attempted to break teaching down into a series of simple statements describing the skills, attitudes and knowledge that a teacher might display. Teaching was judged as to the extent that these were then achieved. The connoisseurship approach went beyond this. It argued that successful teaching was more than the sum of its constituent parts, that there were some elements of successful teaching that could not be simply articulated in behavioural objective terms and that these were recognized by the experienced teacher's intuitive judgment.

This debate had a significant effect on the way in which students were introduced to curriculum planning and in time also informed the framework used for the assessment of their classroom performance. At this time students were supervised and assessed by college tutors who visited schools on a weekly basis. The students were supported in school by a class teacher who would often contribute to assessment decisions but the final responsibility for the assessment rested with the college tutor. This led to the situation where the outcome of a school placement could fail to reflect, fully, the views of the school i.e. a position where the views of the most immediate representatives of the profession, the class teachers, were not the final arbiters of who should enter the profession.

In addition to having responsibility for making the assessment, the responsibility for deciding what should be assessed also lay with the college. Teachers and headteachers would often be involved in discussions about what it was appropriate to assess but the final decision was in the power of the college. At this time in the mid-eighties students' classroom performance was assessed against a series of behavioural categories. In the main these categories focused heavily on generic classroom skills, 'planning', 'classroom organization and management', 'instructional skills', 'control' and 'general professional qualities'. In addition there was a token category that addressed the students' competence in teaching the major areas of the primary curriculum. Each of these categories was further sub-divided into a series of more focused elements such as, 'effective allocation and use of time', 'management of resources' and 'display of children's work'. For each of these more specific elements tutors were required to grade using a five-point scale ranging from 'unsatisfactory' to 'excellent'. In addition to the grading there was also the opportunity to include written comments on each section. Hence students were given feedback in the form of both written comments and grading.

These two approaches to assessment were grounded in the two contrasting traditions described previously, one relying on the 'objective' assessment of specific areas of teaching skill and the other on a professional assessment of more general elements of the overall teaching performance. The tension between these two aspects of the assessment process led to a growing dissatisfaction with the process in general. There was also a growing recognition that the moderation of the grading process was a significant problem. The wide variety of teaching situations and the range of tutor expertise made comparability of judgment difficult. The response to this was to modify the assessment process by removing the grading of more specific elements. This had the effect of focusing the assessment on professional judgment of the whole teaching process with the generic categories now becoming the unit of analysis rather than the smaller elements. The smaller elements now acted as descriptors of the categories rather than the unit of analysis. Whilst this allowed for the assessment of teaching in a far wider sense the major focus remained generic teaching skills.

It was at this point in the late 1980s that the national agenda for teacher education began to have an increasing influence. The emphasis on partnership and the political initiative to move the control of teacher education from HE to schools had several effects. Probably the most significant of these was the increase in mentored supervision of students' school-based work. The supervision of student teachers began to shift from college tutors to teachers and with this a consequent shift of responsibility for assessment. The teacher in school was now seen as being the most appropriate person to make judgments about students' classroom performance. Although this move seemed to be based more on ideology than on evidence, it is now generally welcomed by all those involved in teacher education. There was initial resistance from some tutors in colleges who feared that they were losing control of the process and from some teachers who felt they were being asked to take on even more when they had already to cope with a much increased workload brought about by the introduction of the National Curriculum etc. This in turn led to certain tensions between schools and colleges. The students, however, almost without exception felt it to be an appropriate move, feeling that their assessment was better done by somebody who has a thorough knowledge of their teaching rather than somebody who made a judgment based on a small sample of their overall teaching. One difficulty that the move did raise was that of moderation. Once recognized the difficulty was initially addressed by the development of short 'mentor training programmes' designed to create common practices and expectations.

Towards the mid-1990s there was a general change of focus for the assessment of students. This was brought about by the introduction of the National Curriculum, *Circular 24/89* and then *Circular 14/93*. The major change was the increased focus on the students' subject knowledge and their ability to apply this in the primary classroom. There was now a clear list of competences that students had to achieve. These related to both subject knowledge and general classroom skills. The categories of assessment were modified to focus on the competences which in many respects acted as elements of level descriptors. Mentors were required to comment on the students' attainment of the competences.

Grading the Competences 1996–97

The assessment of competence by mentors was further developed by the introduction of grading as a required element of assessment in order to ensure consistency of judgment across the wide range of teaching situations in which students were placed.

In the autumn of 1996 a new framework for inspection was introduced by the Teacher Training Agency and OFSTED (OFSTED, 1996). This framework made one very significant addition to the assessment of students' classroom performance. In addition to the assessment of teaching competence students would also be graded on three aspects of their teaching of mathematics and English. The competences to be achieved were determined centrally and applied to all students working towards being awarded QTS regardless of the training route they followed.

The Framework laid down a series of cells relating to different aspects of teacher education. Some cells referred to the management of courses, others to the quality of the provision, others to the administration of the courses and three to the work of students in school. The significance of the Framework should not be underestimated. The identification of who was to assess students in school had already been altered with the introduction of teacher mentors and the insistence that colleges move towards using only mentors as supervisors. The Framework and *Circular 14/93* now began the process of defining what should be assessed. The three cells that had to be assessed were:

C1. **The trainees' subject knowledge for teaching in the relevant age group.**

C2. **The trainees' planning teaching and classroom management.**

C3. **The trainees' assessment recording and reporting of pupils' progress.**

These cells were to be assessed on a four-point scale:

1	**Very good:**	— practice of teaching is competent with several outstanding features
2	**Good:**	— practice of teaching is competent with no significant weaknesses
3	**Adequate:**	— practice of teaching is broadly competent but with some areas in need of significant improvement
4	**Poor quality:**	— an unsatisfactory level of competence

* It should be noted that this scale applies to trainees and newly qualified teachers.

With the introduction of the Framework the task for school-college partnerships was clear. Mentors would have to be appraised of the new requirements. Details of how mentors were to carry out the assessment necessary to grade students in respect of the cells would have to be developed. Mechanisms by which mentors could moderate their gradings and by which these gradings could be collated also had to be developed. For some institutions, involved with inspections by OFSTED using the new framework, the timescale for this process was a matter of weeks, inadequate to set up a full consultation between partnership members and raising the question whether it was really desired that the grading of students be an aspect of partnership.

One function of the OFSTED inspections was to assess the accuracy of the gradings given to the students. Should there be a difference between the grades given by the inspectors and those given by the mentors, it was assumed that the mentors were inaccurate in their judgments and this would become an issue of non-compliance for the institution involved. This clearly raised questions about the resources available for the training of mentors and inspectors and the nature and extent of the evidence they each could draw upon to make their judgments. However, as yet, there has not been a public debate of these issues.

There were several other difficulties inherent in the grading process. The descriptions of the grade categories were open to interpretation. This raised the question of how to ensure that the interpretation put on the categories by the mentors would be the same as that of the inspectors. A different interpretation would obviously lead to potentially different judgments. A second difficulty related to the question of when mentors were to judge students. Was the judgment to be made at a point before inspectors see the students, on the same day as the inspectors see the students or was it to be a projection to the end of the placement? Unless there was an assumption that students would not improve their performance throughout the placement the time at which the grading was made was critical. Neither the Framework, nor OFSTED itself, gave any guidance on this issue. There was also the question of how the grading process was to be linked to the final assessment of the placement; if a trainee was given a '4' for any cell did that mean that the trainee would automatically fail the placement? In addition to these major questions there still remained the need to find a method of ensuring comparability across the very wide range of teaching situation and teacher background. All these issues needed to be resolved if the grading process was to be successful.

One college attempted to address these issues in a coordinated way. Rather than attempting to address each issue separately, an overall package was developed which was designed to cover the further development, clarification and monitoring of the process. The package adopted five main elements:

(i)   All mentors would be given a training session where the situation would be explained to them and some basic training would be given. At these meetings it would also be made clear that all mentors had access to their link tutor (a college-based tutor with responsibility for supporting a number of mentors in their role) should they have concerns about any aspect of the mentoring process.

(ii)   A sample of students would be visited by a team of tutors with a very clear brief relating to the grading of the students.

(iii) There would be a detailed consideration by college tutors of the programme that the students had followed and this would then lead to a prediction of the overall pattern of grades that would be expected from this year group.

(iv)   There would be a statistical analysis of the distribution of the grades to ensure this was consistent with the other information being gathered.

(v)   Link tutors, who by the time of the final grading, would have visited all schools involved in the placement and also have had copies of weekly mentor observation notes and weekly tutorial reports would also ensure that the grading was consistent with the information they had received.

There was a particular concern over the assessment of cell C1 the subject knowledge cell. This concern arose mainly from the fact that this detailed assessment of trainees' subject knowledge was new to many mentors. When the assessment of subject knowledge was first raised several mentors had been quite firmly of the belief that this was a matter for the college and that they were not in a position to carry out this task. A clarification of what was meant by the term subject knowledge as the accuracy of the knowledge being used in their teaching by the trainees, reassured mentors that they were able to make this judgment. Because of this concern a final element of the overall package was added.

(vi)   A booklet was prepared by the subject teams in college that for each subject gave what amounted to level descriptors for teaching that would be regarded as unsatisfactory, competent and very good.

The different elements of the package were then implemented and every student graded and those gradings collated (Table 17.1).

An examination of Table 17.1 raised several interesting issues. Not least amongst these was the distribution of grades within cells. Between the C2 and C3 cells the

Table 17.1: The percentage of grades allocated to each cell

	Mathematics			English		
Grade	C1	C2	C3	C1	C2	C3
1	6%	10%	5%	8%	10%	5%
2	71%	57%	57%	68%	57%	56%
3	22%	31%	33%	21%	31%	33%
4	1%	2%	5%	3%	2%	6%

distribution of the 2 and 3 grades was remarkably similar. There was some variation in the 1 and 4 grades but this was minor when compared with other variations in the table. When the distribution for these two cells is compared with that for the C1 cell there were clear differences. There was approximately a 10 per cent difference in the distribution between the grades 2 and 3. Mentors seemed to have consistently graded students subject knowledge higher than assessment, reading and report or classroom management. There were several possible explanations of this. It might have been that the students' subject knowledge was actually better than their competence in the other two areas. Given that this area was being graded for the first time and that the students had been focused on the other two areas for each of their previous block placements this would seem an unlikely explanation. It could be that mentors were less competent in their ability to assess this element of practice as they had so little time to consider the process or to share ideas with other mentors or to carry out shared moderation. It was possible that mentors felt less secure in their own subject knowledge than they did in the other two areas and therefore tended to overestimate the subject knowledge of their students. Another possible explanation could be that due to the lack of specific detail of what each grade represented mentors were erring on the side of generosity to support and encourage students, avoiding a punitive approach and interpreting the term 'in need of significant improvement' in respect of a student in their final year of training rather than in relation to a newly qualified teacher. A final possible explanation is that mentors were accurate in their judgments but defined subject knowledge differently to the other cells. Whilst mentors could and should be expected to assess the accuracy of student subject knowledge and how well they apply that knowledge in the classroom they cannot be expected to assess students' subject knowledge and understanding in terms of the criteria in the National Curriculum for ITT. Whatever the explanation the fact remained that the C1 cell required further consideration.

A second issue that emerged from the distribution of grades was the overall distribution pattern. The general distribution clearly indicated that the trainees were divided with approximately 60 per cent being given a grade 2 and 30 per cent a grade 3. This was at variance with the other estimates of the appropriate distribution of grades. Both the tutors' general estimation of how the students should be distributed, and the feedback from tutors that visited the sample indicated that the distribution of grades would be more appropriate if the percentages for grades 2 and 3 were reversed, leaving 30 per cent in grade 2 and 60 per cent in grade 3. Given this apparent discrepancy a sample of mentors was asked to reconsider the grading and were given the opportunity to discuss their grading with other mentors. The outcome of this exercise further indicated that the revised distribution better reflected the competence level of the students. This was further confirmed by the scrutiny of mentor observation and tutorial report by link tutors. The outcome was that the moderation process regarded as 3 a number of trainees that were originally graded at the lower end of the grade 2.

Again it is interesting to speculate as to why this might have been. What seemed to be the most likely explanation lay in the lack of specificity of the descriptions of the four grades. At one level mentors may well have been reluctant to give a grade of adequate to a student who seemed to be performing reasonably well, preferring to think of the student as good. At another level the use of the word significant in the description of grade three again tended to seem rather severe. Whilst accepting that the student might well have areas in need of improvement it was a completely different matter to say a student was in need of significant improvement. One way in which this difficulty could be, at least in part, overcome would be by giving mentors clearer information about the sort of distribution of grades that would be expected. In this instance the moderated grading was confirmed by the inspectors.

Issues

One college's experience raises a number of important questions including the issue of who is in the most appropriate position to make the judgments about grades. Clearly mentors are in an excellent position to make this judgment if time is available for them to undergo training and be involved in moderation. This will be particularly true of cells C2 and C3. It may be that cell C1 should be assessed by a combination of mentor and college tutor, the college tutor contributing information about the students' subject knowledge as assessed through their college-based courses and the mentor contributing their knowledge of the ability of the student to use their subject knowledge accurately and effectively. However the accuracy of the grading process will be determined by OFSTED on their visits to schools during inspections.

The introduction of the grading process raises several other issues that the profession need to debate. One such issue relates directly to the reintroduction of the grading of students. The inclusion of the grading in the Framework for Inspection seems to indicate a belief that the grading process as an element of the assessment of the professional competence of students is unproblematic. The experiences described above would seem to indicate that at a practical level this is simply not the case.

Grading the Standards 1997–98

The introduction of *Circular 10/97* and a new 'Framework for the Assessment of Quality and Standards in Initial Teacher Training 1997–98' again made significant changes to the way in which students were to be assessed. *Circular 10/97* replaced the existing 'competences' with a series of standards which all students had to achieve before being awarded Qualified Teacher Status. The standards, in the way in which they are worded, appear to be criteria. The process of assessing students by these standards would appear to be criterion referenced. Students will achieve the standard or not for example,

> For all courses, those to be awarded qualified teacher status must, when assessed, demonstrate that they:
> are aware of the breadth of content covered by the pupils' National Curriculum across the primary core and foundation subjects and RE
> OR
> know pupils' most common misconceptions and mistakes in the subject
> OR
> establish a safe environment which supports learning and in which pupils feel secure and confident.

Unlike the competences outlined in *Circular 14/93* the standards are specific criteria to be achieved rather then elements of a level descriptor. Hence the students must now be assessed in terms of their ability to achieve the standards. They will either achieve all the standards and be awarded QTS or fail to achieve one or more of the standards and not be awarded QTS. This does raise again the question of whether it is appropriate to reduce the assessment of teaching to a simple, if extensive set of criteria. However, *Circular 10/97* makes it clear that this is what is to take place. The new Framework for Inspection redefines the cells that are to be graded. As with the previous framework there are cells relating to the quality of training, the selection of trainees, the quality of staffing and management and quality assurance. The cells relating to the quality of trainees' and NQTs' teaching have been significantly modified. The cells relating to subject knowledge (formerly C1), planning, teaching and classroom management (formerly C2) and monitoring, assessment, recording, reporting and accountability (formerly C3) have been renamed ST1, ST2 and ST3. An additional cell ST4 has been added relating to 'other professional requirements'. The most significant issue is not related to the renaming of the cells but to the fact that they have been redefined in terms of the standards. It is intended that each student is graded for each cell on a four-point scale not dissimilar to that in the previous framework. Unfortunately the new framework does not provide any clear guidance on the issues raised by the previous framework and discussed earlier but does raise an additional issue. By defining the cells in terms of the standards mentors are being required to use a criterion-referenced assessment (nominal data) to make judgments on an ordinal scale. Conceptually this is confused and confusing. Is the assessment meant to be criterion-referenced or norm-referenced? Without clarification those making the judgments will be very unclear about the distinction between the apparent criterion-referenced judgment as to whether the students have satisfied the criteria or not and the apparently norm-referenced judgments relating to the grading process. This is clearly demonstrated with the use of the grading scale. It would appear that a student may be given the grade '3' having some significant weaknesses in elements of their teaching and this would be viewed as compliance with the Secretary of State's criteria but at the same time would indicate that they had not achieved all the standards. This throws into very sharp relief the need for clear definitions between cells and how the grading process links into the overall assessment of the students' teaching.

Conclusion

The reality of the present situation is that those involved in the training of teachers will be required to grade the students in certain aspects of their teaching. The definition and assessment of this process is in the hands of OFSTED. The partnership between HE and schools must continue to develop in such a way as to allow this grading to be as accurate and as consistent as possible but also to have an appropriate place in the total professional assessment of the next generation of teachers. The DfEE should be encouraged to allow sufficient time in the implementation of change for the different partners involved with the education and training of teachers to work together to reach shared understanding, to dispel confusion, to agree on assessment procedures and best implement those changes for the good of the profession. Grading of trainees must not be allowed to become a simplistic instrument which is used to measure the supposed effectiveness of schools and colleges in the overall professional development of would-be teachers.

References

DES (1989) *Initial Teacher Training: Approval of Courses (Circular 24/89)*, London: DES.
DFE (1993) *The Initial Training of Primary Teachers (Circular14/93)*, London: DFE.
DfEE (1997) *Teaching: High Status, High Standards (Circular 10/97)*, London: DfEE.
OFSTED (1996) *Framework for the Assessment of Quality and Standards in Initial Teacher Training 1996/97*, London: OFSTED.
OFSTED (1997) *Framework of the Assessment of Quality and Standards in Initial Teacher Training 1997/98*, London: OFSTED.

Part 5

Beyond Initial Teacher Education

18   The Induction of New Teachers: The Road to High Status and High Standards?

Neil Simco

At the current time there is widespread political debate about standards in many aspects of teacher education. The arrangements for the induction of new teachers are a critical part of this debate. This has expression in the Government's White Paper *Excellence in Schools* (DfEE, 1997a) where the notion of 'structured support' (p. 47) in the first year of teaching is cited. Clear implications for the development of practice are seen in the White Paper such that the experience of newly qualified teachers (NQTs) is more rigorous, focused and related to individual targets. Yet at the same time this drive to raise expectations needs to be reconciled with a professional experience which many NQTs find to be demanding, exhausting and for some overwhelming. There is little doubt that induction arrangements are coming under increasing scrutiny and this in turn leads to the importance of speculating on the consequences both for NQTs themselves and for schools and providers of initial teacher education. The current chapter provides and justifies one such speculative framework.

Induction Provision 1988–1997

Before building towards a speculative framework for induction, it is important to acknowledge the gradual development of previous provision at national and local levels. This is important because the starting point for a new framework has to understand the issues of past practice. The HMI survey of provision for newly qualified teachers suggested that arrangements for the professional development of NQTs, probationers at that time, were poor in terms of both school and LEA support and monitoring (HMI, 1988). There were also detailed findings which related to the generally low quality of subject knowledge for teaching, relatively poor classroom management and control and match of tasks to learning. This survey was significant in that it clearly suggested a pattern of poor quality support and low expectations, even though three–quarters of lessons were judged to be at least satisfactory. Yet there is a sense it which this is not surprising. The complexity of teaching and the necessarily slow rate of professional development have been noted elsewhere in this book. Additionally Calderhead and Shorrock (1997) and Carre (1993) both note the huge demands that are faced by the new teacher in school. Effective induction frameworks had not been defined at national level and at local level there was a muddled and patchy picture of support. Also the demands and opportunities of the first year of teaching had not been fully recognized. Put simply the culture in the profession was not right for effective rigorous induction.

This culture began to be developed in the early 1990s when the DES published new detailed guidance to both schools and LEAs on induction arrangements (DES, 1990). This was built on in *Circular 2/92* (DES, 1992a) which established the importance of induction and the shift from probation to induction. 'Induction should be a planned extension of initial teacher training . . . it should refine the skills and build on the knowledge new teachers have gained in this pre-service training. It is clear from the HMI report that statutory probation does not guarantee induction' (DES, 1992b, p. 2). It was here that central priorities were established, the need to improve links with initial teacher education and continuing professional development (CPD); the need to improve coordination of induction and to encourage documentation on induction.

As a result of this legislation increased importance was attached to induction and this had expression in LEAs beginning to develop and disseminate portfolios for professional development in the induction year. Earley (1993) outlines the urgent activity in which LEAs were engaged through GEST funding. One example of the products of this activity was the Surrey New Teacher Competency Profile (Surrey Educational Services, 1992) which contained menus of competence that NQTs would use to track and focus their development. Perhaps for the first time there was a formal recognition of the need for induction year arrangements to be focused primarily on specific elements of the teaching-learning process, rather than on general support. However the Surrey New Teacher Competency Profile also reflected the dominant culture at the time which was to use lists of competences as a starting point for professional development and to 'tick' when these have been achieved. Arguably this process played down the role of the individual by not defining her/his needs as a first step.

Other professional development profiles had other strengths and weaknesses. A draft version of the Cumbria Newly Qualified Teacher Portfolio tried to link individuals' awareness of their own classroom practice to the competency framework defined in *Circulars 9/92* and *14/93*. This was achieved by the notion of 'storyboarding', identifying and describing significant classroom incidents over a period of weeks and then relating these to a competency framework. In essence this contrasted with the Surrey materials which appeared to start with the competency framework and then relate this to individuals' experience. However the draft Cumbria materials were flawed as the amount of material made the document unmanageable and compromised the quality of professional development. The final version of the materials (Burdon et al., 1996) is streamlined and encourages intensive dialogue at certain times of the year whilst at other times acknowledging the constraints represented by the day-to-day demands of the induction year. At national level the notion of a career entry profile (CEP) was beginning to come into focus as a way of fulfilling the underpinning ethos of induction namely to make effective links with initial teacher education. Yet the original primary and secondary CEPs (TTA, 1996) were seen as problematic. Competences and strengths were defined in great detail. The language of the competences was not always helpful in the setting of targets nor in generating understanding of individual professional development. The principle of using the CEP as a basis for induction was there but its complexity limited its usefulness for student teachers and NQTs.

Alongside these developments at national and local level there was a range of evidence which suggested that induction was quite frequently seen as support for survival rather than rigorous professional development. This contention is supported by empirical evidence which suggests that whilst many NQTs felt warmly welcomed into their first schools, few were involved in intensive interaction between mentor and NQT. It is this interaciton that is arguably of real importance in professional development (Carre, 1993). Simco (1995) and Simco et al. (1996) also reported that induction overemphasized support as opposed to challenge and intensive dialogue. The experience of the induction year is extremely demanding and the provision of support is important. However what is equally important is the provision for NQTs to understand elements of their teaching at depth. Perhaps it is the case that effective induction needs to have support and challenge for individuals in different ways, but if individual induction is to be effective the balance needs to change so there is an expectation of challenge through intensive interaction based on specific classroom incidents.

This is illustrated through Carre's (1993) study which describes four broad patterns of mentor–NQT interactions, only one of which provides an appropriate context for effective professional development through the analysis of specific classroom incidents. This is described as the 'listening and discussing pattern of mentoring'. Other patterns lead to support to varying extents but do not have the potential for close analysis. Here the 'open-house arrangements' leads to NQTs being able to approach their mentor as and when they felt they needed support whilst the 'model role' involves the mentor merely providing advice and recipes. The 'many mentor' role is concerned with the whole staff acting as a supportive whole.

Calderhead and Shorrock's (1997) research provides further evidence of the lack of systematic professional development in the induction year. Their case studies of student teachers followed through into the first year of teaching suggested that 'contact with the official mentor was infrequent and it was usually the case that it was left to the new teacher to seek help if and when they felt it was needed and from whomever they found available or approachable. The close mentoring relationship that some of the students had experienced during initial training was absent' (p. 179). This last point seems particularly significant. If a move towards individual programmes of induction is imminent then this is largely dependent on the quality of professional discourse between mentor and NQT. Lack of this could be the most serious obstacle to effective induction.

A focus on programmes of professional development in the induction year customized for individual NQTs is a feature of national development in the piloting of new arrangements. The new CEP (TTA, 1997) is fundamentally different from its predecessor. This is because the framework offered by the standards for QTS is separate from the CEP which is used by student teachers at the end of their course and into the induction year. There is no longer a mechanistic response to standards (previously competences) but rather that the standards are related to an individual's development in the induction year. In this way the emphasis is on the characteristics of an individual's teaching in relation to a broad framework related to nationally defined standards. This approach is likely to be beneficial because it is individual, straightforward and provides, or has the potential to provide, an effective bridge between initial teacher education and induction.

In sum, the 1990s have seen a gradual move towards creating more effective induction. The shift to school-centred initial teacher education has also been of potential help because of the enhanced role given to mentors in that context. Edwards and Collison (1996), for example see that 'mentoring is not simply the provision of situations where students can pick up craft knowledge. It is an active process and requires mentors to consider students as another set of learners in their classroom' (p. 158). The proliferation of this model of initial teacher education should help inform the quality of induction and yet, as is seen from the literature above, there is little evidence to suggest that as yet intensive professional dialogue is occurring in the induction year.

The Development of a Manageable System at National Level for the Linkage of Initial Teacher Education and Induction

How can induction policy and practice move forward?

The new CEP (TTA, 1997) offers a promising way ahead. The standards for the award of QTS (DfEE, 1997b) are used as a background for identifying strengths and priorities for further development. Targets are defined at the beginning of the induction year and action plans are developed. The CEP has the potential to be standardized across all new entrants to the profession yet can also encourage flexibility and individuality.

The clarity of the new CEP undoubtedly raises its status and currency. It is clear and straightforward and is likely to be manageable and meaningful. The advent of a detailed structure which bridges ITE and induction raises the issue about when QTS should be awarded. This issue is given further momentum by the increasing importance given to the assessment of standards for QTS at the end of final placements in ITE. From 1996–97 the inspection framework for initial teacher education (OFSTED, 1996) has the assessment of the standards as its centre. If an institution is allowing trainees to enter into the profession who are judged by OFSTED inspectors to be not competent then this is an issue of non-compliance with the Secretary of State's criteria for ITT. This then has potentially serious consequences for that institution. Sixsmith's chapter in this book (Chapter 17) provides an overview of this issue of assessment for the award of QTS.

Taken together these two factors lend weight to the argument for assessing QTS at the end of the induction year. The gateway to the profession should not be at the end of a course of initial teacher education but after a period of induction. If one of the main aims of the CEP is to bridge ITE and induction then it seems illogical for the summative assessment of competence to be in the 'middle of that bridge'. The assessment having been made there is then diminished motivation for a student to be involved in the depth of individual professional development required by the new CEP. Additionally if the assessment of standards is so critical to the inspection framework, then it seems appropriate, especially given the literature on the slow rate of professional development, for this to take place after a full period of teaching. The assessment is more likely to be informed if it occurs after one year than a final block placement. Judgments made by inspectors about the readiness of students to enter the profession are likely to be more valid.

It is interesting to note that the Government proposed at the end of 1997 that QTS should be confirmed at the completion of an induction period. This provides evidence that the Government wishes to enhance the place of the induction year as the gateway to the profession. However the argument presented here goes one stage further. Confirmation of QTS implies that it has already been awarded at the end of a course of initial teacher education. The contention here is that there are advantages in making the initial award of QTS at the end of a period of induction.

If this argument is accepted then there are other implications. It reduces the power and responsibility of teacher education institutions and schools to make summative assessment at the end of courses of initial teacher education although it does not alter their role to make formative assessments to inform future employers about the competence and performance of students. There is then the issue of who should be responsible for making summative assessments at the end of the induction year. Clearly the employer would have a major role here but teacher education institutions should also have a part to play. If assessments were made on a sample of NQTs by the institution this would have the potential to achieve a number of things. It would be a measure of the long-term effectiveness of the preparation and a mechanism for quality assurance. If relatively large numbers of NQTs were performing less well at the end of the induction year than as suggested by the formative assessment at the end of the course of initial teacher education then this would rightly be a serious issue for the institution. It would also create the potential for moderation of the summative assessment of standards by the employing schools and the institutions and in this way dialogue would be created between both parties.

There are logistical reasons why this would need careful management, given especially that NQTs from any one institution are spread all over the UK and abroad. However the increasing regionalization of teacher education provision may well make this kind of proposal more practicable. If there are logistical obstacles these must be overcome. If the assessment of the standards is so paramount then due consideration should be given to the potential for valid and reliable assessment to be made. It is arguable that assessment will be significantly more valid at the end of a full year of teaching.

A move to have the assessment of the standards at the end of the induction year may also encourage providers of induction programmes to become more focused. If a culture is developed which sees the assessment of the standards as central, critical and individual then it is equally right that NQTs should have equal entitlement to professional development towards the fulfilment of individual targets.

If this does not ensue, the adverse summative assessments made at the end of the induction year are open to challenge and appeal. It would be difficult to standardize this entitlement across all LEAs and institutions but it would be possible (given the availability of funding) that a certain amount of money is attached to the NQT which the school decides how to use for the professional development of that NQT. The arrangements made for induction could be recorded on the career entry profile alongside the assessment of the standards. Any assessment of the standards would, in this way, be able to be contextualized by the extent of provision for induction. The induction credit scheme piloted in 1997–8 by the TTA appears to have significant potential because it earmarks funding for individual induction.

The notion of an integrated approach to induction and ITE is cited in the Sutherland Report (1997) and in the Government's White Paper *Excellence in Schools* (DfEE, 1997a). The former states that '. . . an integrated programme has the potential to strengthen teacher education and improve the preparedness of trainees. It could also build upon the TTA's proposal for the development of career entry profiles for NQTs' (p. 11). Indeed Sutherland goes further suggesting that the integration of ITE and induction should be different according to the different characteristics of the different programmes of initial teacher education. The White Paper suggests that 'we believe there is a case for confirming Qualified Teacher Status after the successful completion of the induction year' (p. 48). There is an implicit recognition that the quality of provision for NQTs and the validity of summative assessments for entry to the profession will be enhanced if QTS is confirmed at this point. The use of the word confirmed is interesting as it implies an initial summative assessment at the end of ITE. The argument presented here goes somewhat further advocating that the only point of summative assessment for the award of QTS would be at the end of the induction period. In this model no summative recommendations would have been made prior to this point. This may have advantages in terms of maximizing the rigour of professional development in the induction year.

The system outlined above is based on entitlement and assessment being mutually important. The assessment of the standards is fair; it makes reference to the standards for career entry and it also standardizes entitlement. Moreover there is an implicit recognition of the slow growth of professional competence. It also creates a framework for teacher education institutions to gain feedback on the quality of their provision and the accuracy of formative assessments at the time of final placements.

Target Setting

The concept of target setting is gaining increasing currency. The TTA's CEP uses the notion of target setting as central to individual professional development; it also had expression in earlier LEA support materials for induction. However within this there are issues which need to be addressed about what kind of targets are appropriate for the induction year. Care has to be taken if target setting is to be used to its potential. In particular the setting of long-term targets in the first few weeks of the year may prove to be a fruitless exercise. Decisions about what can be achieved during the year may be based on ill-conceived judgments given the complexities and demands of the induction year.

One model would start with the NQT tracking significant classroom incidents over a short period of time in the form of a storyboard. Detailed discussion of these events with a mentor could lead to the definition of short-term targets which are grounded in the fabric of classroom life (Burdon et al., 1996). The idea of the 'individual' is acknowledged. Over a period of time the identification of individual short-term targets could be related to the standards framework for the assessment of the standards for QTS.

Another model begins with the NQT identifying short-term targets in discussion with a mentor at the beginning of the year which may reflect immediate concerns, for example, behaviour management or the assimilation of the mass of information from the employing school. Only at a later stage would long-term targets covering the remainder of the year be defined and broken down into manageable goals.

A third way of approaching target setting involves the identification of certain periods of the school year when specific targets are identified and considered in intensive ways. At other times there would be little target setting in any formal sense.

The point is that if target setting is seen as central to the induction process, then further definition, informed by empirical research needs to occur if the process is to be used effectively. The idea of target setting needs to be problematized. It is not in itself a panacea for good practice. It seems that the timing, scope, frequency and intensity of target setting need to be carefully considered. Moreover methods of target setting need to be clearly specified so that there is link between targets, observations of practice, dialogue between mentors and students, reflections on teaching, pupils' work and formal external reports by the LEA. It may well be that the quality of target setting, the definition of success criteria and processes of working towards these are the most influential factors in the quality of professional development in the induction year.

Ownership of Professional Development

The location of summative assessment of the standards at the end of the induction year throws into sharp relief the ownership of professional development. Put simply the issue is whether the location of final assessment will compromise the honesty of admission of areas for development in the induction year on the part of individual NQTs. It seems that there is a danger of the quality of professional development being compromised by individuals' over-emphasis on their professional strengths.

The existing TTA CEP has not been constructed in such a way that this issue of ownership is addressed so that NQTs can have confident ownership over sensitive areas of their professional development. In the profile it is clear that the NQT and others — college tutors in the review of initial teacher education, mentors in the induction year — have obligations to complete target setting, review and then set new targets. Yet it is also apparent that the profile is available for OFSTED inspection and TTA audit purposes and by implication to others in the school.

If the assessment of the standards is undertaken at the end of the induction year the records pertaining to this need to be carefully constructed. One way forward is to firstly record the end statement about whether the NQT has passed the induction year. Alongside this would be a detailed statement of the process of professional development that has occurred. This may include information about how any induction credit had been spent, the frequency of formal meetings between mentor and NQT, the number and kind of professional targets and a record of opportunities that the NQT has had to observe others' teaching. It might also include records of formative assessments, particularly formal observations. It would not include the details of target setting, nor the listing of professional strengths and weaknesses on entry to the school. These would remain in the ownership of the NQT who would have shared them with the mentor during the course of the year. This clear separation of summative assessment from the processes of professional development is important if the NQT is to feel a sense of freedom to engage honestly and openly with professional development.

Another issue related to ownership is the extent to which the agenda of professional development lies with the NQT. There is, inevitably, a tension between the needs and targets of the individual and those related to the school development plan, the standards for the award of QTS and national priorities in education such as literacy and numeracy. This is illuminated by small-scale research evidence which demonstrates that the degree of ownership which an NQT had over the agenda for her/his professional development varies widely between schools (Simco, 1995).

One resolution to this tension is the grounding of professional development in the NQT's individual experience of the classroom. Time taken to identify critical incidents (Tripp, 1993) through description of classroom events is of real importance if these descriptions are appropriately used. Having identified targets it is then important to relate these to the defining frameworks for the induction year but to start from these has the potential to take ownership from the NQT and undermine confidence in the process of professional development. In this way the rich fabric of the individual's experience is linked to the broad frameworks which define the boundaries of professional development.

Conclusion

Induction is at a threshold. There have been considerable developments and improvements both locally and nationally throughout the 1990s. To take this forward moving the point of assessment of the standards from the end of ITE to the end of the induction year could provide a catalyst for further development. It has the potential to trigger new relationships between ITE institutions and employing schools. It may define entitlement for professional development as well as criteria for the assessment of the standards. It has the potential for issues such as target setting and ownership of professional development to be addressed. The growing concern about induction over the last 10 years has led already to debate and improvement. To assess the standards at the end of the induction year would arguably enhance the quality of professional development as well as retain the rigour increasingly apparent in the granting of the award of QTS.

References

BURDON, M., PRENDIVILLE, F. and SIMCO, N. (1996) *The Cumbria Newly Qualified Teacher Portfolio*, Carlisle: Cumbria Country Council.

CALDERHEAD, J. and SHORROCK, S.B. (1997) *Understanding Teacher Education*, London: Falmer Press.

CARRE, C. (1993) 'The first year of teaching', in BENNETT, N. and CARRE, C. (eds) *Learning to Teach*, London: Routledge.

DES (1990) *The Treatment and Assessment of Probationary Teachers, Administrative Memorandum 1/90*, London: HMSO.

DES (1992a) *Induction of Newly Qualified Teachers, Administrative Memorandum 2/92*, London: DES.

DES (1992b) *DES Press Notice 96/92*, London: DES.

DfEE (1997a) *Excellence in Schools*, London, HMSO.

DfEE (1997b) *Teaching: High Status, High Standards, (Circular 10/97)* London: DfEE.

EARLEY, P. (1993) 'Initiation rights? Beginning teachers' professional development and the objectives of induction training', *British Journal of In-Service Education*, **19**, pp. 5–11.

EDWARDS, A. and COLLISON, J. (1996) *Mentoring and Developing Practice in Primary Schools*, Buckingham: Open University Press.

HMI (1998) *The New Teacher in School*, London: HMSO.

OFSTED/TTA (1996) *Framework for the Assessment of Quality and Standards in Initial Teacher Training*, London: OFSTED.

SIMCO, N. (1995) 'Professional profiling and development in the induction year', *British Journal of In-Service Education*, **21**, 3, pp. 261–72.

SIMCO, N., BURDON, M., COOPER, H., HUGGINS, M., PRENDIVILLE, F. and SIXSMITH, C. (1996) 'Support of development: The induction of newly qualified teachers', paper presented at the annual meeting of the British Educational Research Association, Lancaster.

SURREY EDUCATIONAL SERVICES (1992) *The Surrey New Teacher Competency Profile*, Guildford, Surrey Educational Services.

SUTHERLAND, S. (1997) *Teacher Education and Training: A Study*, London: National Committee of Inquiry into Higher Education.

TRIPP, D. (1993) *Critical Incidents in Teaching; Developing Professional Judgement*, London: Routledge.

TTA (1996) *Career Entry Profile for Newly Qualified Teachers* (draft documentation), London: TTA.

TTA (1997) *Career Entry Profile for Newly Qualified Teachers*, London: TTA.

19   Turning Round the Titanic: Changing Attitudes to Professional Development for the Teaching Profession

*Meryl Thompson**

Who is Accountable for the Lifelong Learning of Teachers?

Why, when education is seen as so central to economic prosperity, social equity and individual fulfilment and when 'learning organizations' and 'lifelong learning' are vaunted as the absolute prerequisite for the post-millenium society, is no-one responsible for the strategic direction of professional development — lifelong learning — for the teaching profession? Why is no-one held accountable — except, it seems, the individual teacher herself — for enhancing the capacity and motivation of teachers to continue to learn and for providing accessible learning opportunities? (Brennan and Little, 1996, pp. 21–22). Why was it that there was no comprehensive, national programme of professional development to precede or accompany the introduction of technology in the primary National Curriculum, the simultaneous expansion of the subject content in science, history, geography, art and music, or at the point when the code for special educational needs (SEN) was introduced or when the responsibility for initial teacher training was transferred to schools? Why are the concepts of human capital, human resource management and people management not applied in the teaching profession? The result is that a managerial climate which dispirits, demoralizes and disaffects a newly-qualified teacher (NQT) carries no odium if she leaves the profession, thus wasting both the national investment and her personal investment in her education and training as a teacher, and the culpable neglect of an employee's level of competence over many years results in fast-track capability procedures for the teacher, but neither naming or shaming of the successive management omissions which highly probably contributed to the situation. Why does no-one see the teacher as an internal customer of the education system, the inspection process or of senior management? Why does no-one think in terms of 'delighting' teachers with opportunities for personal and professional growth? (West-Burnham, 1992).

These, and many other questions, have plagued me as I have followed a series of initiatives related to professional development, starting with membership of the National Steering Group for School Teacher Appraisal, which reported in 1987,

---

* Meryl Thompson is writing here in a personal capacity

and continuing currently with the implementation of the Teacher Training Agency's (TTA) national standards and the legislation on reinstating an assessed induction period and on establishing a General Teaching Council. My conclusion is that teachers' professional development is dominated by the same set of fundamental, often unexamined, assumptions about the nature of the world — and also the role and proper place of the teacher, the value of young children and their education — which others have identified as a world-view or paradigm limiting our capacity to change — even though it is imperative that we do so as the impact, speed and scope of change accelerate (Beare and Slaughter, 1993; Caine and Caine, 1997).

Assumptions About Teachers' Professional Development

The prevailing assumption — the world-view or paradigm — that dominates professional development planning and strategy in English education — is mechanistic. The assumption is that we can control the world like a big machine. 'In a machine, causes and effect can be clearly identified, separated and measured, and related to each other' (Caine and Caine, 1997). We can, therefore, on this assumption, change professional development by working out what each part does and then changing that part so that it works better. For example, the assumption was that a mechanism of regulations relating to teacher appraisal would put into effect improved performance management for teachers and promote improved teaching and learning: even though headteachers may not have believed in or understood the importance of investing in people; despite the competing workload demands of the National Curriculum; and without any strategy to disseminate best practice on effective teaching and to provide effective in-service education. National standards and target setting related to appraisal seem to be ideas informed by the same paradigm.

But attitudes to professional development also seem to be influenced by a vast range of less paradigmatic but just as pervasive '*memes*' — a term coined by Richard Dawkins to describe a cultural belief or 'unit of cultural information', the social counterpoint of genes in physical organisms. 'Initially we adopt memes because they are useful. But after a certain point they begin to affect our actions and thoughts in ways that at best are ambiguous and at worst definitely not in our interests' (Csikszentmihalyi quoted in Caine and Caine, 1997, p. 33). Amongst these memes appear to be the following. Teaching, particularly primary teaching, is about self-sacrifice, about putting the children first. Why else do we in schools 'spend a great deal of time placing oxygen masks on other people's faces while we ourselves are suffocating'? (Barth, 1990). Other memes are that learning, and continuing to learn, to teach is rather a simple process and that affective factors — related to morale and self-esteem — do not, or should not, apply to teachers. If our understanding of, and attitudes to, professional development are to change for the future — and they must — then these underlying assumptions must be challenged and reversed. To turn round our Titanic we need to find the lever — the 'trim tab', the 'rudder on the rudder', which Buckminster Fuller used as a metaphor for high-leverage activities which can bring big results from small changes (Senge, 1990, pp. 63–5).

What is Professional Development and Whose Responsibility Is It?

First, however, for the avoidance of confusion it is necessary to clarify two points. What constitutes professional development and what is the extent of the individual teacher's professional responsibility for their own development? It is perhaps indicative of the low level of understanding of professional development that we have no shared understanding across the teaching profession of the complexity of the concept. A useful definition shared by other professions is that it is: *'the maintenance and enhancement of the knowledge, expertise and competence of professionals throughout their careers according to a plan formulated with regard to the needs of the professional, the employer, the profession and society'*. Its functions are updating and extending the professional's knowledge and skills related to new developments and new areas of practice to ensure continuing competence in the current job; education and training for new responsibilities and new roles by developing new areas of competence; and developing personal and professional effectiveness and increasing job satisfaction by increased competence (Madden and Mitchell, 1993). Professional development is, therefore, conscious and intentional, work-based and job-embedded, dynamic and continuous, formal and informal, professional and personal and in the interests of the employer and the employee. It is synonymous with the blueprint for the principles of lifelong learning which leads to the systematic acquisition, renewal, and upgrading of knowledge, skills and attitudes, necessary in response to the constantly changing conditions of modern life, with the ultimate goal of promoting individual self-fulfilment; is dependent on people's increasing ability and motivation to engage in self-directed learning activities; and acknowledges the contribution of all available educational influences — formal, non-formal and informal (Brennan and Little, 1996, p. 20). In the future all professional development for the teaching profession must recognize the significance of the continuous, the intrinsic and the personal or it will fail — again challenging some of the most basic assumptions of both policy makers and the profession.

A teacher's responsibility to be committed to the systematic maintenance, improvement and broadening of their knowledge and skills and for the continued development of the personal qualities needed to undertake their teaching role is, and should be, regarded as one of the fundamental ethical imperatives of the profession. Furthermore, so should working collaboratively with colleagues as critical friends and working collectively as a professional community to develop and transmit professional knowledge and raise standards (Thompson, 1997, pp. 48–50 and 52–4). Regrettably, the current social meme, which appears to affect our understanding of professional development too, 'enthrones independence . . . Most of the self-improvement material puts independence on a pedestal, as though communication, teamwork and cooperation were lesser values'. What is missed is an appreciation of interdependence, which gives access to the vast resources and potential of other human beings (Covey, 1992, pp. 50–1). Futhermore, primary teachers cannot exercise this professionalism unless their work environment supports professional learning and professional collaboration. This depends not only upon management decisions to support developmental opportunities but crucially upon historical assumptions about the funding of primary education, which have meant that non-contact time is minimal and which currently favour the reduction of class sizes more than the provision of time for professional collaboration. Regrettably, too, although few teachers would deny outright this professional responsibility, it is too easily overridden by the dominant, socially-approved principle that teachers, and especially primary teachers, should always be in contact with children. Today's children always take priority over tomorrow's. Thus a future strategy for professional development that relied only on calling on teachers to demonstrate this aspect of their professionalism is doomed to be moralistic not realistic, unless a different climate is created.

What Malaise?

In a recent article, in the first edition of *Professional Development Today*, Anthea Millett (1997) speaks of tackling a long standing malaise — a poor career structure and the lack of development opportunities — of the teaching profession and of the TTA's success in integrating all aspects of its remit — teacher supply and recruitment, ITT and induction — and continuing professional development and research. Yet as of March 1996 61 per cent of full-time teachers in our primary schools was over the age of 40. Certainly they had all completed their own full-time school education before 1976 and the majority would have completed their tertiary education, including initial teacher education, by then (DfEE, 1997, table 27). From thenceforward their continuing personal education and continuing professional development were largely by happenstance, dependent upon their own curiosity, ingenuity and survival tactics and the inconstant and variable provision and access from their multiple employers, local education authorities (LEAs) and governing bodies. An idiosyncratic and random list of events and trends since 1976 that have affected the role and nature of primary teaching might include the introduction of equal opportunities legislation, the appreciation of gender stereotyping in education and the possibility of male and female learning styles; the revelation of the widespread nature of child abuse, including amongst those who would be expected to protect children; the Children Act; the rise of the Pacific Rim and the fall of the Berlin Wall; Thatcherism; the National Curriculum and its assessment; reading recovery and assertive discipline; the greater integration of children with SEN and the code of SEN; the publication of *School Matters* (Mortimore et al., 1988) the rise of information technology, the video, fax and mobile phone and the decline of mining; and appraisal, OFSTED and New Labour.

Surely these have constituted development opportunities? The majority of these teachers will also have become subject coordinators and many SEN coordinators (SENCOs); a sizeable proportion are likely to have become mentors and appraisers; and many have entered senior management. Surely these have resulted in career development? Although it may not have been formally recognized, the skills of teachers and the nature of teaching have changed.

But the TTA's solution to the perceived malaise is its framework of professional standards, of which more shortly. The framework of professional standards will address the problem 'by establishing clear expectations at different points in the profession'. Its main objectives are to help teachers at those different points to plan and monitor their development, training and performance effectively, and to set clear and relevant targets for improvement; ensure that the focus at every point is on improving pupils' achievement and the quality of their education; provide a basis for the professional recognition of teachers' achievements; and to help providers of professional development activities to plan and provide high quality training which makes effective use of teachers' time and brings maximum benefits to their pupils.

To me, the malaise appears to be more the result of the inability to acknowledge the learning and development that have taken place within primary teaching, despite unsupportive management and systemic structures.

The consequence is to enhance both the negative view of the profession and, perhaps unsurprisingly, the allegedly transformational role of the TTA. As Brennan and Little (1996) argue can be seen in others' conceptions of the 'learning society', the TTA 'may have a greater concern with the certification of learning than with learning itself', (p. 22) and with its own extrinsic functions, its own concern with 'social engineering' and with meeting the needs of an ever-widening set of clients than with the pursuit of knowledge for its own sake. This seems to be borne out by the TTA's underlying assumption of what underpins the purpose of professional development. Its purpose is not, it seems, because of the importance of enhancing the skills of all our teachers, since as Michael Fullan (1991) says 'educational change depends upon what teachers do and think; it's as simple and complex as that'. It is not because professional development plays a central role in school improvement, although it does. It is not to put enhancing the morale, motivation and commitment of the teaching profession at the centre of the management role. It is because, Anthea Millett (1997) says: 'Effective professional development plays a central role in convincing potential teachers that teaching bears all the hallmarks of an established profession, including clear progression routes and professional status. It should convince them that it is in an intellectually challenging profession, worth joining'. So there we have it. The purpose of professional development is instrumental, mechanistic. It is not to nurture and enhance those in the profession but to achieve the TTA remit.

She also justifies the development of the national framework on the basis of research the TTA commissioned in 1995. This found that professional development was often ad hoc with insufficient linkage across school development planning, personal development planning and appraisal; that there was little consistency in how much schools spent on professional development; that very few teachers believed professional development activities had any impact on their work in the classroom; and that schools rarely had systematic methods in place to evaluate effectiveness. I find it difficult to see how the national framework solves these problems and I see no way in which it can enhance professional development while it ignores other structural problems.

What Does the National Framework of Professional Standards Contribute to the Quality of Professional Development?

Of course, the immediate answer is that we simply do not know what the TTA's framework of professional standards contributes to the quality of professional development and since like most policy directions it will not be evaluated by comparison with equally well-resourced and researched alternatives, we shall never know. Also since it is not yet in place a great deal is hypothetical. But the standards developed so far are for the award of Qualified Teacher Status, for SENCOs, for subject leaders, and for aspiring, new and serving headteachers.

There could scarcely be a greater consensus that the headteacher plays a key role in the effective school — of which teachers' continued development is a critical factor — and that this is crucially dependent upon creating a culture, where teachers work together, never stop learning to teach, give and receive help, because teaching is seen as inherently complex and not with an implication of incompetence or inadequacy, and where the headteacher supports this with mutual respect, openness, praise and celebration, shared decision-making, involvement, leading by 'standing behind' and all those features now described as 'transformational leadership' (Fullan and Hargreaves, 1992; Stoll and Fink, 1996; Blase and Kirby, 1992).

I believe, therefore, we could reasonably have expected the standards for the National Professional Qualification for Headteachers (NPQH) to have recognized these attributes of leadership because of the inextricable links between organizational improvement and individual improvement. On balance they do not. The TTA has never backed up its standards with evidence from research. We do not know the rationale upon which the standards are based, except by inference. We do not know, therefore, what concept or paradigm of 'leadership' the TTA is using. We do not know, for example, what are the political, economic, social, religious and technological influences which the TTA believes have an impact on strategic and operational planning in schools. Presumably the various training programmes may interpret these in a manner which more or less promotes teachers' lifelong learning and which recognizes the impact of a learning society. But the management standards are unpromising.

Neither of the key outcomes of headship related to a positive ethos or to teachers emphasizes a collaborative and participative culture and there is no hint or suggestion that some outcome related to high professional self-esteem or indeed continued professional learning might be a reasonable expectation of effective headship. The ethos-related outcome, though, does include commitment to high achievement and teachers' accountability for success. Significantly the key outcome for teachers concentrates exclusively on the individual teacher. There is no reference even to effective team-working, commonplace in almost every other management standard. The NPQH seems unlikely to alter the paradigm of teachers' lifelong learning. Indeed it seems to be permeated by an outdated vision of the head as hero or charismatic leader, where the followers are not capable of much originality or creativity. Unless it is implemented with a different vision it seems likely to be seen by teachers as instrumental, alienating, conformist and impersonal, exhibiting the very characteristics that are inimical to a culture conducive to professional growth and learning.

If primary school teachers cannot look to the TTA's headship standards for a different future for their professional development what is offered by the standards for subject coordinators and SENCOs? The TTA appears to have shown peculiar insensitivity to the primary sector in both sets of standards. The original standards for subject leaders amounted to highly inappropriate proposals for coordination roles often held on a short-term and intermittent basis, and were based on assumptions that teachers have distinctly differentiated subject expertise and that non-contact time is available. This fails to give primary school teachers the confidence that their professional growth was the focus of these standards. Nor is the revised draft of July 1997 any more convincing when it says: 'While the standards apply to all schools, they will need to be applied and implemented differently in schools of different type, size or phase. For example, they will need to be used selectively in smaller primary schools where headteachers may retain more of the defined role than in larger school primary schools. The degree to which subject-coordinators in primary and special schools can use the specified knowledge, understanding, skills and attributes in order to carry out their key tasks in these standards will depend on their experience and opportunities to develop their role'.

What is perhaps more surprising in view of the headship standards is that the outcomes for effective subject leadership include teachers who 'work well together as a team', 'are involved in the formation of policies and plans and apply them consistently in the classroom' and 'make good use of guidance, training and support to develop expertise in their teaching'. But they are not outcomes of the headship standards. Why not? Particularly when teachers who 'regularly mark and assess pupils' work and reinforce and extend pupils' learning and achievement through setting consistent and challenging homework' are. Could it be that the TTA's conception of professional collaboration, growth and development is that it is created not by headteachers but only by middle management? If that were so, although it would be utterly inconsistent with the literature on effective schools, it would be consistent with the TTA's standards for SENCOs, for these appear to confuse effective SEN coordination with the overall management of SEN within the school. The SENCO is to be deemed effective when teachers 'communicate effectively with the SENCO', and when teachers 'have high expectations of pupils' progress', recognize and reward success and 'foster pupils' self-esteem and confidence'. The interface between managerial and coordination responsibilities for teachers' attitudes and development appears to have become confused. The model the TTA is still using appears to reflect the expectation that there can be dramatic and profound changes in schools based solely on using individual teachers as 'change agents' and on staff development programmes intended only to help them do their jobs more effectively. Such a model is manifestly insufficient to produce the desired result.

Why the Future must not look like the Past

So far, as the TTA research found, most teachers have not had positive experiences of professional development. The laudable ambitions at the introduction of teacher appraisal — to make professional development continuous and an integral part of school management, to promote professional collaboration by enhancing the training and role of appraisers, to recognize the achievements and success of teachers — seem to have foundered on the rocks of history, suspicion, the distractions of devolved management and a competitive environment, poor human resource management, and repeated undermining and denigration from Her Majesty's Inspectorate (HMI). The LEA infrastructure and advisory personnel has largely gone, translated into inspectors and performance indicator crunchers. Earmarked and increasingly delegated funding for in-service training has not proved a solution. Pump priming, for example, for behaviour management and reading recovery, has proved spasmodic and discontinuous. Although the White Paper, *Excellence in Schools* makes a welcome commitment to making sure that teachers understand the best teaching methods and the National Grid for Learning and Virtual Teachers' Centre are exciting ideas with high leverage potential, none are yet practical realities. Teachers sorely need a new future for professional development, which is convincingly permanent, thoughtful and forward-looking and is there for them. In the future professional development must have the oxygen of success and be perceived by teachers as contributing to their ability to operate as professionals. The national framework of standards and the piecemeal approach to professional development now seen in schools are not the high leverage approaches needed. Lifelong learning for teachers is too important for the Titanic to be turned round at leisure.

Making Teachers Professional Development a First Order Issue

Put simply it is time for all those agencies and employers, policy-makers and evaluators, to stop assessing our provision for teachers solely on the assessable educational outcomes of today's children. It is time for the 'customer satisfaction' of teachers to become an active concept in their overall management. It is time for teachers' perceptions of their developmental needs and of their job satisfaction to figure as key data and indicators. It is time for headteachers and governors to be ashamed for not making time for appraisal and collaboration or for not having active professional development policies in place. It is time for real targets for the growth and development of our teaching force to be set nationally, to feature in LEA educational development plans, and to be operational at school level. It is time to make it clear that the quality and welfare of the teaching profession is so critical that all the relevant agencies should be asked not what have the teachers done for you, but what have you done for teachers *and* that they should be able to point to objective indicators of both teachers' enhanced skills and competences and self-confidence and professional satisfaction. Just as children are the clients of the teaching profession, teachers should be seen as the clients of a series of professionals

— senior management, civil servants, teacher educators, and the staff on non-departmental public bodies. It is not enough to enthusiastically recognize and celebrate success — although that is a welcome development (Bichard, 1997). The essential prerequisite — the high-leverage solution — is for *all* those exercising educational leadership to be seen to put the followers first, to believe in the followers (Starratt, 1993). The message to all should be, as Fullan and Hargreaves (1992) advise headteachers — value your teachers; promote their professional growth; promote collaboration, not cooptation. We cannot turn round teachers' professional development until everyone accepts that teachers matter and that undivided concentration on what they need and what sustains them is not provider capture or misplaced liberalism but the new bottom-line.

Of course along with this will need to go a series of other initiatives; a coherent resource management system; the need for an infrastructure; the need for understanding organizations and for constant updating.

A Coherent Resource Management System

As Ewart Keep (1993) argues so persuasively, the high quality education system we need requires 'coherent and accountable management of those major personnel issues which are beyond the control of individual schools' yet 'the human resource management issues confronting education would appear complex and large scale even to the most sophisticated private sector employers'.

There is no body with overall responsibility for the personnel issues which affect the teaching work-force. Salaries and conditions of service related to recruitment and retention are the responsibility of the School Teachers Review Body (STRB). Initial teacher training, induction and promoting teaching rest with the TTA. Effectiveness and improvement, and the dissemination of findings, rest with the DfEE and OFSTED. Keep contrasts this with the Home Office's responsibility for prison service employees and the education service board of management and central education service personnel function of the National Health Service. There is a certain irony in that the latest evidence to the STRB from the DfEE states that it remains worrying that there may not be sufficient candidates for primary headship, possibly because the pay differential does not compensate for the increased responsibility. It says, 'roughly speaking, one in four primary teachers is likely to become a head at some stage in his or her career, whereas only one in 20 secondary teachers will become a head' (DfEE, 1997, p. 24). The TTA's national standards appear to have done little to take this challenge into account. Furthermore, the TTA seems to have a very short-term, limited conception of what should constitute investment in the development of the teaching profession, as demonstrated in the allocation of its INSET funds, monies which previously went into higher education. Despite the direction outlined in *Excellence in Schools* there is no support for the promotion of family learning, leadership in a multi-agency context, for example in Education Action Zones, teaching to improve children's attitudes to learning, the development of study support, or citizenship.

Yet the Government does not now seem to be prepared to hand responsibility for professional development to the General Teaching Council (GTC). But the future cannot be ignored. There must be a national strategy for the future development of the teaching profession, for manpower planning, succession management, the analysis of exit questionnaires, the examination of wastage, and the systematic updating and upskilling through the dissemination of research findings and for professional growth. There should be a body establishing pilot studies and evaluation programmes, mapping out means of implementation, including lead-in times and preparatory training, and monitoring and evaluating their effectiveness. One of its functions should be to identify and assess those 'megatrends', for example, the expansion of basics in education to include problem-solving, creativity and lifelong learning and relearning and the dispersion of the educative function to the home and the workplace because of telecommunications and computer technology, which will influence teaching (Caldwell and Spinks, 1992). Another should be to take account of those 'new professional images', such as the importance of communication and empathy with professional clients to understand situations from their point of view, which have implications for the profession's role and its training (Eliot, 1991). Serious research that helps teachers and teacher educators properly understand the processes by which pupils acquire and use language and mathematical ideas also needs to be directed in a human resource context. 'The need is to understand and support learning viewed in the widest psychological and cultural sense' (O'Shea, 1997) and then to disseminate the findings. Whether or not it assumes this function, it should be self-evident that a GTC will need to concern itself with these issues and will have a critical function in representing and leading the profession and in advising.

The Need for an Infrastructure

The strategy must include the provision of the infrastructure to support professional growth. The main reason why I find the TTA's aspirations for the framework of national standards to be the key to professional development, as at worst unrealistic and at best incomplete, is because it wills ends and pays no attention to the means. In the SENCO and subject coordinators standards there are implicit and explicit references to what amount to skills as mentors, trainers and coaches, for example to securing and disseminating effective teaching methods, to sustaining the motivation of others and to helping other teachers to achieve constructive working relationships with students. These are complex and skilful activities. Not only do we need more development of teachers as mentors, trainers and coaches we need trainers, mentors and coaches to provide that professional development. The TTA appears to have no strategy for this. The only strategy that we have had has been regressive as the advisory teachers and central professional development support teams of LEAs have been disbanded since the Education Reform Act and the introduction of local management of schools. The seminal work of Joyce and Showers stressed the need for a cadre of highly trained personnel. We cannot continue to ignore its significance if we are to transform professional development.

The closest we are getting to the acknowledgment that the professional development of others is a key skill required in the education service is in the outline of the Advanced Skills Teacher (AST) described by the Secretary of State as '*a distinct new role*'. The DfEE's written evidence to the STRB suggests that the AST's particular duties might include participation in ITT and mentoring NQTs; advice on classroom organization and teaching methods and materials; dissemination of best practice and educational research; advice on and provision of in-service training, and participation in appraisal of teachers. It is also envisaged that they should become associate fellows or professors at partner higher education institutions and other research bodies. These aspirations look promising until we read the statement that these skills will be '*such as are possessed only by a small minority of teachers*'. This is far too unambitious if every teacher is to be sustained by lifelong learning.

Similarly we cannot ignore what is known about effective programmes of professional development. Bolam (Williams and Bolam, 1993) for example, argues that research has 'demonstrated convincingly' that learning and applying new teaching skills can only be achieved if training programmes take into account five components: the presentation of the underlying theory and a description of the skill; modelling or demonstrating the skill; practice in a simulated setting; feedback in the simulated setting; and one-to-one coaching when the newly-learned skills are applied in the classroom. Changing professional development means a greater appreciation of what constitutes learning teaching. Teaching is not simple. The TTA and DfEE's assumption that appraisal can lead to professional development, can lead to manifestly enhanced educational outcomes within one or two years, belies or ignores what we know about changing the deeper structures of teachers' understanding. Teachers need to construct their own understanding. They, too, 'learn best through active involvement and through thinking and becoming articulate about what they have learned' (Lieberman quoted in Sparks and Hirsch, 1997). The consequence is that future professional development must be supported by a new style of training and facilitation and by provision of the time to assimilate and implement new practices and to work collaboratively.

The Need for Understanding Organizations and Systems

'Typically, those who introduce educational reforms or restructure educational systems pay scant attention to the school organizations and contexts in which these changes are introduced' (Stoll and Fink, 1996). The TTA appear to be typical in this respect. What is needed is not so much needs assessment and a framework of standards but a radical rethink of how professional development is interdependent with organizational capacity. The first essential is to see that all growth depends upon improvements in the capacity of organizations to solve problems. Deming, the guru of Total Quality Management, estimated that 94 per cent of the capacity for quality lay in the organization. The TTA does not seem to have taken on board that 'unless individual learning needs and organizational changes are addressed simultaneously and support one another, the gains made in one area may be cancelled by continuing problems in the other'. 'Staff development not only must affect the knowledge, attitudes and practices of individual teachers . . . but it must also alter the cultures and structures of the organizations in which those individuals work' (Sparks and Hirsch, 1997, p. 12).

The great proponent of systems thinking is Peter Senge. He has identified organizational learning disabilities including confusing our jobs with our identities, finding an 'enemy', illusory proactivity, short termism, not recognizing gradual but catastrophic changes and the myth of the management team (Senge, 1990, pp. 12–26). The management of teachers' professional development appears to be beset by all of these problems. The solution is to see wholes and not parts, people as active participants and not helpless reactors, and to create the future not react to the past. This whole, he argues, is created by integrating personal mastery, because organizations only learn through individuals who learn; revealing our mental models, because they affect what we see and may impede learning; shared vision, because they derive their power from common caring; and team learning, because seeing each other as colleagues *and friends* is extremely important because we talk differently to people who are friends. Recognizing that we are all enmeshed in organizational structures produces a greater humility to understand better the limitations of some conceptions of professional development.

The Need for Constant Updating

The need for updating teachers' skills comes in a variety of guises. The European group of teachers unions (ETUCE) recognized the point made earlier. 'During teachers' professional careers assumptions concerning the nature and purpose of learning and education; the value systems of schools and of society; and the interests, capabilities and ambitions of children and adolescents will all be very much altered from the assumptions of the professions they entered'. Furthermore, the nature of much social, technological and cultural change is that it challenges previously-held beliefs and assumptions and requires new skills. The personal value systems and professional competence of teachers will, therefore, be substantially challenged. (ETUCE, undated) For example, recent research found that primary teachers most frequently mentioned classroom behavioural problems and working with parents as the biggest gaps in their training. The researchers found teachers 'concerned about how to conduct themselves with children in difficult situations, and with parents in more formal situations. They feel vulnerable in the face of increased parental power, and children's own knowledge and understanding of their rights. Many teachers felt that they needed to be introduced to the kinds of situations that they might encounter, prior to actually encountering them' (Davies and Ferguson, 1997). This seems an entirely understandable example and an entirely reasonable solution, but professional development rarely extends to broader thinking about the changing role of the profession, the impact of social change, or the implications of information technology. Professional development in the future should make such opportunities through teacher-led seminars, problem-solving groups, and reading clubs, even psycho-drama. The GTC has a leadership role in raising questions of the philosophical and social role of the teaching profession.

In addition the future demand will be for even faster dissemination of new information and research findings and for faster learning, as new information and communication technologies, some interactive, are introduced into the classroom. Some US school districts are already broadcasting to their teachers on cable television, providing summer institutes open to everyone on key immediate issues, and using dissemination specialists to identify exemplary programmes and to create special events to promote learning about the ideas. LEAs, the DfEE, TTA and the GTC should all look for innovative ways in which they can serve the teaching profession and should hold themselves accountable for the effectiveness of their dissemination.

Thriving on Chaos

Predetermining standards, knowledge and attributes at different points in the profession and the studious process of needs assessment and working towards awards and qualifications may well prove the wrong method to cope with the continuous and unpredictable needs of faster-moving dissemination. We are likely to need greater adaptability. As subject associations, special interest groups, higher education partnerships and individual schools and teachers create their own web-sites and disseminate their practice, the delusion that anyone can determine and be in firm control of teachers' learning will disappear. With it perhaps we can bid farewell to the last vestige of the idea that teachers' professional development is largely something that must be '*done to teachers*' — a device of bureaucratic control that threatens the very desire to teach itself (Fullan and Hargreaves, 1992). Today this threat of bureaucratic control is our Titanic. It can only be reversed by high-leverage activities which delight their teacher customers by their prescience, appropriateness, soul and credibility and by giving everyone credit, standing behind them in hard times, showing up to support and celebrate, and attention to detail. '*Who comes first? Don't be silly . . . ; its employees. That is — and this dear Watson is elementary — if you genuinely want to put your customers first, you must put employees more first. You get it, right?*' (Peters, 1994, p. 55).

References

BARTH, R. (1990) *Improving Schools From Within*. San Francisco, CA: Jossey-Bass.
BEARE, H. and SLAUGHTER, R. (1993) *Education for the Twenty-first Century*, London: Routledge.
BICHARD, M. (1997) 'Professionalism', *Education Journal*, **18**, December, pp. 5–6.
BLASE, J. and KIRBY, P.C. (1992) *Bringing Out the Best in Teachers; What Effective Principals Do*, Newbury Park, CA: Corwin Press.
BRENNAN, J. and LITTLE, B. (1996) *A Review of Work Based Learning in Higher Education*, London: DfEE.

CAINE, R.N. and CAINE, G. (1997) *Education on the Edge of Possibility*, Alexandria, VA: ASCD.

CALDWELL, B.J. and SPINKS, J.M. (1992) *Leading the Self-Managing School*, London: Falmer Press.

COVEY, S.R. (1992) *The Seven Habits of Highly Effective People: Restoring the Character Ethic*, London: Simon and Schuster.

DAVIES, R. and FERGUSON, J. (1997) 'Teachers' views of the role of initial teacher education in developing their professionalism', *Journal of Education for Teaching*, **23**, 1, pp. 39–56.

DfEE (1997) *School Teachers Review Body: Written Evidence from the Department for Education and Employment: Statistical Tables: September, 1997*, London: DfEE.

ELIOT, J. (1991) 'A model of professionalism and its implications for teacher education', *British Educational Research Journal*, **17**, 4, pp. 309–18.

ETUCE (undated) *Teacher Education in Europe*, Brussels: European Trade Union Committee for Education.

FULLAN, M. (1991) *The New Meaning of Educational Change*, London: Cassell.

FULLAN, M. and HARGREAVES, A. (1992) *What's Worth Fighting For in Your School?; Working Together for Improvement*, Buckingham: Open University Press.

KEEP, E. (1993) 'The need for a revised management system for the teaching profession', *Briefings For The Paul Hamlyn Foundation National Commission on Education*, London: Heinemann, pp. 17–29.

MADDEN, C.A. and MITCHELL, V.A. (1993) *Professions, Standards and Competence: A Survey of Continuing Education for the Professions*, Bristol: Department of Continuing Education, University of Bristol.

MILLETT, A. (1997) 'Tackling a long standing malaise', *Professional Development Today*, October, pp. 5–8.

MORTIMORE, P. et al. (1988) *School Matters*, Wells: Open Books.

O'SHEA, T. (1997) 'Innovation versus control in teacher education: The role of new technology', paper presented to the SCETT Annual Conference, Dunchurch Rugby, November.

PETERS, T. (1994) *The Pursuit of Wow! Every Person's Guide to Topsy-Turvy Times*. London: Macmillan.

SENGE, P.M. (1990) *The Fifth Discipline: The Art and Practice of the Learning Organization*, London: Century Business.

SPARKS, D. and HIRSCH, S. (1997) *A New Vision for Staff Development*, Alexandria, VA: ASCD.

STARRATT, R.J. (1993) *The Drama of Leadership*, London: Falmer Press.

STOLL, L. and FINK, D. (1996) *Changing Our Schools*, Buckingham: Open University Press.

THOMPSON, M. (1997) *Professional Ethics and the Teacher: Towards a General Teaching Council*, Stoke-on-Trent: Trentham.

WEST-BURNHAM, J. (1992) *Managing Quality in School; A TQM Approach*, London: Longman.

WILLIAMS, M. and BOLAM, R. (1993) 'The continuing professional development of teachers', paper prepared for the General Teaching Council, England and Wales, GTC (England and Wales Trust).

Part 6

Primary Education and Primary Teacher Education

20 Conversations and Collaboration: Primary Education as a Community of Practice

Anne Edwards

Partnership in Initial Teacher Education

Carolyn Horne was a child-centred teacher in the late 1960s and later became a student-centred teacher educator. As an early years specialist, she placed considerable emphasis on ensuring that the contexts for learning gave every opportunity for learner development. Passionately committed to initial teacher education (ITE) partnerships between primary schools and higher education, she saw them as a way of providing the best learning opportunities possible for students. But creating strong learning environments is not easy; as any early years specialist would confirm. Labelling a relationship between a school and a university a 'partnership' is not enough. Indeed partnership is perhaps a weasel word; able to mean so much and so little. Carolyn did nothing half-heartedly. Training partnerships mattered. They absorbed a great deal of her energy and were always worth the effort. But what makes an ITE partnership worthwhile? Partnerships which are more than loose couplings or simply contractual relationships need a number of conditions or attributes. Firstly they should allow members to contribute their own distinctive strengths to the partnership. This condition demands a respect for differences and a recognition that partnerships will themselves develop through the interaction of different ways of seeing and being. Secondly, partnerships should be aimed at a common set of purposes. Initially that might be ensuring that a particular student reaches the required standards, but I shall argue that these purposes might usefully embrace wider goals. Next, all partners need to feel that they are benefiting from active membership. Partnerships in ITE cannot accommodate sleeping partners, interested only in their unearned income. Active membership is demanding and can only be engaged in by those who see it as personally worthwhile. Finally partnerships need to be flexible with the capacity to accommodate changes in context and in the development of individual partners.

Partnerships are therefore more than business arrangements based on a form of technical rationality which identifies distinct roles and responsibilities and links these through systems of accountability. Partnerships are complex. Partnerships which are aimed at supporting the learning of student teachers in primary schools are certainly so (Edwards, 1995). But partnerships which are aimed at ensuring that students achieve specific common standards within a required timeframe under stringent inspection procedures are particularly demanding. The temptation to limit partnership to the definition of narrow roles and responsibilities located within a tight accountability system is bound to be strong. But what a lost opportunity that would be. This is not the form of partnership which inspired Carolyn and our school-based colleagues in the pilot training partnerships at St Martin's in the early 1990s.

John Goodlad, writing of the benefits of school-university partnerships in the US (Goodlad, 1991) emphasizes the mutual benefits for both schools and universities to be gained from close links. His 19 postulates for sound teacher education address the need for strong university involvement through high status, intellectually independent programmes which ensure high quality field-based learning opportunities for students. Importantly he argues that a focus simply on mentoring is an insufficient basis for improving the US school system; good mentoring will occur in good schools. Schools, he suggests, can find support for school development in their relationships with universities and universities can benefit from the opportunities for field-based, practice-oriented research which partnerships provide. Goodlad therefore identified a multifaceted form of partnership which demands adjustment from all partners and considerable preparation. We may not achieve all that partnerships might offer us in English and Welsh primary education. However if we are to make them worth the effort we do need to consider at least the distinctive contributions of partners and the kinds of benefits that are likely to sustain them.

A Framework for Conversational Collaboration

The framework for thinking about partnership draws on the work I've recently undertaken with Lynn Ogden at the University of Leeds. We have been exploring how students acquire the capacity to teach mathematics, science and religious education in primary schools. Our view of student learning leans heavily on sociocultural psychology and its close relation situated cognition. James Wertsch and his colleagues describe the sociocultural approach to the study of human action as follows.

> The goal of the sociocultural approach is to explicate the relations between human action, on the one hand, and the cultural, institutional, and historical situations in which this action occurs, on the other. (Wertsch et al., 1995, p. 11)

We are particularly attracted to a sociocultural perspective on learning because it focuses our attention on both the learner and the learning opportunities available in a context which is in turn shaped by its own history. Primary schools are complex institutions and we need to try to do justice to that complexity when considering just how students learn to become teachers. The key features of a sociocultural approach are the relationship between learning and identity, the construction of knowledge in use, communities of practice and the importance of conversation. I shall look briefly at each and consider their implications for how we might think about teacher education partnerships.

Learning and identity are interdependent. Our sense of who we are, or would like to be, provides a blueprint for how we respond to events. However, as we learn to see, interpret and respond to both new and familiar events we can change from being someone who does x to becoming someone who does x+y. Consequently our identity shifts. A corollary of this view of learning is that one way of changing thinking is to change practices. Sociocultural psychology and situated approaches to learning do emphasize the importance of action to learning but most also give a great deal of attention to how that action is supported by the expertise of other participants (Rogoff, 1995; Wertsch, 1991). Mentors certainly have a role in supporting students in action in classrooms.

A focus on student identity reminds us of the extent to which students come into schools with ready-made identity projects they want to enact. They often know what kind of teacher they want to be even to the extent that they are resistant to information which disturbs their pre-conceptions and their acting out of these projects (Desforges, 1995; Edwards, in press). Students' pre-conceptions about teaching can therefore present a considerable challenge to teacher educators. If these pre-conceptions act as blinkers, preventing students from seeing and responding appropriately in classrooms, mentors need to help students see in more informed ways. The actions of experienced teachers depend on their capacity to see knowledgeably in classrooms and to respond intelligently. Jill Collison in her chapter in this volume (Chapter 16) discusses ways in which experienced teachers are able to see so much more and respond more appropriately than can novices. Clearly student teachers need to learn to interpret classrooms through the lenses that are used by more expert practitioners.

One challenge to initial teacher educators lies in the extent to which students can be assisted in that seeing and responding while they learn to become teachers. It may be that one way forward is greater emphasis on team teaching enabling mentors to overtly interpret events and model immediate responses. The efforts of Cathy, in one of the examples provided by Collison, were largely unnoticed by the students who may have gained more had they recognized that they might be learning from her interpretations and actions.

Knowledge informs our identities and therefore our actions. Luckmann (1982), for example, talks of the stocks of knowledge which inform our identity projects and hence our actions. Importantly a sociocultural perspective on learning and knowledge asks us to see knowledge as something developed and owned in the communities in which it is used. Consequently we acquire and use the knowledge which is valued in the communities in which we are participating. Therefore when thinking about how students learn to become teachers in schools, this perspective leads us to focus on how knowledge is used in action, in response to informed interpretation of events.

One of the problems vexing a number of people who want to make the most of school-based teacher training is the extent to which mentors' knowledge about teaching and learning is tacitly held and not easily made available in conversations about practice (Edwards and Collison, 1995). Polanyi (1958), however, reminds us that we draw on our 'subsidiary knowledge' when our 'focal awareness' demands it. In other words, external events will stimulate our use of our stocks of knowledge as we respond to the events. Again the emphasis is on knowledge use in action.

This view of knowledge use in action certainly challenges the idea that conversations about practice after a teaching session has finished provide the best way, or at least the only way, of making the most of what mentors can offer students. Lynn Ogden and I have found that the highly supportive conversations about recently observed practice that we analysed tended to reveal that mentors confirmed students in their existing stocks of knowledge rather than replenished them with additional insights. We have therefore concluded that more attention needs to be paid to how knowledge about teaching is constructed in the act of teaching (Edwards and Ogden, in press).

Communities of practice are the places where knowledge is used and developed into forms that are acceptable to the community. According to Lave and Wenger (1991) a community of practice shares a common history, values, meanings and anticipations. There is consequently a case to be made that primary education is a wide-reaching community of practice. Practitioners in schools, local education authorities and higher education share similar beliefs about children as learners, how children are best brought into contact with curricula, the importance of sound relationships with parents and so on.

But primary specialists who work in higher education usually belong to more than one community of practice. As teacher educators they find themselves working as practitioners in the teacher education community. As researchers they are members of a wider research community with privileged access to the products of research. In schools, arguably their participation is largely what Lave and Wenger term peripheral (see Twiselton and Webb, Chapter 14 in this volume). Similarly local education authority (LEA) advisory staff are practitioners in the advisory service and peripheral participants in schools. Teachers also, while confidently situated in the community of primary teaching may be peripheral participants in research or advisory communities. In addition, through school-based teacher education, they are being asked to participate as teacher education practitioners.

Such an array of communities may seem unnecessarily confusing. However, once one starts to see knowledge as something developed in use and closely tied to a specific set of values, the dangers of closed communities are immediately evident. Readers would, for example, perhaps agree that midwifery has benefited from association with a developing medical science. Primary education therefore may be seen as richly endowed with a number of overlapping communities each able to inform the other for the benefit of all.

Conversations about practice in the community of practice are important sites for the development of knowledgeable practice. Twiselton and Webb (Chapter 14 in this volume) have used the work of Tharp and Gallimore (1988) to outline how pupil learning is supported by conversational forms of contingent interactions. Students too need contingent support which is conversationally provided. In addition Kay Mills, also in this collection (Chapter 12), has indicated just how mentors might manage more difficult interactions with students conversationally and inclusively. Therefore, despite any reservations about an overreliance on post-teaching conversations in mentoring, it is clear that we do need to consider how students are brought conversationally into the professional discourse in use in primary schools and importantly how that discourse is refreshed so that students do find themselves in lively learning environments which at times challenge their preconceptions.

We therefore need to consider how mentors are supported in their own learning. A sociocultural view of mentor professional development suggests that if mentors are to be assisted while they develop identities as teacher educators support needs to be provided in the context of their own practices as mentors. Mentors may then be helped in interpreting the actions of student teachers and in finding effective ways of responding. Such a view calls for opportunities for fairly frequent conversations between novice and expert mentors and between mentors and higher education staff about the practices of mentoring and teaching.

Paul Hirst (1996) has argued that conversations about practice are important sites for the development of teacher knowledge and as such serve as probably the most important interface between research and practice. He sees the role of those of us who have privileged access to research-based knowledge to be to inform the practical reasoning of practitioners with theoretical reasoning. He is not advocating a one-way process. Rather he also sees how theoretical reasoning might be informed by contact with the messy realities of the world of practice. Though he does not use the terminology of sociocultural psychology, he describes a lively overlap between the communities of research and classroom practice for the benefit of both.

Opportunities for conversations across communities of practice about the practice of teacher education would seem to be one prerequisite for a partnership that lives up to the term.

The framework just outlined in the examination of the key features of sociocultural approaches to learners and learning provides a way of conceptually linking student learning to the contexts in which their identity construction, i.e. learning, occurs. In addition it allows us to see how flexible partnerships which are based on strong mutual respect can benefit students, mentors and tutors. But how do we move from framework to practice?

Conversation, Collaboration and Research-based Practice

The relationship between research and practice, as Colin Richards has reminded us earlier, is currently a vexed issue. While most would agree that the profession of teaching should, like many other professions, be informed by research; there is little consensus on what teaching as a research-based profession might mean. For some it appears to suggest there should be a linear link between research and practice where the outcomes of research are presented as neatly packaged by researchers for general application by practitioners. This perspective is at odds with, for example, scientific research which adds an additional phase in the chain between research and practice. In the additional stage, research findings are field-tested in a development process which involves both users and researchers. However one could go further and argue that generalizability of all educational research findings, however carefully field-tested, is an unrealistic aim.

A sociocultural view of knowledge construction certainly suggests that a more constructivist view of knowledge use would be wise and that it should be acknowledged that the outcomes of educational research can not be applied like paint to a wall. Schools are not blandly receptive surfaces but complex organizations engaged in their own processes of knowledge construction and use. Paul Hirst's notion of connecting theoretical reasoning with practical reasoning in conversations about practice certainly offers a way of seeing how research-based knowledge might inform the development of practice.

If we are to ensure that students do find themselves in stimulating environments where practice is questioned and discussed and where knowledge in use is not taken for granted, we need to consider how this might be achieved. In Leeds we have received three years funding to establish a research consortium based on a partnership between the School of Education at the University, Leeds LEA and six of the primary schools involved in the primary initial teacher education partnership. These schools are linked to the other partnership schools through the Leeds Primary Research Panel which was established earlier and operates as a forum for the discussion of educational research amongst interested practitioners. The consortium is focusing on the promotion of pupil learning in literacy and numeracy. The research partnership is in its early days but the intention is that teachers undertake systematic evaluations of their own practices with support from university and LEA staff. The work of the first year of the consortium is outlined in 10 stages. Stages one to six occurred in the first term. Stages seven to 10 are to take two terms.

1   The identification by schools of the area of practice to be developed in each school.
2   University staff supply and discuss relevant research with participating teachers.
3   The research focuses are fine-tuned in discussions between teachers and university staff.
4   Teachers identify the new teaching and organizational strategies to be used.
5   The evaluation of the impact of the changed strategies is designed in discussion between teachers and university colleagues.
6   Relevant data collection methods are identified by university staff and guidance is provided on their use.
7   The new strategies are tried out in classrooms and their impact monitored by teachers with help from LEA and university staff.
8   Regular discussions are held between teachers, university and LEA staff about the data gathered in classrooms.
9   University staff monitor the processes of knowledge in use as their research project in collaboration with teacher colleagues.
10 Final evaluations of impact are made and discussions about future research focuses identified.

Conversations are a feature of every stage. Sometimes the triggers for fresh ways of thinking are provided by university staff and sometimes by classroom practitioners. The focus is always how, between us, we might understand practice better, whether we are looking at children's mental mathematics or their narrative writing. Each of us is augmenting the stock of knowledge that serves us as we work out our own identity projects in our own communities of practice. We are all gaining.

We cannot create stimulating learning environments for pupils and for students by fiat. We need instead to ensure that we are able to place students in contexts where they will learn to become learning teachers able to set themselves and achieve high standards of pupil learning. Goodlad's eleventh postulate proposes that teacher education programmes are

> . . . conducted in such a way that future teachers inquire into the nature of teaching and schooling and assume that they will do so as a natural aspect of their careers. (Goodlad, 1991, p. 290)

If this is also, even implicitly, an aim of professional preparation in England and Wales we need to place students in school communities where enquiry is a way of being. Carolyn and I worked together over a number of years on action research-based professional development projects in partnership with early years practitioners in schools and nurseries. For her the most important feature of that form of enquiry-based professional development partnership was how, in her terms 'it moves our thinking on' and how that process helps to inform practice.

Collaboration between higher education and schools has been outlined in more complexity by Huberman in an attempt to counter what he terms the *bricolage* of so much classroom practice by connecting theoretical insights to practical problems in a context of constant conversation among teachers and with key outsiders. His description of 'networks that alter teaching' (Huberman, 1995) demonstrates the power of overlapping communities of practice and the importance of informed talk about practice within school communities. Both the Leeds Consortium and Huberman's analysis of effective networks encourage us to, at times, shift our focus from students, and from students and mentors to find ways of supporting schools as learning communities.

Conversations with Carolyn

Conversations with Carolyn were rarely brief. They were always premised in her strong belief that everyone had something to say that was worth hearing. She was an intensive listener and a challenging conversationalist who probed meanings and used conversations enthusiastically to construct fresh understandings. Planning meetings invariably started from first principles, but so rapid has been the recent pace of change in teacher education that the detail sometimes had to be worked out in action and she trusted the experts in schools and in college to do so. She certainly contributed, and ensured that others contributed, to the high standards of teacher education achieved at St Martin's.

These features of professional life with Carolyn, though I did not recognize it at the time, connect directly to why partnership mattered to her. All partners have a great deal to offer each other. We do need to listen intensively. We need to find time for the conversations that allow us to construct improved understandings of teaching and learning in primary schools. We also need to recognize quite how much can be learnt in action and even find time for joint action. Partnerships which can accommodate relationships of these kinds won't simply be business arrangements. But they may be contexts in which pupils, students teachers and teacher educators can all learn.

References

DESFORGES, C. (1995) 'How does experience affect theoretical knowledge for teaching?', *Learning and Instruction*, **5**, 4, pp. 385–400.

EDWARDS, A. (1995) 'Teacher education partnerships in pedagogy?', *Teaching and Teacher Education*, **11**, 6, pp. 595–610.

EDWARDS, A. (in press) 'Mentoring student teachers in primary schools: Assisting student teachers to become learners', *European Journal of Teacher Education*.

EDWARDS, A. and COLLISON, J. (1995) 'What do teacher mentors tell student teachers about pupil learning in infant schools?', *Teachers and Teaching: Theory and Practice*, **1**, 2, pp. 265–79.

EDWARDS, A. and OGDEN, L. (in press) 'Constructing curriculum knowledge in school-based teacher training in primary schools', *Teaching and Teacher Education*.

GOODLAD, J. (1991) *Teachers for our Nation's Schools*, San Francisco, CA: Jossey-Bass.

HIRST, P. (1996) 'The demands of professional practice and preparation for teaching', in FURLONG, J. and SMITH, R. (eds) *The Role of Higher Education in Teacher Education*, London: Kogan Page.

HUBERMAN, M. (1995) 'Networks that alter teaching', *Teachers and Teaching: Theory and Practice*, **1**, 2, pp. 193–211.

LAVE, J. and WENGER, E. (1991) *Situated Learning: Legitimate Peripheral Participation*, Cambridge: CUP.

LUCKMANN, T. (1982) 'Individual action and social knowledge', in VON CRANACH, M. and HARRE, R. (eds) *The Analysis of Action*, Cambridge: CUP.

POLANYI, M. (1958) *Personal Knowledge*, Chicago, IL: University of Chicago Press.

ROGOFF, B. (1995) 'Observing sociocultural activity on three planes: Participatory appropriation, guided participation and apprenticeship', in WERTSCH, J., DEL RIO, P. and ALVAREZ, A. (eds) *Sociocultural Studies of Mind*, Cambridge: CUP.

THARP, R. and GALLIMORE, R. (1988) *Rousing Minds to Life*, Cambridge: CUP.

WERTSCH, J. (1991) 'A sociocultural approach to socially shared cognition', in RESNICK, L. LEVINE, J. and TEASLEY, S. (eds) *Perspectives on Socially Shared Cognition*, Washington, DC: APA.

WERTSCH, J., DEL RIO, P. and ALVAREZ, A. (1995) (eds) *Sociocultural Studies of Mind*, Cambridge: CUP.

Notes on Contributors

Charles Batteson is a Principal Lecturer in Education at the University College of St Martin working on a range of pre and in-service teacher education programmes.

Jill Collison is a Senior Lecturer in Education at the University College of St Martin where she has course leadership for the Information Technology PGCE.

Hilary Cooper is Head of the Research Programme in the Education Department of the University College of St Martin.

Rob David is a Principal Lecturer in History and Education at the University College of St Martin.

Anne Edwards is Professor of Primary Education at the University of Leeds.

Tony Ewens is Head of Primary Initial Teacher Education Programmes at the University College of St Martin and teaches religious and moral education courses in ITE and in-service programmes.

Robin Foster is a Senior Lecturer in Mathematics at the University College of St Martin where he teaches a variety of courses including undergraduate, postgraduate and in-service provision.

Kevin Hamel is Senior Lecturer in Music and Education in the Performing Arts Department of the University College of St Martin.

Paul Harling is a Principal Lecturer in Mathematics at the University College of St Martin where he is the coordinator of primary mathematics courses for ITE and CPD.

Jack Hogbin is Quality Manager at the Didsbury School of Education, Manchester Metropolitan University.

Rob Hyland teaches in the Education Department at the University College of St Martin on a range of courses in ITE.

Kate Jacques is Head of the Education Department at the University College of St Martin.

Karen Jarmany is Coordinator of Primary Core English at the Didsbury School of Education, Manchester Metropolitan University.

Kath Langley-Hamel is a Senior Lecturer in English and Education at the University College of St Martin, Ambleside.

Bob Leather is a Senior Lecturer in English at the University College of St Martin where he teaches on a variety of undergraduate and postgraduate ITE courses.

Kay Mills is a Senior Lecturer in Education at the University College of St Martin with responsibility for managing elements of an undergraduate programme in ITE.

Dave Murray is a Senior Lecturer in IT and Education at the University College of St Martin where he has responsibility for primary IT within ITE and in-service courses.

Francis Prendiville is a Senior Lecturer in Drama and Education at the University College of St Martin where he teaches on undergraduate, postgraduate and in-service courses.

Colin Richards holds a Personal Chair at the University College of St Martin, is Honorary Professor of Education at the University of Warwick and is visiting Professor of Education at the Universities of Leicester and Newcastle.

Chris Rowley is a Senior Lecturer in Geography and Education at the University College of St Martin.

Neil Simco is a Senior Lecturer in Education at the University College of St Martin where he has responsibility both for aspects of an undergraduate course in ITE and for primary mentor training programmes.

Chris Sixsmith is a Principal Lecturer at the University College of St Martin and is responsible for managing a BA (QTS) course in Primary ITE.

Meryl Thompson is Head of the Policy Unit at the Association of Teachers and Lecturers.

Nigel Toye is a Senior Lecturer in Drama at the University College of St Martin where he has responsibility for ITE and in-service courses in drama.

Sam Twiselton lectures on a range of professional English courses at the University College of St Martin where she has responsibility for the English element of mentor training.

David Webb is a Principal Lecturer at the University College of St Martin where he is responsible for coordinating academic and professional English ITE courses.

Glynis Wood is a Principal Lecturer in Primary Education at the University College of St Martin and is the Coordinator for Continuing Professional Development.

Author Index

Subject Index

Advanced Skills Teacher (AST), 211
algorithms
    in the teaching of mathematics, 85–8
appraisal, 202, 208
assessment of pupils, 112, 146–7, 158
    by students, 80–1, 84–5
assessment of student teachers
    criterion–referenced, 188–9
    in English, 72, 77
    formative, 166–7
    grading, 182
        distribution of, 186–7
        and inspection, 183–7
        level 7 requirements, 90–3
        level 8 requirements, 100–2
        moderation, 186–7
        pre 1990, 182
    in Spiritual, Moral, Social and Cultural,
        114–15
    standards, 129–30
    in subject knowledge, 185–7

BA/BEd Courses *see* Undergraduate courses
behaviourism, 181

Career Entry Profile (CEP), 44, 72, 194–5
Circular 3/84, 5, 17, 38
Circular 24/89, 5, 17, 38, 91, 107, 83
Circular 2/92, 193
Circular 9/92, 7, 17, 173
Circular 14/93, 7, 8, 38, 62, 90, 107, 115,
    173, 179, 183
Circular 10/97, 8, 20–1, 25, 26, 37–8, 40–1,
    43–4, 47–9, 66–9, 78–9, 90, 91, 107,
    109, 113, 115, 178–9, 187
Cockcroft Report, 79
collective worship and ITT, 113–14
communication, interpersonal, 130–2
communities of practice, 219
competences for the award of QTS, 8, 32,
    43–4, 70, 124, 188
complexity of classrooms, 121–4
connoisseurship

Continuing Professional Development (CPD),
    193, 201–13
    definition of, 203
    as mechanistic, 202, 204
    responsibility for, 203–4
    role of LEA, 210
    role of TTA, 204–5
Council for the Accreditation of Teacher
    Education (CATE), 5, 6, 17, 38
Council for National Academic Awards
    (CNAA), 36, 46
Cox Report, 56, 57, 73
cross-curricular links in ITT
    between Core and Foundation subjects,
        95–7
    and drama, 147
    and geography, 96, 97
    and history, 96, 97
    and IT, 103–4
    in spiritual, moral, social and cultural
        (SMSC), 111–13

discipline, 144–5
drama in ITT, 58–9, 137–48

Early Years ITT, 42
Education Action Zones, 209
Education Reform Act (ERA), 109, 210
English as an additional language, 59
enquiry approaches in ITT, 93–4
entry to ITT courses, 55, 68–9, 78, 81
    in IT, 100–1, 104
European Group of Teachers Unions
    (ETUCE), 212
Excellence in Schools, White Paper, 12, 25,
    26, 27, 29–31, 192, 197, 208, 209
explanations in classrooms, 118–19, 121, 123

fiction, use of, 140–1

General Teaching Council (GTC), 210, 213
geography in ITT, 92, 94, 96
grammar, 60–1, 69, 70–1, 75–6